On the Green Hill of Tara

ROBERT ADAM

CONTENTS

Preface

'It was though in those last minutes he was summing up the lesson that this long course in human wickedness had taught us - the lesson of the fearsome, word-and-thought-defying banality of evil.'

1

Chapter One

The black, red and gold flag flapped idly from its staff, uplit by the orange glare of sodium spotlights, as it hung outside the darkened main building of the college. At some point during the night, the wind had picked up, soughing through the pines of the surrounding woods, setting up a clink-clink sound in the halliards of the flag.

Whether it was the noise of ropes slapping against the metal pole or the muted roar of the trees awakening some primordial German fear of the demons of the forest, I was now fully alert, for I wasn't sleeping well these days.

From the window of the austere single room in the accommodation block I searched the shadows of the main building which stood across from us, over the main road splitting the camp in two. I caught the movement I'd been looking for and heard the shouts of a couple of diehard late-night drinkers returning from the student bar. Cubans rather than Syrians, I guessed.

In the gloom of the room behind me Johannes' daughter was stirring in the gently creaking bed. I let the thin curtains fall back into place, glancing at my watch before peering out into the darkness again. It was three in the morning. Another three hours to go until the optional early morning physical training session - optional for everyone else, that was.

I'd have willingly done the assault course every morning anyway. But I'd got on the wrong side of one of the two charmless staff instructors on the first day and they'd made my attendance compulsory since. I suspected

2

that for today, training would again only be a couple of long laps of the track along the camp's perimeter fence. As we approached the end of the week, even the enthusiasm of the more sadistic of the pair was waning.

But what I really looked forward to with the breaking dawn, after a quick shower and breakfast, was squeezing in yet another half hour at the indoor firing range with my *Pistole M*. To my delight, on arrival at Bad Belzig I'd been issued with a brand-new one, menacing in its sleek factory finish, the blued surfaces still unblemished.

Even the physical training instructors couldn't find anything to complain about when it came to the extra time I was putting in on the range, at least a couple of hours each day blasting away under the harsh strip lights. What they didn't know was how good it felt to me to have lethal force at my fingertips, to be in complete control of my situation, even if just for that fleeting moment when I pulled the trigger. Shooting the Makarov, known as *'Pistole M'* in East German service, was a small act of defiance in my mind for another reason. When I hefted it in my hands, I was reminded that the Russians couldn't come up with anything materially better than the Walther PP which the Makarov had been derived from.

For the truth was, a year after my entrapment by the Stasi and the fallout from the events in Brussels which had followed, I was still discovering just how deeply entangled I was in the webs of the different intelligence services. It was what happened when you were forced to play for both sides in the Cold War at the same time. Overlaying the persistent, latent fear that one day I'd be exposed to my family and friends as an informer for the Ministry and a traitor to West Germany was the boredom of my day-to-day job at the EEC. The resulting cocktail made me more depressed than I cared to admit to myself.

It had been the suggestion of my Stasi recruiter, Major Johannes, to come to the East this summer and join one week out of a longer training programme in counter-surveillance techniques and agent running. Favoured foreign intelligence agencies from other socialist brother-states had been invited too. There was no pressing need for me to be here, and I wondered if he'd simply sensed my disillusionment from a distance and was now trying to make my work for them more interesting as a low-level mole in Brussels' own embryonic intelligence organisation.

As it happened, though, he was also honouring a strange promise to me. When I was arrested in East Germany last year on an assignment for a senior official at the EEC, which had taken me to the other side of the Iron Curtain and then promptly gone wrong, Johannes had tried to sweeten the pill of my forced recruitment. Unlike the amateur efforts of the EEC, he promised to turn me into a real professional by giving me Europe's best training in espionage. It had seemed a pointless inducement to treason at the time, principally because I had no choice in the matter. But perhaps as he had hoped, with the passing of a year and more, my own attitude to the other Germany had also slowly changed. By the spring of this year, when he made the offer again, I was open to the idea of coming onto the course and being trained alongside regular Stasi personnel, even if some of them had proven to be real *Schweine*.

For I had also come to the realisation over the last few months that there were many East Germans at all levels of the hierarchy who genuinely thought they were building a socialist system which was benign at heart. Even if its visible outworking in the form of a giant prison camp was a perversion of the Party's own avowed ideals.

I myself hadn't come around to Johannes' point of view to the extent that I now believed in Marxism-Leninism. This wasn't just because of a lifetime's indoctrination growing up in the West. Even if you forgave the Party's instinct to control the activities and attitudes of a whole society - for the people's own benefit of course - I saw no practical proof that their economy would ever catch up with that of the Free World. At least not in the everyday things that mattered to ordinary people such as being able to purchase a colour television, rent a telephone line or, especially, own a car. Even as part of the feared Ministry, the college campus was small and undistinguished, its buildings left over from before the war, when it was a training facility for leaders of the Hitler Youth and the League of German Girls.

But I rationalised my informing for them - my reports on West Germany's and France's manoeuvres to control the future direction of the EEC - with the idea that I was lessening the chances of the East misunderstanding the Community's long-term ambitions. The logic of how a defective East German appraisal of EEC treaty negotiations might somehow lead to a shooting war between the Americans and the Russians I skated over quickly in my mind. In answer to my own question, I told myself that the political assessments made by the Soviet satellite states such as East Germany eventually found their way to the Kremlin. And the more that the Russian comrades knew of the West, the better for all of us.

Another part of my maturing outlook this past year was that given it would be the Germanies where the fighting would take place, if the Cold War ever turned hot, neither one of us intended to do anything to risk that happening. This was why I'd voted in the October 'sixty-nine West German federal elections for Willy Brandt and his 'Ostpolitik' policy of détente, and probably with greater assurance than most of the members of his own Social Democrat Party, too. Given that all my living relatives, bar my mother, were in East Germany - my aunt, uncle and two cousins - I had a personal incentive to promote peace. A meaningful one, over and above the suggestions of their persecution if I betrayed the Ministry, or simply, if I didn't deliver the information they demanded.

Back in the present, despite my attempts to forget my situation by shooting endless rounds of pistol and challenging myself to beat the wiry Cubans in our five-kilometre runs, the past two nights I'd been presented with another complication to deal with. One that was now lying twisted in clammy bedsheets, her face obscured by the lurid shadows cast by the sodium lights outside. As the luminous hands of my watch ticked on, my mind slowly wound down. After a while, I went back to make space in the narrow bed and waited for dawn.

The pine needles were soft under my running shoes. Next time I wouldn't bring my Adidas to avoid the half-contemptuous, half-jealous glances from the East German staff. As I'd guessed, the instructors simply set us off at twenty second intervals to complete the circumference of the camp at our own pace, not even intending to keep a record of our times. That suited me - it gave me a little while on my own to think about my fresh entanglement with the Stasi family as I pounded the circuit, counting off the deer hides just visible in the trees outside the wire, each one a miniature one-man wooden watch tower.

Last year Johannes had told me that his daughter from his first marriage worked as a trainer at The Firm, but hadn't said exactly where. I was still uncertain as to whether her presence on the course was intentional on Johannes' part or not. With the Ministry, you never knew these things, it was how they kept seventeen million people on their toes day and night.

I'd seen her name on a noticeboard on my first day at the 'Edkar André Main College of the Society for Sports and Vocational Training', as the Bad Belzig training facility was snappily known to the outside world, and guessed immediately who she was related to. Then, as I later realised, I'd seen her in the student bar every night since the start of the week; and each night, as far as I could tell, I'd seen her leave with someone different. But on Wednesday evening she came over to where I was drinking with some of the Syrians, a group of them who spoke good French, coolly introduced herself and then quizzed me at length. I answered her in kind, but the identity of my handler wasn't asked for or given. Her short-cropped black hair matched her no-nonsense style and her blue denim jeans marked her out as someone who was so confident of her place in the system that off-duty she could afford to dress as a subversive without any sense of embarrassment. For sure, the first night together had been fun, but when she followed me back to my room again this morning, I started to worry a little. I wasn't looking for even a casual relationship this side of the Wall. And certainly not with the daughter of someone I absolutely needed to stay on good terms with.

However we'd both ended up at the college, I was deadly certain that if anything, observation was all her father had intended. From my conversations with my aunt, I'd discovered that unlike the image of socialist free love projected by certain sections of the Left in the West, East German society was in many ways still surprisingly conservative - even if that was changing in the new decade. At least for the sake of my vestigial sense of propriety, I wasn't going to meet Johannes again this trip. And by the time I saw him next, I was counting on his daughter having long forgotten me, given the number of targets of opportunity available to her from among the students passing through on courses.

When I got back from scaring the deer on the far side of the chain-link fence, she was already gone, as she had been the previous morning. As I showered, I resolved to put her to the back of my mind for the rest of the day. Part of me was hoping she'd already be moving on to someone else tonight so that I wouldn't have to tell her 'no', or worse, be interrogated as to why not.

In the cafeteria, I polished off my rye bread with processed cheese, eating quickly to avoid the smirks of my fellow students before making my way over to the low brick-built building by the gatehouse.

I drew my weapon from the armoury and signed for another box of fifty in the school exercise book hanging from a nail in the wall, using the stubby pencil which dangled alongside it on its short length of grey string.

As I took the approved stance and started to pump bullets into the silhouettes of American GIs, the ghosts of former students from an earlier time, who'd graduated to a mean death among the hedgerows of Normandy, once again looked on in irony - or so my imagination told me.

I'd only just emptied my first magazine when there was a sharp rap on the wooden side partition of my cubicle.

I placed the Makarov carefully on the bench, slipped off my ear defenders and turned around to see my nemesis from the first day's physical training session, wearing his burgundy Dynamo Berlin tracksuit and a cynical expression. I stared back at him, standing erect in my black track top with its death's head on the left-hand side. The name of my own club, 'St. Pauli', was stitched underneath, just to make sure that people didn't confuse it with an older uniform that also carried a skull. Maybe that was what attracted the ghosts. Maybe they'd forgotten how to read.

'You're coming with me to see the director. Right away,' he said with a mirthless grin. He held the ammunition logbook down by his side and stretched out his free hand for my pistol. 'Give it to me now.'

I cleared the gun in silence, proving it was safe whilst I held him with my eyes. Reluctantly, I handed it over and he snatched it with an air of triumph.

'Last time you'll see this,' he said smugly. 'This way.'

He marched behind me up the road from the gatehouse back to the main building. Once inside, I studiously looked past the other course attendees coming down the stairs as we climbed them, up to the second floor.

The college director's office had a view over the accommodation block and the surrounding pine forest. The director, a major, was at the window contemplating nature when the instructor rapped on the side of the permanently wedged open door. The director ignored the knock and remained standing there for a few deliberate seconds, legs planted shoulder-breadth apart and hands clasped behind him, as if he'd just been given *'Rührt Euch!'*

After he'd let me sweat just a little, he slowly turned around, a caricature of the Prussian military type despised by left-wing students in the West, with his close-shaven head, trim field-grey uniform jacket and spotless jackboots. The latter, outside of a formal parade, were a little too much, even for the Stasi. His tunic wore the cuff-band of the Ministry's own Felix Dzerzhinsky Guard Regiment - highly trained, well-equipped, and above all fanatically loyal to the regime. From his get-up he clearly wished he was back there in the Stasi's own private army. Born thirty years earlier, he might well have wished he'd been in the German security service's private army then too, so maybe the students were right to be worried about all the dressing-up.

The instructor went up to the desk, placing my gun on top of the logbook.

'It's all there, sir,' he said, tapping the cover of the book, 'one thousand, one hundred and fifty.'

He went back to stand by the door, on guard. The director motioned me to sit. I did so slowly, wistfully eyeing my Makarov the whole time.

He went up to stand by his desk, tossing the gun to one side and picked up the exercise book to flick through it. He discarded that too and leant over the desk on outstretched fingertips, his nails pressed white and stared at me coldly.

'Did you know that prostitution was banned in the Republic two years ago? It's strange, because Major

Johannes is coming to collect you shortly. Delicacy prevents me from saying what I really think his relationship is to you, but I am sure it's illegal these days.'

I raised my eyebrows in surprise.

'But don't worry. We're going to make sure he hears all about your various performances here this week.' My eyes widened in alarm.

'And when we send you away from here, after our report to Johannes, we'll ensure you're never allowed back. Ah, here comes the Comrade Major himself. *Herein!*'

I turned around in my chair and saw Johannes, large as life, framed in the doorway wearing his own uniform - the unofficial one of a light grey lounge suit, beloved by the Stasi's foreign intelligence service, the HVA.

'Take a seat, Comrade Major,' the director said. 'We were just about to ask Lenkeit for an explanation of his behaviour this week gone past.'

Johannes said nothing, but I saw Sigrid's cool appraising look again in the set of his eyes, which didn't make me feel any better.

The director tapped the table to get our attention. 'Did you hear just now how many pistol rounds you've fired over the past four days?' I shook my head in surprise at the unexpected line of questioning, but also in relief, given what else he might conceivably have asked.

'One thousand, one hundred and fifty. That's dangerously obsessive. Not only are you blowing through my monthly ammunition allowance, you can't even be shooting straight by the end of each session. I suspect at best you have an unhealthy fascination with guns - and that's my opinion as a former sniper champion of the Felix Dzerzhinsky regiment. Or you have some other, undetected, psychological problems. What do you have to say?'

'I've taken part in all of the voluntary activities and had the highest score in the counter-surveillance exercises. If there's been some problem with my participation on the course, the Comrade Major will make sure it doesn't happen again,' I replied frostily.

The director continued to glower at me. 'He's not your "Comrade Major" and you're not an East German citizen, let alone an officer in the Ministry. And I'm glad of that, because your conduct this week has been a disgrace, even for the morally degenerate Nazi successor state you come from.'

Johannes coughed, 'I'm sure anything that needs to be recorded formally will go on Lenkeit's completion report for the course.'

With a start, I realised that somewhere, someone had started a Stasi personnel file on me and was adding to it with each of my official encounters with the Ministry. Which was a little late in the day for the penny to drop, fifteen months into my new career.

'Yes, but we're not finished yet,' said the director. 'His attitude is all wrong. He thinks he's God's gift to the socialist revolution; thinks he doesn't need to listen to instructions; talks back to the staff. I've explained his dangerous love of guns and to that you can add a fondness for alcohol and excessive fraternisation with the female comrades.' My eyes almost stood out of my head as I willed him to stop there. 'From the other socialist republics on the course,' he finished. I gave an inaudible sigh of relief.

'I'm sorry he's been a disappointment,' said Johannes, even though his tone didn't. For although Johannes, like the director, was also a major, he effectively outranked him. The HVA was the true elite branch of the Stasi. It was certainly the most politically reliable one. Its officers had to be, given their greater opportunities to escape to the West. That was why a transfer out of the HVA at the same rank into any other department within the Ministry was seen as a demotion, as Johannes had told me on a previous occasion.

'As I said, please include everything relevant and it will

go into his file. I need to ask you to formally release him from the course, as we have to travel up to Berlin this morning for a briefing.' Another look appeared in Johannes' face, saying silently to me: 'not here and not now'.

My ears pricked up. When I'd met Johannes at the border last Saturday, he'd made no mention of this. Almost anything would be more interesting than what they'd had me do so far - meet every three to four months to report banal office gossip from the Berlaymont to one of the East German foreign trade office staff in a backroom bar in the Stalingrad neighbourhood of Brussels.

Johannes stood to leave, shaking hands with the director who pointedly didn't shake mine. At least he hadn't expected me to salute him, about-turn and march out.

'Go clear your room. We'll talk more on the way,' Johannes said once we were out, as if he were a parent collecting an unruly schoolchild from the Rector's office.

I was born at the end of nineteen forty-five, the year before Johannes' daughter, and had been brought up alone by my mother. However, over the past year, as I'd got to know Johannes, a small, subconscious part of me couldn't help but to start treating him as a replacement for the father figure I'd never known. Which made Sigrid's attention over the past two days doubly uncomfortable when my mind roamed free in the small hours of the morning.

'What was all that about?' I demanded as he returned his vehicle pass to the guard at the gate through the rolled-down window of his Wartburg.

'I'm not a conscript in the army anymore.'

He smiled to himself as he leant forward on the steering wheel, twisting his head to look for oncoming cars as he turned out of the main gate onto the highway.

'Sometimes, Oskar, things simply are as they are. Good as the Stasi is, we don't control everything that happens to people over here. You probably got on the wrong side of an instructor, so the college director simply enjoyed putting you in your place, and me in mine for taking you away a day early.'

He rubbed the light stubble on his chin. I wondered how early he'd got up this morning to come and fetch me, if he'd had to shave the night before.

'I can guess at what they teach you in school and during army conscription over there. And I know what Axel Springer prints in Bild. But over here, when the Party tells people that West Germany is the successor state to the Third Reich, some people really take it to heart. They really do believe it and end up hating Westerners. Even those working for us, the ones they're meant to be training. There, I've told you something about our propaganda that I shouldn't have - in case you use it against me.'

He drove on in silence until after we'd rattled down the sharply-curved cobbled slip lane onto the old pre-war Berlin-Munich autobahn.

His earlier comment regarding annoying an instructor was why I hadn't mentioned meeting his daughter on the course there and then, as soon as we had got into the car at the college. And now after fifteen minutes of his polite questions, those that hadn't been asked earlier this week about my aunt's family in Wismar and my return enquiries on his fourteen-year-old son - second place in the regional gymnastic trials - it was too late to bring it up without obvious embarrassment. By the time the conversation had lightly tripped along and reached our only other mutual acquaintance, apart from Sigrid, I was sure there was the faintest of grins when I caught sight of his side profile from the passenger seat.

In the surreal world of the secret police, that

acquaintance was the person he'd arrested alongside me in March nineteen sixty-nine, my associate at the time, I suppose you would call her, Sophie von Barten.

I listened carefully to the wording of his questions about her and his responses to my replies. Because while I didn't think she'd been turned last year and had also agreed to work for the Stasi in Brussels, you just never knew. However, there really wasn't much I could tell him. She still worked in the Agriculture Directorate, and I still occasionally saw her name on internal memos. That was it though. After the disaster of the trip and its aftermath, she and I had stayed out of each other's way, to put it politely, and hadn't seen each other again.

We skirted West Berlin on the orbital autobahn and stopped at a rest area, just before the turn-off to drive up into the capital. On the way, I'd kept looking carefully to the north, but we were still too far away to see anything of the Wall, or to give it its full title, the Anti-Fascist Protection Wall.

We sat at a wooden picnic table by the side of the parking lot and Johannes poured coffee from a flask.

'Private supply,' he explained, 'much better than what you can get from the official sources.' He stretched out, crossed his legs and lit a cigarette. Whatever had happened in Bad Belzig was obviously staying there for the time being.

'When we get to Berlin, we're going to see my boss to brief you on an investigation we want carried out. And if time permits, we'll get to see his boss in turn.'

'You didn't mention this on Saturday when you picked me up at the border.'

He drew on the cigarette, tilted his head back and slowly exhaled the smoke.

'Something's come up and we think you're in an interesting place to help us.'

'Is it to do with the EEC?'

'It's to do with where your job there can get us into. We're short of options right now and we want to try something out.'

'What are the details of the assignment?'

He tapped his ash onto the grass.

'Nothing more that we'll discuss now. But the usual still applies - if you do a good job and help me, the more I can do for you and your family.'

'I thought I was helping you to keep things just the way they are for them?'

He ignored this. 'How do you fancy going to places no-one in the West gets to go to? I hear that learning to ride a camel in South Yemen is virtually a rite of passage these days for junior HVA officers. Cuba is a possibility too and always Russia of course.' In a different life he could have been a recruiter for the US Navy.

'Somehow, whatever this new job involves, I don't get the feeling it involves drinking mojitos in Old Havana whilst puffing on a genuine Cohiba.'

He smiled to himself. 'Well, it still might involve a lot of drinking, based on the reputation of the people we're hoping you'll get to meet.'

'Tell me again what really went on back at the college there? Thrown out early for practicing too hard on the range?' I asked bitterly.

'Bah, don't take it to heart. But seriously, tone down the aggression. It doesn't become you. It's not how the real world of espionage operates and playing the hard man is one certain way to get yourself into more trouble out in the field than you can handle.'

'Okay.'

He stubbed out his cigarette. 'Time to get moving. One last thing. I said there was a chance, depending on his diary schedule, that we'll get to meet my boss's boss. If we do, that will be a deadly serious meeting because he doesn't see just anyone. Especially not Westerners as a rule - only a trusted select few. I've only met him occasionally myself so it's a rare chance for me to show you off and make a good impression. Don't mess it up, for my sake and for yours.'

'There's more than a chance though, isn't there?'

He gave a wry smile. 'As it happens, I know that one of his appointments for today is going to be unexpectedly cancelled and I'm hoping his secretary will give us the slot.'

It sounded more like we were headed for the Berlaymont than the headquarters of the Eastern bloc's second biggest intelligence agency. He had said last year I would get the chance to learn from the best, and maybe I was. In any case, part of me was already wondering what it would be like to ride a camel.

As we came back onto the autobahn, Johannes had to immediately pull out to overtake a Soviet military convoy.

'Here we go again, Circus Aljoscha, driving to the capital to give a performance, three nights only at the Friedrichs-Palast.'

'Circus Aljoscha?' I asked.

'Look,' he pointed as we drew alongside the rear vehicle, a jeep with a red warning flag hanging out the back. On its driver's door was a symbol, a circle split horizontally in two with "CA" in white letters painted on the red background of the lower half.

'Recognition mark for the Group of Soviet Forces in Germany. "CA" are the initials for "Sovetskaya Armiya" in Cyrillic.'

As we slowly overhauled the convoy, truck by truck, I peered into the back of each one. The complete spectrum of the peoples of the Soviet empire was there to see: brown-haired Europeans, stocky peasants from the Ukrainian black earth region, swarthy Georgians and Caucasians all the way east, east to the Siberians, narrow-eyed tribesmen of the tundra.

Wherever they were from, they all swayed in unison back and forth, holding onto their AK-47s, butts grounded on the floor bed of the trucks, upright between their knees.

'Do you hate them?' I asked. He turned his head to look at me for a moment.

'They're the reality we have to deal with. West Germany has to keep the Americans happy, and we the Soviets. What choice does either part of our country have?'

'As much choice as Czechoslovakia you mean?'

'That wasn't down to these guys,' he said, pointing with one finger lifted from the steering wheel. 'They almost certainly didn't go in. The invasion was two years ago next month, which is the current duration of Soviet Army conscription. Whatever the Red Army did in the past, Oskar, I will say this in Russia's favour - they're also trying to build and maintain a socialist society, just like us.'

It was the gentlest reminder of where we both stood.

Chapter Two

Berlin - Friday, 17th July 1970

We pushed on through the Berlin traffic which got heavier as we neared the Ministry's beating heart, the Normannenstrasse headquarters complex - forty buildings containing ten thousand rooms spread over four normal-sized city blocks, according to Johannes.

As we approached from the south-east down the Frankfurter Allee, the complex came up on us gradually. Johannes pointed out a long row of nondescript four and five-storey office buildings. Then, as we drove further along the southern side of the extended block, a fourteen-storey tower suddenly shot up at the corner of Ruschestrasse with a very definite statement of purpose.

'That's our one,' he said with a proprietorial air, 'the headquarters building of the HVA.'

As we turned into the staff car park, I couldn't believe I was actually here. I couldn't have imagined, not in a thousand years, that when I left Hamburg for Brussels back in 'sixty-six, that my new job would one day lead me in the other direction, to the real centre of the East German regime and very much on the wrong side of the Wall.

Coming here also brought home to me the seriousness of my situation yet again. I'd met Johannes in the East two times since my first arrest, once late last year and once in the spring of this one, each time under the cover of a family visit to Wismar. On both of those occasions, I'd simply travelled the short distance to the small HVA office in Rostock, the neighbouring city along the coast, for a meeting that was more social than professional.

But the Normannenstrasse was where the serious plans got made and life-changing tasks were handed out. I had the sense that Johannes, too, was walking even more smartly than usual, as we progressed down endless beige-floored corridors to Department III - Third-Country Operations. That was 'Third-Country' in the sense of everywhere outside West Germany and the USA.

We eventually stopped outside one of the ten thousand doors. Johannes checked his watch and rapped twice under a name engraved in bakelite. To the shouted command of *'Herein!'* we entered an office painted in a sickly yellow-green colour, overlooking a dusty interior courtyard.

Johannes' direct boss was a lieutenant-colonel, not that anyone could immediately tell, given that he was dressed much like the major in another light grey lounge suit. He was a dour man with a cynical twist to his mouth when he spoke, rising from his desk to greet us with a few curt words and to point us to our seats around the veneer conference table by the window.

If the college director reminded me of certain of our training sergeants during conscription, ex-Wehrmacht and with a permanent air of disdain at the soft German youth of the sixties, then Johannes' boss reminded me of a particularly nasty police captain from my time on the force in Hamburg, sycophantic to his superiors, toxic to those under him. For following my compulsory fifteen months in the army, I'd chosen to join the city police, hoping to make it to the heady rank of Constable after three years. That was until one day at the start of 'sixty-six, before my probationary period was over, when the call came in from an ex-Hamburg policeman, a friend of a friend, who persuaded me to join him instead at the Internal Affairs department of the EEC in Brussels.

The colonel watched Johannes and I with accusing, beady eyes as he waited impatiently on us settling ourselves at the table. Like the Hamburg police captain, he didn't believe in long preambles either, when talking down to people.

'The overall head of the HVA, General Wolf, is travelling to Moscow in three months' time to attend a conference of foreign intelligence agencies. He has given me the task of recommending a strategy for the socialist states regarding the current situation in Ireland and the attempt of the Irish government to destabilise a member of NATO. To assist me, Major Johannes has volunteered you to make discreet contact with the intelligence service of their military, under the guise of your position at the EEC.'

He watched my face for a couple of seconds, looking for a reaction. 'You are to find out their government's intentions as regards the insurgency in Northern Ireland, specifically if they still intend to intervene up there, either directly or indirectly. We want to know how far they're prepared to go.'

Johannes remained silent, watching his boss in turn as he continued. 'It's now July and General Wolf needs to know no later than the start of September,' he peered up at the calendar on the wall behind me, 'in just over six weeks' time, what on Ireland he's going to brief our friends in Moscow. In good German army tradition I've given you your high-level objectives and how you execute them is up to you.'

Well, I hadn't been expecting that. I frowned a little, just to let him know I was taking it seriously, for I was. The pause lengthened as he waited for me to say something clever in response.

'What makes you think they're planning to interfere with the British in the north of the country?'

In answer, he slapped down a file of newspaper cuttings and flicked to the second page.

'It's here in black and white, taken from Petzold's file, so it must be true,' he smirked as he pushed it across.

The cutting was from the front page of The Irish Times of the twenty-eighth of May. 'Three Arrests in Arms Case' was the headline of the article. I scanned the report as fast as my English allowed.

'It says here they are charged with importing arms illegally and that one of them is an Irish Army officer,' I informed them.

'In Army intelligence. However, you don't need to have attended the course in Zittau to work out that secret importations of arms to Ireland today are only going to one place.'

'But they're going to put him on trial, so supplying the terrorists can't be their official policy.'

'Keep up Lenkeit,' he tutted and glanced with narrowed eyes at Johannes.

'Okay,' I said. 'So you want me to find out if it's their unofficial policy?'

He gave me three slow handclaps.

'Something's happening and right now, this week, Ireland is what the leadership wants to know all about.'

'Generals tend to get what they want.'

The colonel ignored my interruption and carried on. 'Since before the last war, the Irish security organs have seen the IRA as a low-level threat to their own state, repressing them during times of crisis. That's despite them both notionally wanting the same thing, the reunification of their country, and despite the fact that the IRA seem happy enough to do the necessary dirty work in Northern Ireland and England to achieve this.'

Johannes tilted back on his chair. He'd heard all this before and stayed quiet.

'But to further confuse the picture, Comrade Lenkeit, the IRA have split into factions, again.'

'Why?' I asked.

'You'll get to that later. We have informal contacts with the Communist Party of Ireland, the CPI, but we want a German view from on the ground in Dublin.'

'You said only to find out the intentions of the Irish government and their Chekists,' I said, using a term I thought might please him because if I was now a 'Comrade' then why not?

He only partially suppressed the sardonic smile which rose involuntarily from the corners of his mouth. Even Johannes had to cough.

'Yes, but the split in the IRA must be influencing the decision making of the security organs. Or the split itself may even have been engineered by the same security organs in the first place. So you'll need to understand that from first hand too.'

I wasn't overly enamoured with the implication that I might have to get close to the terrorists to do so.

'What's the likely outcome of Wolf's visit to Moscow?'

'He's a bold one, isn't he Johannes?' My handler nodded, but somewhat noncommittally.

'Why do you ask?' demanded the colonel.

'To anticipate the next set of questions the Russians might puzzle him with. So when he arrives back off the Interflug flight at Schönefeld, you'll be waiting with the answers as he walks down the steps.'

'You misunderstand. You're not here to probe us,' he said sharply. 'Think back to what I said at the very start - we want to know whether the Irish are going to play the fool and disturb the balance of power in Europe. What happens if the CIA claim the Irish are supporting attacks on NATO territory and use it as leverage to force them to join their imperialist alliance or face the consequences?'

I shook my head in disagreement. 'What would it matter if Ireland joined NATO? They're a tiny country. Anyway, I think the CIA are busy right now in other parts of the world, what with having to watch the backs of half a million American troops in Vietnam.'

'The real number is lower than that and it's falling,' he snapped. 'Anyway, I'm not here to debate with you.' He paused to collect himself. I knew Johannes well enough by now to sense he wasn't happy with that little exchange either.

Johannes tried to pour oil on troubled waters. 'Find out which of the factions of the IRA is expected to win the power struggle, the further ahead of time the better for us. These guerrilla movements are always falling out amongst themselves. And the factions which come out on top aren't necessarily the ones best placed to win the war against their actual enemies. Sometimes we have to intervene to ensure the right outcomes to these internal conflicts.'

He spoke as if he had personal knowledge of these things. I wondered where else in the world he'd been dispensing his expert advice.

'And if you can tell us if there's a corresponding split in the Irish government aligned to those different factions, and who either in government or in their intelligence service we might wish to acquire as an asset to keep the information flowing, we'll take all of that information too.'

The colonel interjected. 'We don't have an embassy in Ireland yet. We don't have the easy access we usually have to get the answers to these kinds of basic questions. Otherwise I wouldn't be letting you anywhere near the Normannenstrasse. I still might send you away this afternoon if you annoy me any further.'

After this morning's performance by the college director at Bad Belzig I was no longer in the mood to care what senior officers in the Stasi thought of me.

'By "acquire" you really mean who in the Irish government is open to be bribed or blackmailed?' I asked.

'If you put it like that, but we also persuade people too, more often than you think,' Johannes answered firmly. 'But as the Comrade Colonel said, all that is secondary information compared to understanding their intentions. That's the real intelligence gold.'

We sat for a few seconds in silence whilst I digested their shopping list. I looked at the row of certificates and bronze-coloured presentation plaques the colonel had proudly put up on the wall behind him as I collected my thoughts.

My work for them had suddenly become much more serious than handing over tidbits of gossip on EEC power politics in a smoky bar in Brussels. This was me no longer being an observer but becoming an active participant for the first time in the secret side of the Cold War.

'Why don't I just find the IRA and speak to them directly? Come at the problem from that angle?' I suggested tentatively. Because, whether I liked it or not, it might end up being a faster way to a solution.

The colonel disagreed. 'Absolutely not. Although you'll go in under the cover of the EEC, at this stage we can't have anything leading back to us. If you're caught even so much as being in the same room as the insurgents against Great Britain, that's going to derail our efforts to get diplomatic recognition from the West during this window of opportunity of Brandt's chancellorship.'

Johannes spoke up again, softly. 'So now you understand the risks that are being taken. Above all, you're to collect intelligence only. No freelancing, no deals on the side for anyone else, French, West Germans, whomever. Anything your bosses at the EEC might ask of you, which would risk our discovery, don't do it - make up an excuse not to.'

I replied, 'Go to Ireland, make contact with their intelligence service, get them to tell me whether they and their government are still secretly supporting the IRA and which flavour of the IRA that might be. All clear.'

The sheer enormity of the request was beginning to dawn on me.

'Don't get caught because we'll deny we've ever heard of you. And that will be the least of your troubles, given what we've prepared for you and your East German relatives if this goes wrong,' said the colonel.

'How long does he have here?' he asked as an aside.

Johannes flicked his wrist to look at the time. 'Another couple of hours before our next meeting, then he's going back over either this evening or first thing tomorrow.'

Nice of Johannes to let me know in advance, but by now I'd got used to being moved around at the whim of the Sword and Shield of the Party, on this side of the Wall.

'Push that back twenty-four hours. I've had Lieutenant Petzold prepare a package of information on Northern and Southern Ireland, and on the IRA, which your guy needs to study.'

He leant across and dropped a fat folder of papers with a dull thud on top of the file of newspaper clippings.

'How's your English, really?' he asked, acknowledging my presence again.

'It's been getting better. We've been practising in the office.'

This was true. The French boss of our amateur three-man intelligence agency had insisted to Willem, the Dutch associate, and I that we only speak English amongst ourselves. Masson's reasoning being that in addition to preparing us for any eventual international assignments, it might also give us a little extra privacy at the Charlemagne building.

The colonel didn't look particularly convinced though.

'I'll have Petzold come to your office, Johannes, to explain it to him. Get out of here now, and good luck.' But he said it without a smile.

It was also my first time at Johannes' personal office in Berlin too. His door wasn't solid like the colonel's, but had a frosted glass pane. Presumably there was a hierarchy of trust, with Johannes in the middle, because other rooms we passed had clear glass windows in their doors. Just to make sure that the ministry's junior staff weren't tempted to get up to anything unreliable inside.

Once in the room, I was somehow disappointed that it was little different to any of the other blank-walled cubicles which I'd been able to glance into on our travels up and down the corridors. I supposed it underlined that he was just another ordinary Stasi employee.

He cleared a space at a small table jammed up against the front of his desk, fetched a chair from the corner and let me leaf through the file whilst we waited on the mysterious Petzold to arrive.

The index listed the historical background to the formation of the two Irelands, the current state of Irish politics, a summary of events since the riots of August nineteen sixty-nine in Northern Ireland, and what turned out to be the most intriguing section of all, 'Miscellaneous', which contained summaries of old Abwehr files.

Johannes glanced at his watch a couple of times and decided that Petzold wasn't appearing anytime soon. He leaned forward over the desk on his elbows, fingers interlocked together.

'I need to prepare you properly for seeing General Fiedler at four.' He paused to marshal his thoughts. 'The first thing to know is that he's been with the Ministry right from the very start, straight off the plane from Moscow in nineteen forty-five where he and his parents had been living as political refugees since well before the war started.'

'How old is he then?'

'Same age as I am, forty-seven.' He paused to let me digest this. 'Yes, that's right, a golden boy of the regime and not without reason. His family were leading lights of the old-time Communist Party of Germany before they fled. Along with the children of leading Soviet party members and other prominent *émigrés*, he attended the top schools in Moscow, the ones reserved for the sons and daughters of the elite. And despite all the turmoil in Russia in the thirties, he remained and remains a true believer.'

He looked at me to make sure I knew he wasn't using that last phrase ironically.

'However, his greatest skill is that despite his

immersion into the world of the Party, he has an uncanny understanding of the people on the other side, including the motivations, however ambiguous, of our Western supporters.'

Considerate of him to refer to me so delicately.

'So he can read people's minds, is that what you're saying? I asked.

'Treat him like he can. He's a chess player, cerebral. Not for him having fingernails pulled out or having people garrotted with piano wire in the Normannenstrasse basements. Not as far as I know, that is. I think you'll get more inspiration for this assignment from twenty minutes spent with him than from an hour or two spent poring over reports of petrol bombings.'

'Is that why you're taking me to see him?'

'I told you when we stopped by the side of the autobahn on the way over here. I'm taking you to show you off to him. Let him see how clever I've been, to recruit someone in an unusual, but for us, potentially highly valuable role over the longer-term.'

'And what's his position at the HVA? Sounds like he should have Wolf's job.'

'Just as I told you, our boss's boss.'

'"Our boss"?'

'You know this is going to be way more interesting than putting together your own files of newspaper clippings for Masson.'

'Masson is my next headache. I'm going to have to ask him to do something with the External Investigations department its director isn't meant to do under any circumstance - risk being exposed outside the EEC.'

There was a knock at the frosted glass door. The shadow on the other side of the glass wavered, as if its owner was uncertain about whether it really wanted to come in.

The lieutenant who eventually appeared a few seconds after Johannes' command was about my age, maybe a year or two older, wearing wire-framed spectacles with wide oblong lenses and his lank, somewhat greasy hair in a side-parting.

Johannes made Lieutenant Petzold pull up another chair to the side table. He and I eyed each other up as we shook hands and exchanged names. That was the limit of his social interaction, though. He cleared his throat, looked at Johannes to get his permission to speak, and then launched straight in, without any wasteful small talk.

'What have you had time to read in the file so far, Herr Lenkeit?'

'Just the index, really.'

'And what did you already know about Ireland, before today?'

'I read "Irisches Tagebuch" last year.' I looked at Johannes. 'Are Heinrich Böll's works acceptable here?'

'Oh yes, he's very honest about the oppression of ordinary people by the plutocrats.'

Petzold tried to steer the conversation back to facts.

'I read it too, but don't be deceived by all that romantic noble savage nonsense. Barefoot children saying their rosaries and tearful partings in the rain when they later grow up and have to emigrate to find work with the capitalists in England and America. That was back in the late fifties. The reality today is quite different, according to the newspapers at least.'

It was a longer speech than I'd expected from him.

'I hope so,' I replied. 'Because it was a real joyful ode to poverty and misery. When I got to the chapter titled "Skeleton of a Human Habitation" I almost stopped reading. And when I got to "Reflections on Irish Rain" I did.'

But Petzold was right, we had to stay focused on the nineteen seventies.

'What do you know about Ireland, then?' I asked.

'It's one of my specialist countries. I work for Department VII - Data Collection and Analysis,

28

researching enemy minor states and neutrals. You've seen our public sources and we have access to other information through our agents at NATO and the EEC.'

Johannes tapped a forefinger on the desk.

Just then, I felt a little pity for Petzold. At some point in the next few weeks I would be going to Ireland, but Petzold would almost certainly only ever experience the countries he analysed from second-hand.

Presumably there were other junior intelligence officers too, but at NATO headquarters in Brussels, who also had an encyclopedic knowledge of forbidden lands but who also would never see their field of study with their own eyes. Somewhere in that collection of grimy, low-rise prefabricated concrete office blocks under the Brussels airport flightpath, Petzold's doppelgänger was imagining life in the Soviet Socialist Republics of Central Asia - crumbling minarets echoing to the cries of vendors in the bazaars, collective farmers harvesting seas of cotton, herdsmen driving their flocks up winding mountain tracks to pastures on the roof of the world.

'So what are the principal questions you have for me? I'm at your disposal until this afternoon.' I guessed even the Stasi liked to finish promptly on Friday for the weekend.

'Have you ever ridden a camel in South Yemen?'

'Pardon?'

He giggled nervously, smoothed the hair on the side of his head and looked at Johannes, who didn't smile back. 'No, no, I haven't. I just prepare reports on the minor states. Sounds a little dangerous. The camels, I mean.'

'Why are there two Irelands?' I knew the answer to this already. I'd read the newspaper reports and the longer articles in the Belgian press for myself over the past year, as the insurgency had escalated into its second summer. Nevertheless, I wanted to hear how East Germany understood it.

'Oh, that one is easy. It's because at the end of the First

29

World War there was a nationalist insurrection against Britain. But just like Germany after the Reformation, the country was a patchwork of Protestants and Catholics. The Catholics in the south of Ireland declared independence for the whole of the island and fought a partisan action against the imperialist forces. But the mainly Protestant north east did not. When the fighting was over, they remained a part of Great Britain, and were known from that time as 'Northern Ireland'.

'So if Catholics are the majority in the South and Protestants are the majority in the North, why are there riots now? What do the Catholics hope to achieve?'

'Oh, that's also an easy one. They want to reunite Ireland.'

'But what if the people in the North don't want to be reunited? Where do they go? What if a minority of subversives in East Germany, supported from the West, demanded the end of socialism and a takeover of the Republic by West Germany?'

'You know that's impossible.'

'But how do you answer the question? Do we agree with the IRA's fundamental aims in this capitalist civil war or do we oppose them?'

Johannes' palms were resting flat on the table, but now he shrugged and turned them upwards in an expression of ambivalence.

'Let's ask an official source.' He got up, went across to one of the cabinets in the corner of the room, unlocked its door and pulled out a volume from the middle of a row of heavy turquoise-blue cloth bound books.

Petzold looked on in frustration at this amateurism.

'Here, the nineteen sixty-nine edition of Meyers Neues Lexikon. Might need updating,' said Johannes, laying the book down between Petzold and I, open at a page in the middle.

'*Irish Republican Army: an illegal combat unit founded in 1919. Its bourgeois-nationalist rump tried after 1923 to achieve the reunification of Ireland by partisan warfare and acts of individual terror. It officially ceased its struggle in 1962.'*

'Explain it for him, Petzold.' He moved back to lean against the wall, watching us put our heads together.

Petzold cleared his throat. '"Bourgeois-nationalist" is self-explanatory. In nineteen thirty-four some left-wing members of the IRA either quit or were expelled when they tried and failed to get the movement to adopt a socialist outlook. Some of the expellees later went to fight for the Republicans in the Spanish civil war.'

Johannes broke in, 'And that's the second-most important historical test for us. The Minister for State Security, Erich Mielke, fought against the fascists in Spain. His predecessor supplied the Republicans with arms and his predecessor in turn, the founder of the Ministry, also fought alongside Mielke. Go on Petzold.'

'"Partisan warfare" has positive connotations, but "individual acts of terror" has a negative one, because individualism is the opposite of socialism.'

The implication, that it was the individualism which was the problem, rather than the terror, seemed to have passed him by.

'Really, you get all that from two sentences? But the description in that entry ends eight years ago. How has this new split come about?' I asked.

'After the failure of their last partisan campaign, in nineteen sixty-two, the IRA leadership tried to move the organisation toward a strategy of greater engagement in mainstream political life, which came with a push towards Marxism-Leninism, according to our local Communist Party contacts from the CPI. However, the same petty-bourgeois tendency as in nineteen thirty-four reasserted itself and over last New Year the movement split again, both the political and the terror wings.'

'So one faction you, or rather we, are well disposed to, the other not?'

'It's not so black and white. That's partly why you're

going there for us,' said Johannes as he came over to collect the encyclopedia and relock it in his cabinet. I wondered why it needed to be.

'And outside of creating trouble for Britain, how important is Ireland to East Germany, really?'

Petzold swung back into action. 'We export much more to them than we import, but even that's not much. It's not as if we get access to advanced technology through the imports. It's mostly butter and pedigree sheep.'

Butter and pedigree sheep. The lieutenant was leaving no stone unturned in his effort to put me in the picture.

'What personnel or personal connections does the Ministry have in Ireland?'

Back behind his desk, Johannes tapped his forefinger on the wooden top once more.

Petzold took the hint. 'We don't have an embassy. I doubt we'll ever need one, given the volume of trade and the size of the country. Despite that, First Secretary Ulbricht was determined a while back to get early diplomatic recognition for East Germany from any minor state whom we could persuade, including Ireland.'

Johannes picked up the thread. 'He wanted us to negotiate by offering to repatriate the corpse of Frank Ryan, one of the breakaway IRA socialists from nineteen thirty-four, who'd gone to fight in Spain but somehow washed up here as a tool of the Nazis, dying from illness in Berlin in 'forty-four.'

It was Petzold's turn again. 'But, anyway, now that the new West German chancellor is going to recognise us, the other class enemies will soon follow along behind. When we get diplomatic recognition from Great Britain, we'll handle Ireland from there.'

'So a metaphor for Ireland's entire history then, as an adjunct to England?' I asked.

'I don't think they see it that way, but I take your point.'

'And what of the country since Böll visited? You say

things are better for them now, economically?' I asked the oracle once more.

'They were in a death spiral of emigration. Hit their lowest ever population in nineteen sixty-one.' Suddenly he pursed his lips, clamping his mouth shut so as not to let any other dangerous utterances escape.

I realised the comparison he'd just unconsciously made. The nine-year-old Anti-Fascist Protection Wall had been put up to solve a similar problem of population decline.

'Okay, Lenkeit, keep the questions focused on the task in hand,' Johannes reminded me. 'I'm sure every country's done better economically this past decade.'

'Very well.' I turned my chair round to face Petzold properly across the little table and stop the crick in my neck getting worse.

'What do you know of the security organs of the Irish state? What's the best way to approach them?' I flicked through the file to the relevant section. 'Who are "G2" and the...,' here I stumbled over the first two words, '... the Guarda Ci-o-channa Special Branch?'

'The first part is "Police" in their language. And "Special Branch" is their name for the part of the Kriminalpolizei which has the special task of fighting terror gangs. "G2" is simply the name for military intelligence, the same departmental staff number as used by every other army. They don't have a separate civilian agency, but then many other small states don't have one either.'

'How big are they? The Ministry is what, forty thousand people for seventeen million people? How many agents do the Irish have to cover their three millions?'

'Perhaps fifteen or twenty in G2. It's very secretive. The whole Irish Army has only around a thousand officers. The head of G2 is a Colonel Delaney, and I believe Major Johannes has some extra information for you regarding other names.'

'So how did at least one of their number end up

supplying arms to the IRA? And to which faction? And how in such a small department could that have been kept quiet from Colonel Delaney?'

'It doesn't seem plausible to us that it was. Although as far as we can tell, it was only the Captain Kelly mentioned in the newspaper article who actually travelled to the Continent to try to buy arms, in Hamburg. The first plan was to ship them in by sea and then they later tried to fly them into Dublin Airport. We suspect they were double-crossed by their dealer who took the money and didn't deliver the goods.'

I wasn't surprised at the mention of Hamburg. As Germany's largest port, it saw all kinds of black-market activity. In the late fifties the French had even exploded a limpet mine under a ship in the harbour, which had been running guns to the Algerian nationalists, the FLN.

'I assume the real question is, why might the Irish have decided to arm the insurgents and then later change their mind, exposing their own agents?'

Johannes answered for both of them. 'It wasn't just an intelligence officer who was charged but also a member of their politburo, Charles Haughey. The only real question, for me, is how many of the cabinet, as they call the politburo, were also involved and if that number included their prime minister.'

'So a real stink?'

Petzold chipped in with his observation. 'The fact that they were arrested obviously means that the Irish government doesn't want to be seen to be officially supporting the insurgents. Someone was foolish enough to get caught so now they have to go through the motions of a prosecution. The actual trial starts in the autumn.'

'Doesn't sound like they're rushing to put a lid on things.'

'The story broke in April and the arrests and charges were made at the end of May, so fast enough or at least that's the impression they're giving.' Johannes tapped out a couple of cigarettes from his pack and offered them us both. I took one to be polite and tucked it into the breast pocket of my jacket for later, after a drink or two.

Little to my surprise, Petzold declined with a 'no, thank you' and a shake of the head. Smoking had been another part of Sigrid Johannes' put-on rebel act. At least, I was guessing it was for show, because I'd hadn't seen many older women here smoking in public. But Petzold, likely with a murky past as a top member of the Free German Youth was still obeying the anti-tobacco indoctrination my cousins had told me about. He probably said *'nein danke'* to strong spirits too.

'You haven't asked the other obvious question which affects all of these considerations,' he said, somewhat disapprovingly.

'Why is it that Ireland is non-aligned, and how do you intend to keep them that way?' I surmised.

Petzold was only too happy to answer.

'It's a legacy of the war. Although I can understand them being neutral back at the start in nineteen thirty-nine and not wanting to help the British, it's less clear why that should have been the case after 'forty-one, once the Americans had joined. Their prime minister at the time, de Valera, was an American citizen himself and had a careful regard for public opinion over there. They've always seen American support as important for securing the return of Northern Ireland.'

'But not so important that they were prepared to fight against fascism back then,' I countered. 'The Spanish were neutral in the Second World War, but they still joined NATO afterwards.'

'You're mixing things up. The fascists in Spain fought a civil war against socialism. Why wouldn't they join NATO? Having said that, the Catholic Church in Ireland is also highly reactionary against progressive forces. In certain areas of public life it's taken on for itself the role of a shadow government.'

'So there's only one explanation left,' I suggested.

Johannes was leaning back in his chair now, enjoying this. 'Go on, enlighten us Lenkeit.'

'Feigheit.'

He laughed out loud. 'I bet you were a real jester as a conscript. What did you do to the stragglers on your route marches, run along behind, prodding them with your bayonet?'

If only he knew.

Petzold adjusted his spectacles and shook his head. 'I think it's a little more nuanced than simple cowardice. Although you can understand their fear of being swept into nuclear war.'

'They sat out the last war, like the fascists in Spain, on the wrong side of history.'

'I think it's the very fact that their choices were illogical is why they took them - to prove they were independent of all the major powers. And they're still doing it. Their foreign minister until last year, Aiken, spent ten years promoting nuclear non-proliferation at the United Nations. He was the driving force behind the treaty signed there a couple of years ago.'

Petzold was nobody's fool, despite his unprepossessing outward image. All the political analysis he'd done since joining the Stasi had probably boosted his original brain power even higher.

As the lieutenant said his piece, something troubled me for a moment or two, but then it slipped away. Johannes nodded approvingly at our exchange.

'Leave it for now Lenkeit. It's just something else to consider. Last question for the lieutenant now, please.'

'The Abwehr, what did they do in Ireland?'

Now Petzold's eyes lit up with what I thought was a suspicious enthusiasm. Out of the corner of my eye, I sensed Johannes watching him too.

'They tried to make contact with the IRA to persuade them to carry out sabotage attacks in Northern Ireland and

England. After all, there was an IRA bombing campaign in England in 'thirty-nine, right up until a week or two before the war started. To get a new campaign going in nineteen forty they sent Frank Ryan and another nationalist, Russell, back to Ireland in a U-boat, but Russell died during the voyage and Ryan returned to Germany without making landfall.'

He knew a lot of details for events that had taken place thirty years ago.

'Wouldn't the Americans and British have invaded Southern Ireland and put a stop to all that, if they had gone ahead and attacked England?' I asked.

'Maybe that's why the Abwehr suggested it, to undermine Ireland's neutrality,' Petzold said more carefully now.

'I don't understand.' I said, despite having a shrewd idea of the answer.

Petzold swallowed and ran a finger round his collar.

'You need to remember that the Abwehr were implicated in the twentieth of July assassination attempt.'

It was a little unfair of me to make him assign any moral ambiguity, however slight, to the Nazi intelligence organisations, as we all sat together in the heart of the Normannenstrasse. I helped him get back onto safer ground, despite my earlier disappointment at his lack of camel stories.

'How would an Anglo-American invasion of a neutral country have damaged the Hitler regime?'

'The British complained bitterly that the denial of convoy escort bases on the west coast of Ireland, which had been available to them in the First World War cost them dearly in the Second.'

'Was that true or could it simply have been a pretext to invade?'

Petzold laughed uncertainly. 'I've never had anything to do with the Volksmarine, so I don't know how important those bases were to the British navy back then. Major

Johannes might know. He used to be in that line of work once.'

'Very good, Petzold. Get out now before Lenkeit thinks of another question to ask,' said Johannes coming around from his side of the desk to show him the door.

Petzold stood up, holding himself stiffly erect, not in a hurry to move as if he was still hoping for that next question. Part of me wanted to shout out *'Stillgestanden!'* to see if I could shock him into standing fully to attention, but the time for playing word games with the employees of Department VII was over for today. With another 'thank you' from Johannes, he left.

After Johannes had made sure the door was properly shut, he turned around to me and wagged a finger, tutting from the side of his mouth.

'I can't let you roam the corridors and lead any more junior officers into ideological danger but if you stay here, I'll fetch some coffee while you study this.' He unlocked a different cabinet and pulled out a thin manila folder.

'In this document you'll find the names of Colonel Delaney's deputies, department heads we're assuming; the gift of a well-wisher somewhere in the West German government.'

Inside, was a single handwritten sheet with a long list of surnames and initials in alphabetical order, more than twenty. The initials were essential given the number of O'Brians and Murphys.

'This page you can take back with you. The names with a dot after the last initial are the ones you want.'

He locked the cabinet again and then left the office, locking the door behind him.

Whilst he was gone, I took my chance for a closer look around his room. On the desk there was a black and white photograph of a smiling Johannes in uniform, standing next to Sigrid in front of a podium, a velvet curtain glinting in the background. Sigrid was also in dress uniform - that of a second lieutenant. She also wore a wide grin, looking smart and confident on what I suspected was her graduation day from the main Stasi college in Potsdam.

Propped next to it in a plastic frame was a colour photo of his current wife and son, a posed picture at the base of the Fernsehturm, the three-hundred-metre-tall pride of the East German regime. Both photos were exactly the kind of politically-safe family snapshots you'd expect a Stasi officer to have at their place of work. They were yet another reminder, should I need it, of whose side Johannes was on.

I got back to my seat well before he returned, rattling the door as he walked in backwards with two plastic cups. The coffee was as awful as he'd hinted at earlier today on the way to Berlin, but I drank it slowly with carefully calibrated appreciation.

The fun was over in Johannes' Department III for today as well. He stared at me with a solemnity I hadn't seen since the day he recruited me.

'So, how do you think you'll break into the Irish agencies?'

'Using my Brussels job as cover all depends on whether the handful of EEC senior officials who sponsor and direct our work are prepared to risk revealing the existence of External Investigations, and what it does to those outside of a highly-restricted inner circle. As I indicated earlier, as of today the department is more secret than the final resting place of Attila the Hun.'

I took a sip of the office coffee, trying not to grimace. 'The last thing they want is for member states to get the impression that the EEC is developing its own state-like capabilities and might one day supersede its component parts. It's much too soon for that, especially now that the accession of Britain, Ireland, Norway and Denmark is back on.'

'Then you need to have a compelling reason to make that trip to Ireland and to make it work in your Brussels sponsors' direct interests too.'

'Your boss said no side-deals.'

Then I went silent for a few moments. Because a deep double game whereby the Stasi got me to go to Ireland and then deliberately blew my cover claiming I was an EEC spy, all in order to undermine the accession talks was uncomfortably plausible. To me anyway, given that I'd be the one chewed up and spat out by both sides.

'So if you can't say who you are, how will you get G2 and the police Special Branch to speak with you?'

I raised my eyebrows and sighed, coming back to the present. 'I'll suggest to the Irish that I have some special new information not available through regular channels which their intelligence officers will want to know?' I ventured, even though I couldn't imagine what that might be.

'I'm sure you can eventually find or make up something of interest to show them, even if it's only partly true. The trick is to get access to the specific individuals on the list, without disclosing you already know who they are.'

'Why would that matter? If I ask for an interview with G2 or the Special Branch and get one, that's what counts.'

'How would you know they had given you an interview with an actual officer there and not a decoy?'

'How would I know anyway, even if they said they were someone on the list?'

'You wouldn't, but at least you'd know you were one step closer to getting on the inside, than if you were just given a meeting with an anonymous person. So what's your excuse going to be for having that list if the police search your hotel room in Dublin?'

I shrugged, 'I'd have to use our emergency cover story - that we're a department which liaises with the member states' intelligence agencies. Or even stretch the story to military liaison and say that that's where the names came from. After all, G2 is a military intelligence service, as Petzold said.'

'Presumably it won't take G2 a day to check with the Bundeswehr if that is the case. The Irish have telephones too. We don't want any suspicion falling on us and our moles as the source of the names.'

It felt like he was setting me an exam rather than giving me advice.

'Okay, have a think about it and keep reading. I'm off now for another meeting for thirty minutes. I'm going to lock you in again when I leave to avoid someone coming in by chance and asking questions.' Because he had the monopoly on those right now.

I chewed it over some more and the outline of an idea or two came to mind, but truthfully, I was stumped. Maybe the chess-playing genius, General Fiedler, might have a game-winning move.

After what turned out to be almost an hour, in which I finished with Petzold's file for all intents and purposes, Johannes came back to unlock the door in a rush. *'Fliegeralarm! Fliegeralarm!* Duty crew to flak positions.' He chuckled at my confusion.

'Come on, leave those files here. Our meeting with General Fiedler has been brought forward. We've got ten minutes to get right to the far end of the block. Let's see if we can do it before the Tommies launch their eels.'

He tapped the side of his head a couple of times as if working out the fastest way to get there. 'This way.' He dived down a couple of corridors, striding purposefully. We exited the building at its corner, and he made us virtually run across the concrete courtyard through a gap in the buildings to the next open area.

He grinned at me as we slowed down again at the main entrance. 'Five minutes still to spare. Up we go.'

As we rode the lift, he gave one last warning. 'Remember, once again, you can't outsmart Fiedler. Also, no back-chat. Show some acknowledgement of his rank. He's a general, after all, even if he's only a Stasi one in your eyes.'

Johannes knocked at the outer office. A secretary with a curious purple tint in her hair opened up for us, closing the door behind her. 'You can go through.'

I was sweating a little, and not just because of our dash in the July heat. It didn't help that the air conditioning in Fiedler's office was none too effective. Maybe it was forced through a filter to exclude radioactive dust or poison gas and lost its power before it got to us.

Otherwise, the interior reminded me strongly of Kramer's office on the top floor of the Berlaymont. Kramer was the senior French official who had sent me east last year when I was still a direct employee of Internal Affairs. In the aftermath of the events in Rostock, he had been the main sponsor for the creation of the brand-new External Investigations sub-department of Internal Affairs, notionally reporting to him. And with Masson as its first director, also French, of course.

Just like Kramer's rooms, Fiedler's office was sleekly panelled to half height with pale coloured wood and was also furnished with soft leather chairs around a low table. Almost as if both technocrats were trying to project an air of stylish conviviality, disguising a ruthless determination to rule their respective fiefdoms, absolutely and unchallenged. As the meeting started, the irony wasn't lost on me that I'd been sent east last year by Kramer and was now being sent west by General Wolf.

Fiedler was a tall, somewhat handsome devil. I wondered if it was his wife who made sure that his secretary was an aging battle-axe. He invited us both to sit, then eyed me up with a searching stare for a couple of seconds.

'Tell me something I don't already know.'

An answer came unbidden into my head. 'When the

Nazis counterattacked through the Ardennes at Christmas nineteen forty-four, some of the Vichy French government officials who'd gone into exile in Germany, to Sigmaringen in Baden-Württemberg, proposed holding a victory concert to celebrate what they thought was the start of the restoration of their regime.'

'How do you know that?'

'I spent some time last year speaking with people who were there.'

Fiedler allowed himself a smile.

'There was greater delusion in Stalin's Russia during the Show Trials. I know because I was one of the deluded. Tell me something else.'

'There is a faction at the EEC which is determined to gradually remove all national-level decision making in the critical areas of government. Instead, they'll concentrate those powers in the Commission where they will be carefully insulated from direct democratic control. They've looked at the way the Communist Party created the Supreme Soviet of the USSR and unconsciously seen it as a model for the government of a future so-called European Union, but in a capitalist context.'

That did make Fiedler stop and ponder for a few seconds. 'Maybe you're right. But that's why the Soviets invested in recruiting elements of the French nomenklatura, to persuade them to leave NATO four years ago and make sure that they keep the EEC from going down the path of full political union.'

'Then your hope is misplaced. The temptation of wielding that kind of influence is too great, even for the most patriotic French nationalists to resist. I know because I've worked for one.'

I sensed rather than heard Johannes' intake of breath and remembered his warnings about my tone.

'Well, you're a real ray of sunshine from the West today. So tell me, in your own words, how did you end up working for us?'

Johannes and I had never revisited March 'sixty-nine during our long, well-lubricated lunches at the Hotel Warnow in Rostock when I came back East for debriefings. Now I was forced to speak aloud the truth of what had really happened, as opposed to the carefully fabricated fiction I'd created for myself over the past year about helping to maintain European peace.

'I came East to retrieve a wartime document, was caught, set up for a serious crime and was told by Major Johannes that I wouldn't leave jail until I confessed to it.' Instinct made me sanitise even that abridged story in front of Fiedler, leaving out the part about Johannes' threat of persecution of my family in Wismar.

The room was quiet for a few seconds. The hazy glare of the summer sun streamed in through the drawn curtains, past the lignite smog hanging over the capital.

'And since then, has the Comrade Major brought you around?'

Often in these situations, the best lie was the truth.

'I was resentful at first, but as I got to know Major Johannes, I realised that our propaganda didn't account for there being real people on the other side, including my family in the East who merely want to get on with their lives here.'

Fiedler nodded his head gravely. 'So have Major Johannes and his chief explained our problem to you?'

'Yes, but it won't be straightforward.'

'That's why you're here now. Which part causes the most concern?'

I glanced at Johannes, trying to explain Kramer and Masson's expected reticence about me even going to Ireland in the first place would take too long.

'How to make contact with specific individuals in the Irish security organs without revealing where we got their names from.'

'Ah yes,' said Fiedler. 'The Russians have a saying: "washing the bear without getting its fur wet."'

44

Now Fiedler looked at Johannes, who replied on the General's behalf. 'You could consider that if the names didn't come from another intelligence agency, they might have come from an individual who's had direct dealings with the Irish security organs in the past.'

'Do you hear what the Comrade Major is saying, Lenkeit?' Well, I did, but it was already sounding like a scripted double act to me and if Johannes genuinely wanted me to perform well in front of Fiedler, it was one he could have shared with me first.

Johannes carried on. 'We need to find a German whose path has crossed enough people at the Irish agencies to make them take notice of you when you claim to have been in contact with him or her.'

'The arms dealer in Hamburg who supplied Captain Kelly, the officer going on trial?' I suggested, grasping at straws.

'Possibly, we were thinking more about the Sicherheitsdienst's biggest rogue, the charlatan liberator of Mussolini and a landowner in Ireland, no less,' prompted Fiedler.

'Otto Skorzeny?' I asked incredulously. I was already worried from earlier that this assignment might be an elaborate set-up. Adding Skorzeny to the plot would be like putting the dot on the 'I'.

'Hear us out,' said Johannes. 'He's tried and failed to get residency in Ireland as he's too tainted, even for them. When he first went there in nineteen fifty-seven, he was an object of fascination, as he remains for many people. Although the official attitude of the Irish towards him has changed over the years, he must have come across enough of their key people in intelligence and in politics too. If you say you've met him yourself, that can be your cover story for knowing those same names. Captain Kelly was assigned to G2 off and on from nineteen sixty, he must have encountered Skorzeny at some point,' Johannes concluded.

45

Fiedler had all the moves planned out, just as Johannes had warned me. There was even a chess board on a side table by his desk. Of course there was.

'Captain Kelly,' said the general in wonderment. 'The Irish putting their own intelligence officer on public trial instead of a secret court and the "unexpected shot to the back of the head" he'd had received here. That's a brave move politically, and I say that as someone who knows the politburos of most of the socialist states. Then, on top of everything else, to expose their own head of intelligence to public view too.' He shook his head sadly at this evidence of Irish impetuousness.

'It's either a grand Russian-style *maskirovka* deception plan for the benefit of the British, or the unavoidable surfacing of a much deeper political dispute within their government.'

He paused for a moment, pursing his lips. 'It would be like Ulbricht putting Mielke on trial.' It took him half-a-second to break out into a smooth, joking smile. And in that short slice of time I realised he wished the picture he painted of his ultimate boss at the Stasi was real.

They were going way too fast for my comfort. I didn't care how important Fiedler was. I didn't like being railroaded into a neat, pre-arranged plan.

'Sorry, I didn't realise Skorzeny had ever been in Ireland, let alone bought property there.' Skorzeny was probably the biggest living Nazi celebrity, the SS-Sicherheitsdienst commando leader who'd rescued Mussolini in an aerial assault on the mountaintop hideaway where the pro-Allied government had been holding him after the country changed sides in nineteen forty-three.

But Fiedler wasn't brooking any opposition to his Skorzeny idea for now and moved the conversation on, ignoring my questions.

'We're not amazingly well disposed towards the Irish, what with them avoiding the struggle against fascism and then closing a blind eye to fascist asylum seekers after the war. Maybe we've forgiven them now though, because they didn't join NATO. And after all, they hate the English.'

Now, in addition to worrying about whether the East Germans were planning to ambush the EEC, I was quickly trying to think through if they were planning to somehow settle historic scores with Ireland by using a smear related to Skorzeny.

'Did you know that they're putting a Belgian Nazi collaborator on trial for gun running, along with Kelly? Someone who helped them source weapons on the mainland,' Johannes said, nudging the discussion in that direction.

I was spared from having to answer his question by Fiedler's secretary, who came bustling into the room. She was an efficient, impatient sort and like her boss, she'd also fit right in on the top floor of the Berlaymont.

'You have a meeting with the head of Department X now, Comrade General. He's waiting outside.'

Fiedler looked at her almost apologetically. 'This is important. Please tell him he'll have to hold on until we're done.'

He waited until she was gone and gave me a wry smile. 'You see who's really in charge here? And Western propaganda says we're a police state.'

I was sceptical. I'd never heard of a German, in either the East or the West, being deliberately late for a meeting. He might not think he was helping run a police state, but they'd instinctively not mentioned the name and rank of whoever it was that he was meeting in front of the Westerner.

Fiedler turned back to me and turned the charm up a notch. 'We have to say goodbye now, so here's my last few thoughts. If it makes your conscience easier, think of yourself as our consultant, helping us understand the West. That's all we're really asking of you. And as you go about this task that Johannes has set, remember Hoshea son of

Nun who searched out the Promised Land for Moses. You're not a bad-looking guy. Make use of it.'

'Sorry, I don't follow the meaning behind your reference. One of the twelve spies in the Bible?'

'Please, the Luther translation uses the word *Kunsthandler*, a simple gatherer of information. Still, there's two lessons from the beginning of history: Moses' use of deception, giving his man the cover name of "Joshua" and the way that Hoshea persuaded Rahab, the woman of ill-repute, to work for him.'

My eyebrows arched at this.

'What are you shocked about? My suggestion or hearing a reference to the Bible in the Normannenstrasse? Well don't be - I'm Jewish. Putting me in high office is one of the things which reminds people that we're the good guys.'

'I do have one last question, General Fiedler, if I may.' Johannes recrossed his legs, nervous of what was coming next. And he should have been, because he was the one who'd talked about intentions being intelligence gold. And if 'General Fiedler' really was Wolf himself, as I had a sharpening suspicion he might be, then this was a chance I couldn't afford to pass up, to bank something for the future, something of real interest and value to the West.

'Will Germany ever be reunited?'

As I tossed my grenade onto the table between the three of us, all the air seemed to be sucked from the room, as if the feeble air conditioning had staged its own workers' revolt and gone into reverse. The next two minutes could either go very well or very badly.

'That's what you really care about, isn't it? You voted for Brandt, Johannes tells me?'

I nodded in agreement. 'Virtually all my family are here. Their wellbeing is what concerns me, above all else.'

He raised his eyebrows. 'You realise that I only answer your question out of politeness?'

'I want to know if there's hope,' I said, trying to inject

the correct amount of plaintiveness into my voice.

'One day, if West Germany fully embraces socialism and détente between America and Russia becomes more certain, then perhaps an accommodation will be found.'

None of us in the room were convinced by his answer. We all knew there could never be such a coming together out of mere goodwill. One system would have to win, and he had the intellectual honesty to acknowledge it, even if in a roundabout way.

'My family fled to Moscow before I was even a teenager. I've lived through the rise of Hitler, the purges of Stalin, the disaster of the fascists' war, the denunciation of Stalin and the building of the Wall which came as a surprise to me too, by the way.'

I tried not to let my own surprise at that last comment show as he continued. 'My life has seen constant change and may still yet. But whatever happens in the future, we have permanently embedded socialist ideals into this society; ideals which will not only survive any form of reunification but will change the nature of the western part of a reunited Germany for the greater good.'

Fiedler, I supposed, could be permitted such latitude in his thinking but the young Stasi officers I'd met on the course in Bad Belzig had no such doubts. 'Enemy-side' was what the border guards called the western face of the frontier defences, and they meant their use of the term.

'Thank you, General. I've never asked for payment from you and I never shall.' I wasn't sure how much real intelligence value was in what he'd just said, but if I had to, I could always try to create a saleable confection from his words.

'I know you won't. I know your type.'

We were well past the point where he could be acceptably late for his next meeting, so I reasoned I might as well carry on squeezing him for as much goodwill as I could in whatever time was left. I tried to soften him up a bit more with a grin.

'I don't want any payment from you, if only because I've worked in Internal Affairs and I've seen what bribery does. I'll end up with an expensive girlfriend and a big flat, and not be able to explain either if l get pulled into an audit.'

Johannes glanced nervously at Fiedler again.

'Pay me instead, by looking after my family in Wismar,' I said. 'Make sure they get what they need, whether it seems trivial to you or not. A car for my uncle, university for my cousins - if they want it, my younger cousin to be kept out of your files because he has a tendency to get himself noticed by the Ministry's helpers. And help me in my own career at the EEC, help me take down my rivals, push me as high up the tree there as my ability will take me.'

Fiedler raised his eyebrows and nodded to himself. 'We can do some of that, perhaps. We need to know better whom we're investing in, though.'

He looked at me more closely now, with colder eyes. 'You haven't done much for us since the middle of 'sixty-nine, or so I'm told. Time to step up a gear again and show us what you can do in Ireland and then we'll see.'

But when he turned to Johannes it was with a polished smile. 'You caught yourself a feisty one that spring day last year. Well done Johannes.'

Johannes beamed in relief, a little too obviously I thought. I expected to pay for my questions to Fiedler and my demands of the Ministry with a scolding from him afterwards, but for now he was focussed on reinforcing success.

'He's a good fit for the Ministry. Should we explain more?' he asked Fiedler.

'Why not? He's not stupid.'

'It's because although you have only one close relative in the West and most of your family are in the East, you lived all your life over there as a genuine West German citizen. You're clean on almost all the indicators the enemy counter-espionage services use. We were just as happy to catch you last year as your travelling companion.'

Well, I was pleased for him and when I wasn't being sarcastic, also a little pleased for my own sense of self-importance too. We all got up and Fiedler walked us to the door with a call to his secretary to send in his next visitor. From the dark look we got from the heavy-set bureaucrat who'd been waiting outside, my suspicions as to Fiedler's real identity only increased.

We walked back to Johannes' office, slowly this time, enjoying the summer warmth. I knew Johannes well enough by now to know that on balance, he was pleased with how the meeting had gone.

When we got into the room and the door was closed, instead of a tirade at my questions to Fiedler, the relaxed Friday afternoon mood continued.

'Okay, take your list of names, make any last notes from Petzold's file and let's have a beer. I can get you into an Interhotel tonight. Or you can probably just make it back to Wismar this evening to stay with your aunt.'

'Sounds good to me. I should probably set off soon for Wismar, though, as originally planned.'

He pulled a Deutsche Reichsbahn timetable off the shelf and tossed it to me. 'Find out when you need to leave. We should have enough time to go to a bar in the centre, away from the Stasi pubs around here.'

He reached back into his desk for a pre-printed form.

'Before I forget,' he explained, setting the sheet up on his personal typewriter and starting to bash the keys, 'best you have an authorisation to take your new toy out of the country. I'm still amazed they let you take it away from Bad Belzig.'

'They didn't trust me with any ammunition, though,' I replied. He sighed and reached back into his desk for a box of fifty.

In the end, I didn't make the train. As I'd also come to learn, if Johannes did have a particular personal weakness, it was an uninhibited enjoyment of alcohol. He wasn't an obvious drunk with slurred or aggressive speech. And presumably you didn't get to become a Major in the Stasi without the ability to conceal the effects of drink, along with the innermost depths of your soul. It was just that he kept going and going, until suddenly he'd consumed beyond what was reasonable, and what in my eyes, was reasonable for someone old enough to be my father with a wife and child waiting at home somewhere.

The afternoon and later, the evening, were pleasant enough despite the outstanding, unspoken question about just how well I'd got to know his daughter in Bad Belzig. We started shortly after four in a bar in Prenzlauer Berg where we sampled Berliner Weisse in two pubs on opposite corners of a crossroads. One had been the local for a unit of the Communist Party's Red Front paramilitaries before 'thirty-two, the other, that of the Sturmabteilung - the 'Brown Battalions' as they were named in the lyrics of that now-forbidden song.

When it was obvious that he wasn't ready to stop, I phoned my aunt from the pub, calling the trade union office where she worked to tell her that I wouldn't be in Wismar until tomorrow after all. Eventually, we moved to the bar at the Hotel Unter Den Linden where I suspected he had a room booked for me all along, and we settled down to see out the remainder of the evening together.

As time slipped by, he became more obviously in the mood to talk, about East and West German football, family holidays in the Tatra mountains in Czechoslovakia and even the prospects for peace in Vietnam. In certain areas, he could be open with me in a way he couldn't be with his real colleagues. I took the opportunity to put some questions to him I'd been meaning to ask for a while, to go fishing some more in his past.

'In that book I mentioned earlier to Petzold, "Irisches

Tagebuch", one of the Irish characters suggests her grandson was killed by an English U-boat. How likely would that have been?'

'You're starting to think like an East German with your indirect question about my time in the navy.' His tone was more amused than annoyed, though.

'If the grandson had been on an Irish ship that was sunk by the English, then he would have suffered from a freak accident of war. Not that the person Böll described could have known the nationality of the U-boat. Maybe just an illustration of how much the Irish hate the English. And, yes, I was in the Kriegsmarine during the war but in the surface fleet, mostly destroyers, in Norway.'

'Did that mean you were more acceptable to the Ministry, than having been in the Wehrmacht, whenever it was you came to join?'

'More acceptable to the Volkspolizei you mean? I was recruited to the Ministry from there in nineteen fifty-five, so we have that career change in common. There's a long revolutionary heritage amongst the sailors of the German surface fleet, which didn't hurt in getting a job with the Ministry during the big expansion after the riots in 'fifty-three.'

He shifted in his seat. 'To be fair, though, it's never stopped growing, so they'd have taken the right person, regardless of background, if they were demonstrably loyal and trustworthy. We were about fifteen-thousand strong when I started. It's around three times that now.'

'The EEC is about four thousand people today,' I said reflectively, giving it a couple of seconds before asking what happened in Norway.

'We mainly served as escort for convoys transporting iron ore to the Reich. We also supported the big capital ships when they ventured out from their bases in the fjords to threaten Allied convoys sailing to Russia in the opposite direction to ours. Tough job all the way through. Either being shot at, torpedoed or rocketed by the English air force. Or being bored to death for the rest of the time. Apart from the very last months of the war, after we left Norway - that was the worst of all.'

He faded into silence and swirled the schnapps in his glass.

'I remember the departure of *Scharnhorst* on her last voyage. Christmas Day nineteen forty-three - gliding like a ghost into the snow flurries. Two thousand men, less than fifty survivors.'

Then somewhat unnecessarily, but perhaps from force of habit, he added, 'Victims of Hitler, like so many others.'

He took a sip and pointed at me with his glass. 'Everyone says it so often, that it loses its meaning these days - but we really do want peace. We Germans just need to be left alone to find our own path. But our big brothers on both sides know better for us.'

I took a sip from my own glass.

'There, I've said enough for tonight. For me, time for home. For you, stay out of trouble until you're back in Brussels. And the usual rule I've taught you applies when you're back at your relatives - if the cover story for your activities this week isn't working, stop speaking and stay silent. They'll get the message to steer clear.'

We stood up and left the bar, past the 'law students' with elegantly crossed legs perched on high stools at the counter. We stood facing one another in the foyer. Johannes was relaxed, even swaying slightly now, although in his case that was probably more from the heat and the closeness of the air than the alcohol.

Suddenly, his eyes hardened, revealing that clarity of perception that sometimes comes upon people with increasing intoxication. He reached out to grip my hand and pulled me in hard towards him.

'One last word of advice. Don't get her pregnant. I like you well enough Oskar, but I'm not ready to have a grandson by you yet.'

It had been a long day and after my session with Johannes I was done for. Despite the nightmarish orange and brown swirled wallpaper on the wall opposite the bed, I went to sleep almost immediately.

I was awoken at two in the morning by the sound of three sharp cracks; at least that was the number I counted after I'd come back from the world of my unsettled dreams. Immediately suspicious, I got up and went over to the window. They had sounded very like the report of a high-powered rifle. For the second time in twenty-four hours, wrapped in a curtain I peered out into the darkness to see what was going on.

About three blocks away there was a dull orange glow and when I looked more carefully, I could see it again between gaps in the buildings, disappearing into the distance in a curving line. With a shock I realised I was looking at the course of the Wall itself. Either the shots or the backfiring car had been close enough to the hotel to be heard up in the rooms. As I looked up and down the line of the lights, my eye was drawn to one gap where I managed to convince myself the glow was moving. Searchlights perhaps? Then suddenly came a sound there could be no doubt about. A three-second rattle of automatic fire. It was the sobering reality of opposition to the society that indulged Fiedler and his little international games of chess.

But I also wondered how insulated Fiedler really was, from what he must know was happening on his doorstep. He clearly wasn't enamoured of Mielke. Maybe the way he did his job at the HVA, without pulling fingernails, was his own unconscious act of resistance.

Chapter Three

When I woke, I fiddled with the radio to pick up the West Berlin station, RIAS, but there was no mention of an escape attempt overnight. At breakfast, tempted as I was to ask the hotel staff if they'd heard the firing as well, I knew not to for their sakes as much as mine.

After the drama of yesterday, the early morning Saturday service to Rostock and then onto Wismar was an anti-climax; a long, hot and stuffy ride for three and a half hours through Brandenburg followed by another hour's meandering along the Pomeranian coast.

The Soviet Army were visible on the way out of Berlin too. A couple of officers were sitting at the end of the carriage, chain smoking their entire time on the train. Maybe they were simply frustrated at having to travel the wrong way on the weekend. Away from Berlin back to duty at one of the hundreds of barracks and airfields scattered across the East German countryside. In military terms, the Republic was one huge assembly area for a future invasion of Western Europe. The other travellers ignored them, stepping past without a glance as they went to and from the end-door to the carriage vestibule. But if they didn't find the tan uniforms of the occupiers disconcerting, I did.

When I eventually got off the train at Wismar and exited the station, a battered Trabant pulled up and the driver cautiously asked me in which direction I was headed. Normally I would have quickly declined the offer, wary of the risk of getting stopped in an illegal taxi and into trouble with the police. Johannes was constantly warning me against drawing attention to myself, even to the Volkspolizei.

But today was different. Having come straight from Stasi headquarters, surely I was untouchable for a while - until after Ireland at least? And in any case, whatever Johannes said, when it came to providing personal services of a temporary nature, the risk of the State finding out was low, regardless of how many laws they might pass against them. Illegal or not, all I would really be guilty of was making sure I got to my aunt's in time for lunch.

When I'd spoken to her last night after it had become clear I wasn't going to make the evening train, she'd said they already had plans for the afternoon - friends from her work and church coming over for a meal. It gave me another reminder to have my cover story well rehearsed.

I'd agreed with Johannes that when I was inside the country, I'd tell people I met that I worked for the EEC promoting trade with East Germany. Conveniently, this would also involve me acting as an export consultant to various engineering firms in different parts of the Republic. Johannes had even provided me with a handful of business cards left behind by West German importers and by the representatives of East German manufacturing combines, which he'd picked up at the last Leipzig trade fair. The semi-annual fair was East Germany's showcase to the world and the Stasi did their bit to help too, by demonstrating their skills at attempting to recruit or entrap Western visitors of interest.

The EEC consultant story not only gave my family a reason for my travels elsewhere in East Germany but also an explanation as to why I seemed to be in official favour with the regime - why my aunt received her unusually frequent permissions to visit her sister in the West.

Despite knowing it was all a big lie, I was tempted to believe it myself. And to enjoy the fiction of having an honoured status within the country as opposed to being someone who'd been compelled to work for the Stasi under extreme duress. I began to understand how even seemingly simple graduations of favour, such as access to special supermarkets and even awards of bronze-coloured plastic plaques to Stasi colonels had their effect on people - the psychology of the prison camp, as I'd come to see it.

And cut off from normality, a surreal facsimile of a Western pluralist society it certainly was. My aunt was a secretary to an official of the trade union federation, logically a pointless anti-capitalist organisation where every firm of any size had a 'People-Owned Business' legal form.

In addition to the ruling Party, there were also other notionally independent political parties too. Copies of the ones in the West, right down to bearing similar names, such as 'CDU'. They even ran in national elections, returning deputies to the Volkskammer. For sure, they were only allowed to exist because they were permanent coalition with the Party, but the point had been proven, that East Germany was a democratic republic. And if the Communist Party hadn't been banned in West Germany, it would surely have been the people's choice there too.

A table had been set up in the scrabbly back yard of my uncle and aunt's ground-floor flat. My aunt was serving food from behind it when I arrived. I went around to greet her with a kiss, surprised once again at how similar she looked to my mother, her elder sister.

Out in the yard, I shook hands with my uncle, but as he was in the middle of speaking with their church pastor, who I'd ended up arguing with at my very first visit in spring 'sixty-nine, I quickly moved on. Instead, I found my cousins as they waited on the adults to finish being served first.

My younger fourteen year-old cousin, Thomas, was, for the want of a milder word, a delinquent, in East German terms at least. I asked him briefly about his studies, tried to encourage him to take them seriously. But he stood there in his gawky hormonal way, looking at me with jealousy as he asked what TV and radio stations I could get in Brussels and even more so when he asked about my car. The last time we met I'd let out that I had recently replaced my original Volkswagen with a Type Three - he obviously still couldn't get over the idea that I'd had two different cars since nineteen sixty-six.

My seventeen year-old cousin, Karin, was by contrast a shy, reserved girl, quiet like her father but sharing the same strong family resemblance with both her mother and mine.

Unlike Thomas, she greeted me warmly, her eyes animated as she laid her hand on my arm and said excitedly, 'Wait here a moment, Cousin Oskar.' After almost a quarter century of living alone in the West with my mother, I still enjoyed hearing myself being called 'cousin'.

She ran back inside and brought out an embroidered shoulder bag to show me, which she'd made herself. It was stitched with a flower pattern that looked suspiciously hippy-like, to my eyes, anyway.

'What do you think?'

Last year she'd told me that she wanted to design clothes one day, so I gave her some vague male encouragement.

'It's very pretty. Who's it for?'

She blushed a little, 'For me. But do you have a camera here cousin? Can you take a photograph to show Sophie in Brussels?'

That gave me a check. When we came for that first visit, Karin had been mesmerised by the window into the world of Western fashion which my companion on that first visit, Sophie von Barten, had given her. I hadn't realised the extent of her ongoing hold over Karin, though.

Then again, Sophie's strength of character drew almost everyone she met into her orbit and trapped them there, long after her own interest in them was gone. It was why the constellation of younger *fonctionnaires* who followed her around the EEC drinks reception circuit only grew larger every year.

'I'm sorry. My camera is back in Brussels. I didn't know you were in touch with her.'

'I'm not. I wrote to her at the EEC the other month, but I didn't get an answer. I hoped...'

I gave a slight frown.

'You could have written to me to make contact.' And I'd have done it for her, no matter what I now thought of Sophie.

She looked down at her feet, making circles with her right toe.

'I didn't want to bother you, cousin. I just wanted to ask her if her trouser suit that day she came was a copy of one worn by Jackie Onassis which I saw last month in a magazine, and if she had a pattern for it.'

I could have saved her the price of postage, for there was no way Sophie would have spent hours with a needle and thread. Not when she doubtless had accounts open with the leading boutiques of Paris and Milan.

'If I see her again, I'll be sure to ask for you.' She smiled at me gratefully, not realising Sophie and I had spent a year and more deliberately avoiding each other.

Our cover story had been that we were on a pre-nuptial visit to my relatives in the East. It was a selfish story devised by the people in Brussels which I'd felt obliged to go along with at the time. And it was stupid too, because it could only be used once unless Sophie really had been struck by Cupid's arrow. Which she hadn't, and definitely not after the return to Brussels.

My aunt had sincerely believed the story, though. She'd naturally wanted it to be true once she'd met Sophie for real, so I'd left it to my mother to tell her the truth afterwards. But whatever story had subsequently been given to my cousins, from the way Karin still referred to her idol on each of my visits, it sounded like they'd been told the 'engagement' had been broken off amicably.

My aunt finally finished serving and we ate as a family unit around one of the tables brought out into the yard for the guests. I'd have thought Karin could have helped serve with my aunt instead of one of the other women but maybe they couldn't see how she was turning into an adult herself. Sometimes, the less seen of certain people, the clearer one's perception of their true selves.

Following my first visit to Wismar, my aunt had gone in turn to Hamburg to see my mother twice within nine months, the only two times she'd seen her sister since the end of the war and the partition of Germany.

No-one had commented, but in a society sensitive to fine graduations of rank, I knew they sensed in their hearts that my aunt's travel privileges hadn't simply been given for me helping East German firms find export markets in the West. The unspoken implication was much darker.

That first time we had met had been a genuine family reunion, fairly unconstrained, even as we caught up on difficult parts of our shared family history. However, by my second visit at the end of 'sixty-nine, and certainly by my third in the spring of this year, the mood had subtly changed. With the exception of Thomas, they had become more careful and reserved when they spoke with me, and my uncle and aunt would now quietly wince when their son made his unguarded remarks.

This I had not anticipated when I first agreed to work for Johannes upon pain of my family being targeted for East Germany's special flavour of state persecution, *Zersetzung*. The supreme irony of my assistance to the Ministry was that by trying to protect them, I had brought the fear of the Stasi right into the very heart of their home.

With their greater age and experience, my uncle and aunt knew what could and could not safely be said in front of known members of the regime. But I was an outsider, in some ways even more innocent than Thomas of the required nuances in speech. Even worse than merely being a collaborator, I might be reporting back their conversations with a Westerner's naivety in a way which made them seem guilty of political crimes, even when they weren't. If Petzold could impute so much about the IRA from a short entry in Meyers Neues Lexikon, who knew what he'd be able to derive from their son's ramblings?

We had a too-short discussion about where Karin would study after high school. Her prospects were apparently good for getting into a vocational college for fashion design. One of the textile industry officials my aunt knew through the trade union federation had promised to sponsor her.

After having heard enough praise for his sister, Thomas took over the conversation with random, haphazard questions interjected to keep my attention. These soon moved from officious queries about Western pop music and rock - were East Germany's Klaus Renft Combo really as good as the Rolling Stones? - to an area that was obviously a bone of contention with his parents.

'Which part of your army did you serve in during compulsory military service?'

'Infantry.'

'What rifle did you use?'

'Heckler & Koch G3.'

'How's that different to the AK-47?'

'The G3 uses a blow-back operation and the AK-47 a gas-operated one.'

He nodded sagely so I continued, wanting to put him back into his box for his parents' sake. 'In the G3 the cartridge acts as a piston, driven backwards by the exhaust gases from the firing of the round. In the AK-47, the exhaust gases are siphoned off into a separate piston mechanism instead so as to eject the spent casing and work the action to load the next round.'

He was as nonplussed as I'd hoped he'd be. 'Which is better?'

I guessed his real question was a political one, but I wasn't going to be caught out that easily.

'They're both based on late-war German designs. The AK-47 was inspired by the Sturmgewehr 44.'

'Come Thomas, Cousin Oskar doesn't want to talk about stuff that's not important.'

'No, it's okay,' I said, trying to be a peacemaker. 'From which age do you do your service here?'

'From age eighteen, for a year and a half. But my parents want me to apply for service in an unarmed Construction Battalion.'

I raised my eyebrows.

My aunt replied patiently. 'We've been over this before, Thomas. We don't want you involved in any fighting if it can be helped.'

'I don't think you'll be missing out on anything, Thomas. I'd bet against there being any war. Only if the politicians are very stupid,' I said to back her up.

But the thunder clouds had already gathered on Thomas' face.

'It's not fair. My friends in the Free German Youth are all talking about going into the fighting units of the Volksarmee.'

Attempting to talk him down would be delicate, whichever side of the Wall he'd grown up on, but I owed it to my aunt to try. Especially after last year's deception with the story about Sophie and an engagement.

'How old are you, Thomas?'

'Fifteen next January.'

'It's hard for you to understand at this age but whatever you end up serving as, it will be over in a flash. Eighteen months seems a long time now but it's not really. Anyway, I spent more time cleaning and doing drill with my rifle than actually shooting it. The whole point of these huge armies in Europe is that they're not meant to be used.'

I paused. At least Thomas was now listening.

'In fact, the year before I joined, the intake who

preceded mine were set to work for weeks building sandbag dams to keep back the worst of the North Sea floods from Hamburg. They were infantry too, but still ended up doing the job of pioneers anyway.'

He didn't look especially persuaded at my attempts to show that all conscripts, in whatever branch of the army, would end up equally bored so I changed tack again.

'When I left the army, I joined the police in Hamburg for a couple of years. That's a fine career, keeping society safe and free from subversion. You should look forward to what you'll be doing after conscription.'

He screwed up his nose a little at this. I regathered my thoughts for a last attempt to bring him back onto an even keel.

'And my life in the West isn't as great as you might think it is. Sure, I had different things growing up to what you have here, but I didn't have a father or a sister. I was quite alone with my mother. We often wished we could come here and see you.'

The latter was a dubious stretching of the truth. The thought had scarcely occurred to me as a child. The East had seemed as distant and alien as the Moon.

'Do you understand what your cousin is saying to you?' asked my aunt. He grunted noncommittally. He wasn't going to back down, in public at least. My uncle now spoke up for the final word, a rare occurrence for him.

'I saw a man during the war once, burnt all over. It's not a game.'

I wondered where that had been, but then everyone of his age at some point had seen something they were unlikely to forget.

My aunt stood up to fetch dessert from the kitchen and start serving. My uncle brought over their pastor to our table - he had apparently asked to speak with me earlier.

I stood up and we shook hands.

'It is Oskar, isn't it? Hilde put on a barbeque for you

last year and you came with your girlfriend. Or was it fiancée?'

I couldn't remember how I'd introduced Sophie to him back then, so I just nodded along. In any case, I assumed his question was only a preamble to the resumption of our somewhat fraught conversation from a year ago.

I indicated to him that we should go inside away from everyone else in the yard. There was a chance we'd end up in an argument in front of my aunt's guests, which might lead her neighbours to start asking careful questions, undoing all of Johannes' good work in collecting business cards for me.

The danger with this pastor was that despite his mild exterior, he would fix you with his eyes, pinning you to where you stood, seemingly looking right into the very depths of your soul. So before he got going on me, I preemptively asked him about his church congregation and what the construction battalions were and why Thomas was so opposed to being sent there - because the best form of defence was attack.

'What are these *Bausoldaten* which my cousin is bitter about being made to join in three years' time?'

His eyes widened with excitement. 'It was a real change in the regime's attitude that came about through the church. About five years ago, the Leipzig theologian, Professor Fuchs, persuaded the leadership of the Party to allow conscientious objectors to serve as non-combatants in the army.'

I frowned, somewhat troubled. Like seeing Petzold's wavering shadow before Johannes' office door, I felt I was glimpsing the uncertain outline of something through frosted glass. I was prepared to accept that there were well-meaning people in the East, that most, if not all of them wanted peace, and that helping their government understand the intentions of the West was no bad thing. But I wasn't prepared to accept that the regime itself had any inherent virtue. Even though allowing conscientious objectors to opt out of the struggle of our times didn't sit easily with the evil image of the Democratic Republic in the West. The USSR as a repressive force, though, no question. Look at Czechoslovakia a couple of years ago.

I shifted from foot to foot. Maybe the regime had simply decided to take the path of least resistance in response to the church's request and cheaply buy off a few dissenting voices. It seemed to have worked from the enthusiastic reaction of this minister, anyway.

'So you see Oskar, God can use the weak things of this world, even a ninety year-old academic, to shame the strong.'

I frowned again, that was the problem with totalitarian systems. They had absolute control almost all of the time. But one day, the most unlikely events might start a crack in the foundations, eventually bringing the whole edifice down with a crash. Just look at Tsarist Russia, fifty-odd years ago.

I wondered if the supranationalists back in Brussels had thought things through properly.

The pastor was a Westerner like me and still spoke with an accent, but he had chosen to come East to the parish in Wismar, or been 'called' as he would have put it. Presumably, turning down a comfortable church career in the West for a poor congregation in the East made him one of the 'weak' too and maybe in his own eyes, spiritually dangerous to the regime.

I felt some disgust at myself for the thought which passed quickly through my head, that I was perfectly placed to get him into trouble with my people at the Normannenstrasse should he push me too far with his preaching.

As if in response to that silent thought, he narrowed his eyes and fearlessly went into combat, regardless of the consequences.

'Do you remember what we spoke about last time, Oskar?'

I did. He'd told me that I couldn't take life for granted and needed to ask for God's forgiveness for my sins. And then I was framed and arrested later the same day, so part of me blamed him for jinxing me with his prophecy.

'Are you content with your life now?'

I stared back at him in silence, angry that he was doing it again.

'What do you know of my life?' I retorted after a few seconds.

He looked a little hurt, as I'd intended him to be.

'I can tell you're troubled. I suspect you know full well whatever the root problem is, but are avoiding the one Person who can actually help you.'

I was frozen into silence, as if from up high I looked down on the pair of us, desperately hoping that no-one else was watching or listening from the next room.

'So Oskar, where do you stand with God?'

'Not well,' I croaked.

'He asks very little of us and at the same time, so much. It says in Romans, "If you confess with your mouth that Jesus is Lord and believe in your heart that God raised Him from the dead, you will be saved." Remember that, Oskar. Whatever situation you've found yourself in, God can help you.'

'He can't. Not me.'

The pastor shook his head.

'No matter how desperate things are, when there seems no way out, you just need to call on Him.'

That really was all I could take for now. But before I could find my full voice again and break his hold over me, a sliver of hope escaped my defences and lodged in my heart.

I looked quickly around the room for an escape of my own and caught sight of the time by the wall clock. With relief, I hastily made my apologies for it was already time to go. I'd only planned to make a passing visit anyway because there was someone I had to meet on Sunday before seeing Masson at work on Monday.

I went to find my family, and we gathered outside the front door for our farewells.

'Goodbye once more, Aunt Hilde. Perhaps I'll see you when you next come to Hamburg?'

'It won't be long now. I have papers for the beginning of September. Say hello to your mother for me when you see her.'

I shook hands with my uncle, kissed Karin to her embarrassment and took Thomas' hand in my grip.

'Be good, young man. Next time I'll bring over my car and we'll go and shoot air rifle in the woods.'

I picked up my bags and wondered how I would find them all when I saw them next.

Chapter Four

I had arranged to meet my true EEC boss Kramer on the Sunday following my return, as I did a day or two after all my trips to the East. I called him in the morning to confirm, and mid-afternoon I presented myself at the door of his apartment overlooking the manicured lawns of the Place du Petit Sablon. The square was a couple of streets back from the Avenue Louise, the wide thoroughfare running from near the royal palaces down to the leafy diplomatic quarter around the Abbaye de la Cambre.

I met Kramer after every trip because through him, in addition to the Stasi, I also worked indirectly for the French intelligence service, the SDECE. It was only one of several reasons why I wished I could turn back the clock to before March nineteen sixty-nine.

That spring, arriving in Brussels off the train from Rostock where I'd just been forced to agree to become an informant for the Ministry, I'd been presented with a dilemma.

As a West German citizen, I could confess my situation immediately to my own country's intelligence service, the BND, because I had a better chance of avoiding prosecution for treason if they found me out at the start of my Stasi career than in five or ten years' time. Against that, the BND had a terrible reputation for being infiltrated by the Stasi's HVA. I didn't even want to think about the implications for my family if it got back to the Ministry that I'd changed sides again.

On the other hand, via Kramer's unofficial links to the

69

SDECE, I could suggest I became their double agent to secretly work against the Stasi and use French sponsorship to claim exemption from any future West German government investigation. I'd just have to hope that the SDECE's counterintelligence efforts were better than those of the BND.

I'd chosen the French as my least worst option at the time but now I wasn't so sure that there'd been that much in it. I wished I'd known back then that Hitchcock was about to release a movie with an apparently all-too-true depiction of how deeply the KGB had penetrated the SDECE at the start of the sixties. Unfortunately for me, *Topaz* only came out in Brussels at the start of this year. Although I'd had a general suspicion about the reliability of the SDECE a year ago, given its parallels with the BND as another second-tier agency, I had no idea quite how bad things had been.

But without me fully realising it at the time, the unreliability of all the Western agencies had been a powerful incentive for Kramer to buy the idea of sponsoring me.

For if you were to create a new, secret department in Brussels, supposedly tasked with working across the Six and beyond to search out the secrets of those individuals, organisations and states who posed a threat to the EEC project, it would be a prime target for penetration by spies from both sides of the Wall - once they'd found out about it.

By putting me in External Investigations, he started the department off in life, already knowing where the Stasi mole was and trusting that the Ministry itself would keep out interlopers from the KGB or their other socialist rivals. And because the mole had been turned, he got to hear what the other side were thinking and saying about the EEC as well.

To my own annoyance, a team of international jet-setting confidential agents wasn't how Kramer had launched External Investigations. Of course, Kramer was working to his own schedule as regards to how fast the department spread its wings, though for now he was keeping his plans private, even from me.

Kramer himself also continued to be an object of puzzlement to me. Johannes, the revolutionary sailor turned policeman I understood. Fiedler the communist aristocrat I understood to a degree. With Kramer, I saw the man. I heard him speak. I watched how he behaved in front of others. But he continued to keep some indefinable part of himself hidden from sight.

His story before arriving in Brussels in nineteen fifty-eight was way more dramatic than the role of boring Berlaymont bureaucrat he had played afterwards and continued to play. He had worked for de Gaulle throughout the war and kept the faith during the President's wilderness years, anticipating his eventual return to office, also in 'fifty-eight. Kramer's last job before the EEC was as a kind of colonial administrator of the Saarland, the border region of western Germany within the post-war French Occupation Zone. The French had run it as a protectorate hoping, unsuccessfully as it turned out, to make the carve-out permanent. They had even gone so far as to create a separate Saarland 'national' team for the 'fifty-two Olympics. Political subterfuge was no stranger to Kramer, and External Investigations was going to be one of his masterpieces.

Even after all his years in Brussels, I knew he was still at heart a French nationalist and opposed to the supranational ideal of the Project. At the same time, as I'd suggested to Fiedler, the temptation for French officials to take full control of the Commission's ever-increasing powers and use these for the aggrandisement of France was a powerful one - even if those same supranational powers in the long term spelled the end of France as an independent entity. That was because the EEC was shaping up to be a political snowball, one which once it started rolling down the hill, picking up national competences on every turn, would be very hard to redirect indeed.

Nevertheless, if anyone could pull off the next big game of double-bluff in post war Franco-German relations, Kramer might well be the man to do it.

Unlike a year ago, he was now only one of the most senior French employees of the Commission. Because just like the Stasi, the organisation kept on growing and growing. But his generally mild manner and unassuming appearance disguised the danger to his rivals. He was neither tall, with an overbearing demeanour of a de Gaulle, nor short with a Napoleon's aggression. He was neither overweight from the long lunches and rich dinners of the power-broker, nor thin through the overwork of the fanatical believer in the Project. Often the deadliest predators were those who looked nothing of the sort.

On top of that, just like Napoleon's favourite generals, he had the quality of being lucky in war.

Sometimes he won his political contests in a straight fight, but at other times the cards simply fell the right way for him. Kramer had given everyone the impression that he'd sponsored the creation of our department as a reaction to the fallout from my trip to the East and the realisation that the EEC needed a proper international investigative capability.

Such a move was going to be on the cards for the Community at some point, for Kramer wasn't its only visionary *fonctionnaire*. But while everyone else thought he'd merely turned a tactical setback into an opportunity to lead the first move in that direction, pre-empting his rivals, I knew differently.

For the notional external investigations role was merely an excuse for the department to be given a secret status. Its ultimate purpose was to make real the suggestion I had made to Kramer last year, that he needed his own loyal team of watchers inside the EEC to spy on his internal rivals who were seeking control of those levers of power at the Commission.

Fiedler had talked about *maskirovka* but Kramer also knew about deception plans. That was why the new department was called 'Internal Affairs (External Investigations)', the name chosen as a cover for a supposed external intelligence agency which, in turn, was a future disguise for an eventual internal secret police force.

And then there was Masson. Poor Masson, in a way. Like the bureaucrats who'd approved Kramer's budget request, he too thought he knew what was going on. He thought he was setting up an embryonic external intelligence agency, one which valued secrecy over ambition. In this job he was simply hoping to spend three or four unchallenging years basking in the attention of the select group of bureaucrats who knew of our existence while lining up his next EEC job. Little did he know that anything he might achieve would merely be used as camouflage by the next department director.

For when Masson moved on, although Kramer definitely hadn't promised it in any way, I was confident he would make sure that I would be Masson's successor - in the interests of sharing EEC jobs fairly between France and Germany, of course.

That was the point, I guessed, when Kramer would expand the department's external remit to include an internal one which would be much more sinister. He would be able to do it because no-one here, especially Masson, knew I was Kramer's man for life. As a young working-class German with no history of moving in the same social or academic circles as he did, I wouldn't trigger any of the warning indicators carefully watched by his bureaucrat rivals. Kramer would catch them all by surprise.

Once you were inside, his apartment looked every one of its four hundred square metres spread over two floors. Because when the game was played at the Kramers' level, it required both of them to put on a serious show.

He invited me through to the open-plan lounge, down into the sunken seating area and poured me a glass of red wine. In a nineteenth-century building, I always wondered what butchery had been done to the room underneath to install that feature.

'We have the place to ourselves this afternoon. My wife is out with friends for gossip and cocktails down the street at the Hilton.'

Of the two of them, Madame Kramer would probably be having the more important meeting in terms of acquiring immediately useful intelligence.

I sank deep into a sofa which was new since the last time I'd been here - pink-beige and sickly horrible, covered with a supposedly artful arrangement of orange macramé throws. The whole ensemble had probably cost a fortune, for little true style. My shoes half-disappeared into the shag pile carpet underneath.

'She likes to redecorate, and often,' he explained.

I cleared my throat and began. 'This time was the big one. As you know, I've met with them a few times in the East and in Brussels over the last year but never had much to offer them, again, as you already know.'

'But this time?' He took a sniff from his glass as he savoured the moment.

'But this time they called me in for a full day's briefing in Berlin, at Stasi headquarters.'

At this, Kramer raised his eyebrows, to my satisfaction.

'They've eventually worked out that my External Investigations job means I ought to be able to search out information in certain Western organisations, which they have no other easy access to. They now want me to persuade Masson to allow me to probe the intelligence services of Ireland, of all places.'

'Eh? Oh, I see. Up to mischief are they, in Northern Ireland?'

'Not yet. They simply - so they say - want me to find

out which faction of the IRA is currently being backed by the Irish government and their security organs, as the East Germans call them. Then they want me to find out who they can usefully subvert within the Irish establishment.' I played back the abridged version of their demand.

'All that? What's suddenly bitten them over Ireland?'

'The Irish have just arrested their own intelligence officer for arms trafficking to the IRA. And it's distressing the East Germans - the idea of the public arrest, not the terrorism. Apparently, the head of the HVA is attending some kind of conference in Moscow in a few weeks' time and he's asked directly for an explanation for what's going on. I expect, like us, they all like to bring some new, exotic piece of information to meetings with their bosses.'

I had learned over the months how to dissimulate in front of Kramer at these initial debriefings. Plain common sense told me not to give him everything at once.

'Markus Wolf himself, eh? Did you know that no-one in the West has seen him, or at least, the Western agencies have no photograph of him?'

'No. How did he manage that?'

'Take your pick. By being very careful about telling people he meets who he is? By never travelling to the West? Because the Western agents of his who do know him by sight are extremely well-chosen and loyal to the regime?'

If Fiedler really was Wolf, then I'd hit pay dirt and unearthed a nugget of genuine intelligence gold to be spent when I really needed it. And not just his identity but his musings on the prospects for East Germany's long-term independence too. I needed to quickly lean on one of my contacts at the Hamburg police and get an artist's impression drawn of the former Stalinist I'd met in Berlin, whoever he was, whilst his face was still fresh in my mind.

Kramer placed his wine down on the table between us and topped up both our glasses.

'And they want you to get Masson to let you go to

Ireland on some pretext?'

'Yes, I tried to tell them that working outside the Six would be something we'd never previously done.'

'Hmm. External Investigations is only meant to remain in being, not to actually be used for any serious assignments. Not yet, anyway. But Masson is getting frustrated. He wants a noticeable success of some kind to help him move onto his next job.'

Kramer ran his free hand through his thinning hair, then rubbed his chin.

'Anything else they wanted you to do?'

'They suggested I go and visit Otto Skorzeny to get some names of Irish Army intelligence officers, reasoning he must have had contact with them during the years he was in Ireland, attempting to establish his residency there.'

Kramer choked noisily on the mouthful of wine he'd been swallowing.

'For real? Otto Skorzeny? As a plan, that part seems to be too complicated for its own good. It's hardly discreet, either. Not what I'd expect of them.' He shook his head and flashed me a narrow look.

'It's because they realised too, that an agency which isn't meant to exist can't just turn up at the Irish Defence Ministry and demand to see their confidential agents by name. Skorzeny was their suggestion for a cover story.'

Nothing in that statement was false.

'Oh, I see. They were expecting French intelligence to provide those names?'

He pulled a face and slowly tilted his head from side to side, turning the idea over. Then came the Gallic shrug.

'Why not, I suppose? However, before we all get too carried away, I still need to decide whether this is the job that I let Masson show his mettle on. If not, you'll have to say "no" to the Stasi,' he said, but not convincingly.

'But wouldn't the SDECE like to know the same things about Ireland as them?'

He frowned at me sharply. 'Why?'

'Because the SDECE are an intelligence agency too. And they also like to collect information, whether it's of any immediate use or not.'

'Maybe. I may make some discreet enquiries tomorrow.'

'Think of this: the Stasi want to use the EEC as their cover for this investigation, but the SDECE could use the Stasi themselves to blame someone if it all came out into the open.'

He snorted at this. 'What a carousel. Still, there's a reason why you might be onto something.'

'How come?'

He gave a secret half-smile and swirled the wine in his glass.

'Very well, don't articulate the implications of this too widely, even though the events in question are no longer a secret. The SDECE is meant to be taking a new direction, now that De Gaulle has retired and the organisation is getting a new boss sometime this year.'

'I was in France the night de Gaulle resigned.'

'So was I, but listen. The Irish on both sides of the border are lucky he retired when he did. Straight after he stepped down and just before it all started in Northern Ireland, he went to the far south-west of Ireland, telling everyone he'd struggled for national liberation too, just like their own revolutionary heroes. In his old age he's become fascinated by the story of his Irish ancestors. But the Irish are lucky because throughout the nineteen sixties, one of de Gaulle's pet projects was the subversion of Canada.'

'Really?'

'Yes. The SDECE supplied funds to the Quebec separatist movement and probably other assistance too which I'm not going to speculate about out loud. Pierre Trudeau, their Prime Minister, expelled a number of our agents, traitor to his ancestral homeland that he is. In fact, the Canadian federal authorities eventually started to treat our embassy with the same suspicion as the Soviet one.'

Probably with good reason, I thought.

'Did your assistance extend to, what were they called again, the Front de Libération du Québec?'

'I've told you all I'm going to, or need to.'

And he had, because why wouldn't the more enthusiastic elements of the SDECE have held back from arming that confused collection of sometime-nationalist and sometime-Marxist terror groups which had evolved into the Front de Libération?

'What did Canada do to deserve de Gaulle's anger?'

'You didn't know him like I did when he was in power. Once a certain idea had taken hold in his head, he would become obsessed with it.'

And Kramer really did know. He'd been with de Gaulle right from his first day of exile. He'd told me himself that he'd simply been lucky to have been in the right place at the right time. When de Gaulle fled to London from the wreck of the capitulation in June nineteen forty, Kramer was already in England, a junior on the French diplomatic staff at the embassy who had ended up with more than a ringside seat during what came next.

'I think it's because he was dependent on the British that he came to hate them. And he came to hate the Canadians more. In his eyes, they were a kind of Anglo-American mongrel state, ruling over a region which he saw as historically and rightfully French.'

'So how is all this relevant now?'

'Because when France's interests are at stake, it acts with determination.'

'Against the Canadian threat?'

'That was just an example of what we do to our opponents. If the IRA are going to keep causing trouble for the British, we might be interested in helping them.'

'Pardon?'

He continued brazenly, 'Tell me this, the Common Agricultural Policy is going to be funded from what in the future?'

Now I shrugged my shoulders, nonplussed at the change of direction. 'Increased levies from the member states, I presume?'

'Yes, but which levies exactly? You don't know, do you? It's in the Luxembourg Treaty signed earlier this year. By nineteen seventy-five, all customs tariffs on goods coming into the Common Market and all other special import levies on agricultural products, currently collected by the member states today, will instead be paid over to the EEC.'

'Sorry, you're losing me.'

'Keep up, Lenkeit. The EEC needs these so-called "own resources" to maintain the Community budget. And furthermore, needs the Six to become Ten. Otherwise we can't carry on funding the CAP to provide the level of production subsidies which our farmers have become accustomed to, because the costs of the system have completely run out of control.'

Kramer showed no remorse at this sorry state of affairs. He leaned forward confidentially over the bottle, waving his glass at me to emphasise his points.

'But thankfully, Great Britain and Norway are net importers of food, and Ireland and Denmark in certain categories too. Because of the customs tariff wall they will be discouraged in future from importing their beef from Argentina and grain from Australia and will buy it instead from France. And if they do import agricultural produce, under the Luxembourg Treaty, the customs tariffs charged on the food bought by their consumers will go to fund the CAP subsidies paid to our farmers. Either way, we can't lose.'

'So France might want to stir up trouble for England to make sure they somehow feel the need to join the EEC? It doesn't sound particularly plausible.'

'You need to understand why their political class want to join. They regret their loss of influence as a former world power and want to claw some of that back by gaining a new imperial role at the EEC. Although Edward Heath is already utterly devoted to the idea that England should join the Community, why leave anything to chance or to one man, even if we know he only has to push at an open door? Humiliation in Northern Ireland won't make him feel any more confident about Britain's importance relative to France.'

He smiled smugly at this prospect, true Gaullist that he was.

'As for the Irish, they're desperate to join the EEC too, but in their case, it's to receive a level of subsidies they couldn't otherwise afford to pay their farmers. They're also terrified that those same farmers will find themselves on the wrong side of the tariff wall from their traditional British market if the English join and Ireland somehow fails to be accepted by the Six. Anything we ask from the Irish they'll give us. They're not the problem in the accession negotiations.'

With a triumphant wave of his wine glass at the checkmate of the Irish he knocked over the bottle. Red wine glugged out over the table and dripped onto the shag-pile.

'*Merde, Merde.*' He stood the bottle back upright and searched around for something to mop up with, giving the macramé knitwear a nasty look as he did so. I wiped up the spill as best I could with my own handkerchief. If the throws had escaped, the carpet hadn't.

'Leave it Lenkeit,' he said frostily. 'Back to what I was saying. Conflict in Northern Ireland gives the British another reason to join the EEC so they can keep up the pressure on the Irish as a fellow member state to help contain the violence.'

I still wasn't very sure. The French sometimes gave the impression of over-thinking things, no matter that Kramer said the same about the East Germans, and their idea of using an unwitting Otto Skorzeny in a deception plan to trick the Irish.

'Besides all that, once the British join, we might want to make sure Northern Ireland stays as a kind of grey and rainy Vietnam, and stop their running sore from healing too quickly. It would be good to take British minds off their contributions to CAP funding in the first few years after they join. Especially when those increase from what they think they're signing up to.'

Even the East Germans weren't intending to pour petrol on the fire in Ireland. Not yet, anyway, as far as I knew.

'So you think you'll get support from Paris? Maybe get some names in the Irish intelligence services from them which I can use?'

'My wife's fiftieth birthday falls tomorrow. I know it's a Monday, but we're having a drinks party here at eight. Flowers, no gifts please.'

I glanced at the red stain, which had spread deep into the thick carpet.

'Don't worry, she'll have had it changed. Or she'll have bought something to cover it up with by then. She'll see it as a fashion opportunity I expect… I hope. Come along tomorrow and we'll talk again during the evening. Oh and by the way, everyone will be there.'

'How do you mean?'

'Sophie von Barten and a few of her crew.'

I caught my breath as bitterness rising to loathing flared up inside me. A few sparks of my old obsession ignited too, but I tried not to notice them. I supposed meeting her again couldn't be put off forever, though. It would be the final test of whether last year's events could be left behind us - or behind me, at least.

Chapter Five

Masson was a young, energetic thirty-something, a true believer in the European project, intoxicated with the dream of a second Rome. He was also a man in a hurry, but in a controlled, disciplined way.

Germans were naturally cautious these days about empire-builders and my wariness about where the EEC was headed was only increased when I saw the professional dedication of its acolytes. The organisation seemed to have been skimming off the best graduates from the top universities and higher administration schools of Europe for some time.

Johannes was a cog in a large, well-oiled machine; an efficient and competent cog as far as I understood their organisation. But Masson had been required to go further and build the machine whilst he operated it. He did so, solving with seeming ease, the equation combining Kramer's demands, his own career ambitions and what he himself thought was best in the Commission's own long-term interests.

Masson had taken the remit Kramer had agreed with the other sponsors - to create a department supporting EEC officials working externally with non-member states on everything from trade negotiations to co-operation in atomic energy. He stretched the definition of 'support' as far as he felt he could. Our sales pitch to our internal customers, so to speak, was that we would help give them an edge through Brussels-based research and intelligence gathering of all kinds, on their counterparts. Masson had

had some success during the fifteen months the department had been operational, if not quite as much or as dramatic as he'd hoped.

Earlier in the year, through Kramer, we'd been approached by a Hungarian émigré who'd fled to Brussels after the Uprising in 'fifty-six, well-connected in their community here. Presumably in a spirit of revenge as well as European civic-mindedness, he'd fingered a crooked trade official at his country's embassy, who was taking part in the EEC-Hungary wine talks.

At that point in the negotiations, just when our people needed to exert pressure, a discreet word had been had in the ear of the head of the Hungarian delegation.

But this was no high stakes game of Cold War nuclear diplomacy. The wine agreement was only one of a series of agricultural deals with Hungary, intended to cover pork and cheese too, which had been under discussion since 'sixty-eight. Such was life in a trade organisation. It was no wonder Masson wanted to get on to the nation-building phase as soon as possible.

Still, the main lesson I took from the episode right now, ahead of any trip to Ireland, was that the gossip which exposed the Hungarian advisor was a warning of how difficult it was to keep secrets in a small national community.

The other lesson I'd realised at the time, was that if Masson's ambition got the better of his prudence, he might be tempted to take us beyond conducting mere research on corrupt rival negotiators and offer us up as the middlemen to arrange any bribes deemed necessary to pay off the other side.

However, our little department wasn't ready to take on assignments with a serious level of political risk yet, and certainly none which were truly serious such as spying on the Americans whenever the next GATT round was due to take place. For that we would need to harness the member states' national intelligence agencies to work on our behalf for the EEC. At some point my name was going to become known to the BND, whether I liked it or not.

Apart from the Hungarian lucky break, our raw information currently came from the usual sources, gossip by people at the embassies of the Six, freelance investigative journalists and foreign correspondents with the national press of the member states. It involved working the EEC social function circuit, something at which I had got vastly better at since last year. Pretending that I was still at Internal Affairs full-time was a story which came naturally, and I could tell it smoothly at any point in the evening, even if I was approaching Johannes' level of alcohol consumption. The story even had a modicum of truth to it - as our camouflage, our department was still nominally part of the same directorate as Internal Affairs and we as individuals were all officially on secondment from that department.

We didn't have any technical means of intelligence gathering, such as planting bugs or intercepting communications. But as every good intelligence agency should, we too had a counter-espionage division - a part-time division of one, consisting of the beanpole-like Willem.

The Dutchman was cut from the same cloth as Masson and Sophie von Barten, a graduate of the College of Europe and definitely of the supranational tendency. I guessed it was the College which indoctrinated them against Kramer's heresy of intergovernmentalism, his belief that the essential levers of power should remain at the national level. De Gaulle's intent, of course, had been to keep them there so that France could work the EEC in its own interests, which was exactly why Monnet and the other founders hated the idea.

Willem's task of investigating our own people could justifiably have gone to me because of my previous employment in Internal Affairs proper. Although one part of me had wanted that job, because spying on EEC staff was, after all, the actual secret long-term mission of the department, Kramer wasn't taking any risks and hadn't intervened there with Masson. Presumably, there was no rush and he was happy for me to keep a low profile for now.

And in any case, given the sensitivity of creating files on the top levels of officialdom in the Commission, letting a Dutchman do it as opposed to someone from the leading countries seemed safer. He spent his time trying to divine if senior staff were working on the side for countries outside the Six, by looking at a combination of political affiliations, personal income levels and networks of known associates. When all was said and done, rather him than me, if I was being honest.

For Masson, the accession of the Four was coming at just the right point to boost his career to the next level. Whilst it was certainly going to provide Willem and I with plenty of work during the next two or three years, for our boss it meant plenty of opportunities to shine, neatly filling up the rest of his expected time in post as department leader.

The enforced slow pace of activity during the first fifteen months, when we were almost dormant at times, had been deathly boring. I was generally frustrated with life anyway and it only dragged me down further. I sensed it was hard on Masson too. However, since the new accession applications on the last day of June, he had been firing on all cylinders. He was now actively planning for our secret background participation in the talks to be held in Brussels, and determined not to lose any more time from his planned schedule for promotion.

To fill up the gaps during our week, six months ago, Masson had started us retyping Interpol reports and combining these with the national most-wanted lists of the member states. From these unpromising ingredients we confected a monthly digest of crime news which he called a 'security briefing'. This he circulated privately to a select distribution list of chiefs-of-staff and deputy directors whom he wanted to impress for his next job, hoping they wouldn't forget him, tucked away at the back of the Charlemagne building.

Today, as on every Monday morning, he came out to join Willem and I in our shared outer office, perched himself on the conference table and conducted what he called 'morning prayers' in English, just as I'd told Johannes and his boss back in Berlin.

'Good morning, gentlemen. What were you both doing a year ago today when the Americans were colonising the Moon?'

He liked dropping in rhetorical questions about America to his little speeches. He probably thought they inspired us to greater things for Greater Europe.

'Whatever it was, forget it now. Tomorrow, as you already know, is the first working session of the accession talks - a bilateral ministerial meeting with the British to discuss protocol for the negotiations.'

Talks about talks, how typical of the diplomacy game.

'Officially, I've been asked to act as an observer during the early sessions in case any questions on security cooperation come up. Unofficially, of course, we'll be noting with care which delegates are actually sent to Brussels and then we'll have to decide who we should invest time digging for dirt on.' He liked to use the word 'we' a lot, even when it often only meant 'Masson'.

As he spoke, I thought of the bachelor Heath - to have no known lady friends was like waving a red flag to attract the attention of the smearers and insinuators. Which was why it was too obvious a route to bring pressure on him. Not that the EEC needed to, by Kramer's reckoning. Perhaps we'd end up working things from the opposite direction, covering up anything that might hurt him.

'Willem, I want you to especially focus on the Danes and Norwegians. And you, Oskar, on the English and also the Irish who aren't due in town before September.'

The division of labour was convenient for me but hardly a coincidence. After all, it wasn't Holland which had occupied those first two countries thirty years ago in April.

There and then I was tempted to bring up the idea of us going to our target countries to find out more but thought I'd have more success if I left it for Kramer to propose.

But if this wasn't the right moment to bring up a trip, I could perhaps get ready for one. For if I was going to go to Ireland, I needed something to take with me.

'Do the talks mean that this month's security briefing is given lower priority?' I asked. 'It's my turn to create it.' Masson didn't get his hands dirty doing any actual day-to-day paperwork, apart from approving our expenses.

'Perhaps we could show it to the delegates as an example of the benefits of membership?' I prompted.

He looked askance at the shallowness of the suggestion.

'You know that's not why we do it. It's to remind people here, from whom we need ongoing sponsorship, that we're a source of intelligence they can turn to.'

'Yes but what if we were to expand it to cover more topics? Ones which are specific to the EEC instead of general crime reports into terror attacks and bank robberies?'

'Such as?'

The idea had come to me just after leaving Kramer's apartment yesterday. There was one aspect of EEC membership which the Irish cared for, above all else, about which they would surely be interested in knowing as much as they could.

'Difficulties in implementing the Common Agricultural Policy and how different national authorities have overcome them.'

'Difficulties? Come Oskar, no bureaucrat-speak amongst us here.'

'You know, give our readers information on fraudulent grant applications, false reporting of subsidy payments, known production scams. Some of these things must take place across borders. Dress it up as I described it, though, as an intelligence briefing.'

'And do you know anything about these things?'

I didn't, but I had a sinking feeling about who it was I might end up being directed to ask.

The first floor of the Kramers' apartment had been transformed for the evening with foil streamers and silver balloons. A jazz quartet softly tootled away in the corner of the lounge to add to the party ambiance. My name was checked off a list at the door and I left my flowers and card next to a growing mountain of blooms on a table by the side.

I'd prepared carefully, all the time telling myself it wasn't for Sophie von Barten's benefit - the shape of my bowtie, the choice of bouquet, my shoes polished until they were mirrors, even the same sandalwood scent as favoured by Masson.

It was the first time I'd been to one of the Kramers' private functions and I was curious to see what Madame Kramer would be like at her own party as opposed to the Bastille Day reception at the French embassy when I'd last seen her a week ago.

The very first time I met her, I'd expected to see someone polished and effortlessly elegant in the way people assumed was the case for all French women of her class. But with Madame Kramer there was a surprising crudeness and abruptness to her speech which jarred with the fashionable exterior, and to my mind, jarred with Kramer's character himself. Either opposites attracted, or Kramer's wife had been changed by the years they'd spent together. Her behaviour was the other side of the balance sheet of Kramer's success, the cost of soaking up the pressure of the constant battle to thrive and survive in the world of high international relations.

I saw her, standing now at the edge of the conversation pit with two friends of a similar age, one on either side of her, champagne flute lightly held in one hand, cigarette holder in the other.

I went over, intending to greet her in the French fashion, but instead of an air kiss I got the same nasty look Kramer had given the macramé yesterday.

'So you're the *maladroit* who cost me three thousand French francs? Don't they teach you how to hold a wine glass, wherever it is you're from?' she said acidly.

Her friends tittered out loud, but one of them was giving me a secret look as she listened to my admonishment, which I didn't feel comfortable with at all.

'*Mille pardons*, Madame.' I didn't bow my head, because the Great War had finished fifty years ago, but I now knew why people used to do so, when speaking to the social class above them.

Just then something prompted me to gaze past her, across the sunken seating area. To my shock, despite Kramer's warning yesterday, I suddenly saw Sophie, large as life, holding forth to a couple of officials with Rizzo by her side on the other side of the room.

To my eyes at least, she still looked as stunning as the very first evening I'd met her at another social gathering of EEC *fonctionnaires* last year. She was wearing a long, pleated dress that, in my mind, would have looked frumpy on anyone else not carrying themselves with her self-assurance. I thought that Karin might have agreed with me, too.

With a murmured excuse I stepped around Madame Kramer's group, down across the new Persian rug and up the other side, sensing a pair of eyes on my back as I went.

As if magnetised, I filtered through the other guests, drawing near to the little knot of people around Sophie, my better judgement fighting against my suddenly aching hunger to hear her voice once again.

She turned, caught sight of me and immediately tunnelled deep into my eyes, the anger fizzing off her like so many little bolts of lightning. The faithful Rizzo, informal leader of her band of male admirers, caught a sense of the strength of her feelings too. He hastily turned his back on both of us, giving his full attention to the people whom Sophie had just been speaking with, shielding her from their gaze.

I walked up to her, gripping the stem of my wine glass as if to snap it, and stopped a metre away. I nodded, moistened my lips and asked her in German how she had been. The anger in her eyes subsided slightly, retreating for the moment behind a wall of impassivity as she answered coldly.

'Much better, all things considering. I've been promoted and now run the export desk for oils and animal fats at Agriculture.' She stopped and deliberately allowed the silence to open up to show she was in control of the conversation. I knew the power game for what it was, but replied anyway.

'Well done. It's no less than I would have expected.'

I only meant the second part of what I'd just said.

She wasn't so strong as to be able to resist flattery, that even older conversational trick.

'If my department successfully negotiates this year's package of market subsidies, I expect I'll be moved up and onto grains.'

No hanging around doing make-work for her then, and she was only a few months younger than me. But that was it from her, a terse reminder to me of how far out of her league I was in professional terms, let alone all the rest. Thankfully for me, that was all she'd brought up after a year of silence, but her brusqueness still hurt.

Well, enough of this, she wasn't getting away with her offhandedness so easily. Not now that I knew a little better where I stood with her. And anyway, putting all personal animosities aside, if she really was a hotshot in agriculture,

I might as well go to her as anyone else for information on CAP fraud. I tapped Rizzo on the shoulder and switched back to French.

'Hello Rizzo, *ça va?*'

He turned around, somewhat nervously.

'Hello, sorry, what was your name again? We met last year, but I can't remember.'

'Lenkeit, or just "Oskar."'

'That's right. And you went on a trip with Sophie to visit some relatives in East Germany?'

'Yes, I took her to see most of my family, as it turned out.'

A ghost of a smile flickered over his amiable face. I'd spoken with him alone only for a couple of minutes last year, at that same function where I'd met Sophie for the first time, placed next to her at dinner. Of all her circle though, I suspected he was the one with whom I'd have got on best, if we'd stayed in contact. He was a naturally likeable person, as she had been herself, until after Rostock that was. In his role as the informal spokesman for her club of broken-hearted admirers, he provided a foil to Sophie's occasional prickliness with her male friends who, to their chagrin, were never more than friends. His own relaxed demeanour, though, might well be because I suspected he was the one unofficial casual boyfriend she did permit herself.

'And where have you been on vacation this year, or is the start of the new Commission keeping you as busy as us?' he asked.

I felt a warm, prideful glow as I imagined telling him that the head of the East German foreign intelligence service had just given me an urgent assignment in person, tasking me to help them upend Rizzo's comfortable world.

Instead, a ghostly smile came over my lips and I shook my head as I replied.

'Sorry, Rizzo. You know how it is with Internal Affairs and confidentiality. Although I think the accession talks are keeping everyone busy in different ways?'

Sophie eyed me suspiciously. I wouldn't be surprised if she had a good idea what Masson's team really got up to, her better-connected background placing her at least one step closer than Rizzo to the people who knew the truth.

'How are your family in Wismar getting on, Oskar?' I restrained my surprise at both her unexpected interest and her politeness.

'They're all a year older. Thomas is already looking forward to military service, if his parents will allow him to apply for the unit of his choice. Karin is hoping to go to Berlin after high school to get an apprenticeship at the Fashion Institute there. She has a good chance of getting in too.'

'If she lived in the West, she could get a degree in fashion.'

'You know that's not possible. Sometimes we have to accept life as it is.'

As I said it, I was reminded again of the differences between us. Not that her attitude was surprising, given her membership of an inner web of influence which included some of the organisation's most senior officials, all joined together by the delicate tendrils of national preference, benign nepotism and loyalty to shared alma maters.

Unfair as it might seem to those on the outside, such as me, it was what guaranteed reliable successors to the trusted servants of the Project, as it slowly but surely evolved over decades, careers and lifespans.

'Have you actually been to see your family again, since we went there last year?'

I eyed her carefully, at her first direct reference to the events of nineteen sixty-nine.

'Yes, I make the effort to get over there when I can. I tend to go on my own.'

She didn't ask when they'd learned that our 'engagement' was a lie and I didn't offer to tell her. That said, if she was asking about renewed contact, I might as well bring up Karin's letter.

'My cousin told me last time I saw her that she'd tried to write to you in Brussels. She's still a little in awe of you.'

Sophie wrinkled her brow. 'What address did she use? I haven't received anything from the East this year.'

As we spoke, my own deep frustration at Sophie started to fade with it being difficult for two people to dislike one another completely, when standing face to face and speaking neutrally to one another.

'Give me her address tomorrow and I'll write to her.'

Rizzo shifted from foot to foot as he listened, perhaps becoming a little nervous of a rapprochement. But Sophie's antennae were very sensitive too. She linked her right arm into Rizzo's left and pulled him in slightly towards her.

'We're going to Apulia shortly, to the heel of the boot in a couple of months' time for the seventy-fifth birthday of Giorgio's grandfather.'

'Everyone's celebrating birthdays it seems,' I replied noncommittally.

Rizzo was looking like the cat who got the cream though, and not just because his *nonno* was about to hit a big number. I'd felt the same way when she and I had been sent off on assignment to East Germany on our own last year.

'Sophie,' I said, more politely now. She started somewhat at the civil use of her name.

She jutted out her chin, tossing her head slightly, 'Yes?'

'I need to write a report on the CAP, on fraudulent schemes out there in the member states which lead back to people in Brussels. People who are of interest to Internal Affairs for the usual reasons. Might my colleague Willem and I meet you this week?'

I smiled at Rizzo encouragingly, as if this was all completely normal.

'I suppose so,' she said cautiously. 'You can come by on Friday morning at eleven, but only if you're both free.'

I was sure Willem would be, one way or another. He might be a weedy analyst without any romantic hopes for Sophie, but even he wouldn't pass up the chance to sit at her feet. Anyway, I'd make him if I had to - hit him over the head with one of the wooden clogs he probably wore around the office when Masson and I were out, getting secretly homesick for the tulips and windmills.

'Thank you,' I smiled pleasantly. 'Now if you'll excuse me,' I pointed vaguely behind me, 'I need to see some other people. Have fun in Apulia.' With that, I turned and left.

I found Kramer on the balcony of the upper story of the apartment. I sipped my champagne as I waited on his conversation to wind up and moved in before anyone else could buttonhole him.

'So apparently I cost Madame Kramer three thousand francs for a new carpet,' I said evenly.

Kramer covered his mouth with his hand as he gave a quick cough.

'Yes, that's how she understood the story of what happened.'

The corners of my mouth quivered with amusement at the thought of his predicament when his wife returned from cocktails yesterday afternoon and how, although de Gaulle held no fears for him, he'd met his match in Madame Kramer.

'I expect I won't get an invitation next July,' I concluded.

He deftly changed the topic. 'Well, did you see Mademoiselle von Barten?'

'Yes, she was civil enough. What did your people in Paris say about giving you the names of the people in Ireland we talked about?'

'They're still discussing it. Even I find it hard to get information out of them fast unless it's an emergency, although our Russian friends didn't seem to have that problem in the past.'

'When will you know for sure?'

'Come to my office at the end of the day on Wednesday.'

'And the Skorzeny idea?'

He lit a fresh cigarette and drew on it slowly.

'Do you want to go to Madrid?'

I looked out over the city. To the south, almost at the far end of the Avenue Louise, its location made famous by an audacious low-level aerial attack by a Belgian pilot during the war, had been the Brussels headquarters of the SS-Sicherheitsdient, Skorzeny's organisation. The man himself must be into his sixties by now. I thought of him in self-imposed exile in Franco's Spain, the last surviving outpost of the spiritual empire of fascism, and wondered why Fiedler was so keen for me to go there.

'When else will I get the opportunity?' I answered Kramer, 'To meet the man whom Hitler admired the most?'

Chapter Six

The top floor of the Berlaymont was almost deserted after five o'clock, but even so, Kramer had turned the air conditioning in his office up high to a constant roar. He sat across from me on one of the calfskin sofas arranged around the low meeting table in the corner of the room under the air vent. A large manila envelope lay on the smoked-glass surface of the table.

I was surprised both that he felt the need to take precautions and at the crudeness of his attempt. If he was really that worried, he should give Masson the electronics technician my boss kept hinting we needed, to sweep for microphones and to allow our department to do its own bugging in turn. Or we should have just met somewhere else.

'I've spoken with Paris. A memo is being drafted, authorising the SDECE to give me special assistance - the names of those government officials in Ireland whom we talked about. How you use the information to develop a relationship with the agencies is up to you.'

I humoured his use of elliptical language.

'And they want research carried out into the national liberation organisations too? For the Canadian reason you mentioned on Sunday? Is that why they agreed to help you?'

He was suddenly sombre now and I wondered if he'd misread the situation in Paris. As the vanguard in Brussels for France, away from the Élysée, it would be impossible for him to know everything going on behind his back.

I shifted closer to Kramer and sat companionably across the corner from him.

'So we can speak more plainly, what with the noise of the fan,' I explained. In my mind's eye, Johannes was looking on, already smiling broadly at the scene that presented itself.

'There's two reasons for their support to get you into the Irish agencies. Firstly, Paris wants me to test the official assurances of the Irish government to our foreign ministry that the arrests in the Kelly case really do mark the end of their adventures in Northern Ireland. And Paris also wants a way to obtain the names of the key players in the IRA today - but for a different purpose from the one I speculated about.'

I'd instinctively thought on Sunday, that his notion of France using Northern Ireland to undermine the British had been a fantasy, but it had been revelatory all the same. He was a fifty-something wartime Gaullist, still occasionally operating as such in the nineteen seventies, all of which told its own story.

'Any specific intelligence on the IRA which you collect will be fed into the Sûreté counter-terrorism operation against the Breton nationalists. We want to see if we can use the Irish terrorists as a backdoor into the Front de Libération de la Bretagne. The connection isn't as fanciful as it seems. Some of the Nazi's Breton collaborators fled to Ireland after the war and got involved in the nationalist scene there and all these terrorist groups have links with each other, even if it's just sharing the same arms suppliers.'

'And testing the political assurances of the Irish?' I asked.

'Remember what I said on Sunday? The Irish are desperate to prove they can be reliable members of the EEC. Illegal importation of arms doesn't fit with that.'

'So, like our friends in the East, you want me to find out if clamping down on renegade elements is still official policy?'

Kramer nodded sagely. 'Talk to everyone you meet over there about it. See what they say in unguarded moments, even if they're not the intelligence operatives you're trying to meet.'

'And the meeting in Madrid to provide cover for the source of those names?'

'Yes. I thought about that some more after you left on Monday evening. I don't know what the opposition's game is with that suggestion, but I can't see the harm. Not yet, anyway. In any case, it's obviously expected of you by them, so why not go there to reinforce your credentials in the East?'

'What's to be the pretext for that meeting? How does it get set up? Won't the person in question be wary of a request to meet a stranger out of the blue? I thought he was a consulting terrorist and part-time arms dealer himself, what with the visits to South America, Egypt and Pakistan.'

'He's only a celebrity to the tabloids. They love to speculate on the rumours of hidden Nazi gold and the salacious stories about him and Eva Peron. The reality is that he's not as successful in that world which you described as he likes to make out, although he has dabbled there.'

Kramer recrossed his legs, feeling better now he was talking about someone else's problems and forgetting to speak in code too.

'He's tried to relive his glory days by asking to be taken on as a military advisor to different regimes over the decades. But Skorzeny has mainly used his wartime reputation to give West German industrial concerns access to right-wing governments around the world who're sympathetic towards him and his politics.'

Kramer adjusted his cufflinks, twisting them straight, the light picking out the design of the silverwork.

'He's just another fixer taking his cut from bigger deals

done by other people. Anyway, the meeting's been set up already because you told me at my wife's birthday drinks that you wanted to go.'

'When?'

He grinned sheepishly and slid the manila envelope over towards me. 'There's a Sabena flight at a quarter to midnight tonight, you land just before two. But don't worry - Madrid's nightlife will still be in full swing when you get there.'

'Okay. And the exact reason he's been given for my visit?'

'The meeting's been set up as you posing as an EEC official seeking to tap his contacts in the Middle East, so we can persuade the right people in the usual way to let us dump agricultural produce into their markets. You'll have to move the conversation onto Ireland yourself.'

It wasn't the cover story I'd have chosen.

'Why don't I kill two birds with one stone and in addition to the names of Irish intelligence officers, fish for what he knows of the IRA directly? Why don't I suggest I'm privately representing a German arms dealer who wants access to the new market in Ireland?'

Kramer shook his head. 'Because he probably knows all of those dealers already. The "old comrades" are well plugged into that demi-monde, even if Skorzeny himself is often only a front man.

He pursed his lips. 'Be careful. That lot keep themselves to themselves. They're highly suspicious of outsiders because even if nothing's yet stuck to Skorzeny, plenty of the rest of them did things during the war that different national prosecutors still want to ask questions about.'

I was even less happy now about the lack of warning of the trip and the lack of time to prepare a credible story. I suspected I was risking exposure before I'd as much as seen a shamrock.

'So what other inside information do you have on

Skorzeny? Does the SDECE have a file on him? Because if the French don't, why would the Irish have bothered tracking him either? In which case this whole diversion to Madrid will have been for nothing.'

Kramer nodded to the table. 'Take a look inside the envelope. There's something on him in there for you. But I'll let you into a little known secret: in nineteen forty-nine he lived for some months in Paris under the protection of the Sûreté whilst he wrote his memoirs.'

'What? How did that come about?'

'The short version is that we suspect his German girlfriend at the time, later his wife, had been known to the Sûreté during the war.'

'You mean known to the Sûreté of the French State?'

'French State' had been the official title of the regime. It was labelled 'Vichy France' by the Gaullists to delegitimise it because they had needed to use all the tricks available to them when trying to replace the legal successor to the Third Republic, with their own one-man regime based in London.

Kramer shrugged. 'Whatever. He was vouched for by a senior British intelligence officer who'd worked with the Resistance and moved to France himself after the war.'

'How is this the short version of the story?'

'No, listen. I'm trying to explain something. The British guy was someone who, completely unknown to Skorzeny, had been recruited by his defence lawyer to be a witness at Skorzeny's war crimes trial. His defence was trying to show that both sides bent the rules on occasion.'

Kramer raised his eyebrows quizzically, making sure I understood the metaphor. 'After the trial the wartime enemies got friendly, compared notes on missions. The Englishman gave the Austrian advice on other legal issues that came up later. But the point is, Skorzeny has that draw on people. Even on people like Yeo-Thomas, who'd been captured and tortured by the Gestapo.'

'Where's all this going, Kramer? Are you warning me

now about seeing him? I've nothing in common with a Skorzeny.'

'That's up to you to find out. However, remember this too. Skorzeny got away with living in France for eight months because the Sûreté went behind the back of the SDECE, making fools of them. It's the usual story, our agencies often spend more time fighting each other than the enemy. What's the lesson for you there, do you think?'

I thought for a moment, picking up the envelope to test its weight.

I shrugged. 'That even in a country as small as Ireland, with only a couple of agencies which we know about, I might well find them on opposite sides?'

'Someone had to arrest the unfortunate Captain Kelly and it wasn't the Irish Army's military police.'

'Now that we have the promise of names and a deception plan for how we got them, who makes the first call to the Irish about me paying them a visit?'

'What did Masson say about the ceremony yesterday? Were any Irish there?'

'It was a British-EEC bilateral meeting. The Irish aren't due here until September.'

'Hmm. So, what ideas do you have for a reason to visit Dublin? After all, it's you who's asking to go there.'

'My plan is to tell them about CAP fraud with the intent that I should at least get access to the police as a starting point.'

He got up to turn the air conditioning down.

'Stupid idea anyway,' he said. 'Everyone else has gone home.'

'I need that trip to Madrid now, just to get warm.'

'You young guys born after the war have no idea how soft your life is.' He was only half-smiling as he said it.

'Okay, let me think about your idea. It seems reasonable enough. We'll need to write a letter to propose a visit to their justice department or maybe the agriculture ministry. And then we'll have to wait for a reply. Maybe I'll get Masson to go directly to the negotiators. I need to talk to him soon, anyway.'

He rubbed his temples, then took his pocket book from his jacket and unscrewed the top of his Mont Blanc.

'All this will take time. If you're in Ireland by the end of next week, we'll be doing well.'

'Do you think this effort will be worth it for France? What will the Sûreté really get out of one trip to Ireland?'

'The first question you should ask is what this trip means for your department. If you're the one to go there, Masson needs the credit for any positive results. He can't be seen to have been sitting back in Brussels twiddling his thumbs while you get all the glory.'

'What glory is there in telling agriculture ministry officials in Ireland about false invoicing for overripe plums?'

'You know what I mean. Masson needs to come back to the other sponsors and I, able to claim he was the one who managed to gain access to the Irish intelligence agencies, without them realising it was the EEC's own agency who did so - and all before accession too.'

He jotted a couple of lines in his pocketbook, flicked forward to the calendar at the front and ringed a date, before continuing.

'I'll suggest it's time he sent you and your colleague on fishing expeditions to meet police and customs officials at the Four, to see what gossip External Investigations can get from the inside. Every politician has enemies and you know how often those enemies can be in the police.' He paused, until I acknowledged with a toss of the head.

'But before that, I need to get to him first thing tomorrow to say I've sent you out of Brussels for a day on an errand. You're flying back tomorrow, by the way.'

'Staying with Masson for a moment,' I replied, 'if he finds out that we've been doing more than talking, and that I've been using you to steer him, he's not going to take it well.'

Kramer grinned, 'You're using me? I like that. Masson is a hazard of your job. Honestly, if you'd been at de Gaulle's court-in-exile in London and Algiers you'd know what intrigue means.'

He smiled again. 'That hitherto unknown French monarchist faction who assassinated his rival power-broker, Admiral Darlan, didn't just spring up fully formed from the desert sands. A story for another time, perhaps.'

He snapped together his notebook and slid it inside his jacket. Stretching out his legs, he pushed the coffee table away with his feet and crossed them.

'If you want to have a longer career in External Investigations, you need to start planning yourself for Masson's eventual exit and his succession.'

He looked at me inquiringly, expecting a comment or a request for advice. It was the biggest hint he'd made so far about who the future director of the department might be. I quickly weighed it up, judging I'd be in a stronger position to set out my demands if I actually achieved something in either Madrid or Dublin first.

'Back to my earlier question,' I said, changing the subject. 'If the Sûreté are serious about getting and staying close to the IRA, it will take more than one visit to the Irish agriculture ministry to do it.'

'They have to start somewhere and if your trip is a dead-end, then they haven't lost anything. We have to start thinking the way the people in the East do, with patience,' he said, looking grave. 'They plant moles and leave them for years and years. And they can do that because they've had the same leadership for decades. It's a luxury the democracies don't have, so we have to fight differently from them.'

'That's why everyone here at the Commission is so keen to build a technocracy instead, I suppose.'

He didn't have an answer to that.

Chapter Seven

Skorzeny's office was in the Calle de la Montera, halfway between the Gran Via and the Puerta del Sol, the square right in the heart of the city centre where all road distances in the notional kingdom were measured from. So the concierge at the hotel had told me when giving me my directions to the office just before I rolled out after my third shot of espresso at the breakfast bar.

I stood in the dusty street in my heavy northern European suit, getting hot even at ten o'clock. I buzzed the bell with a little trepidation as to who I'd find inside and how I was going to get him to trust me enough to open up about Ireland. I'd had to do it with middle-ranking Vichy collaborators for Kramer last year but Skorzeny would be the first hardline Nazi I'd met - or at least the first one I knew of. Life held all kinds of little surprises like that, such as when the world found out that the previous West German Chancellor Kiesinger had been a Nazi Party member, much to the delight of East Germany.

Despite the passage of time, Skorzeny was still the partly-acceptable face internationally of the Nazi regime. The glamour of his wartime commando raids and other famous exploits, such as his escape from a US Army prison after the war, had nothing to do with death camps or other such unpleasantness. But as the most famous Nazi in public life, he was inevitably the subject of every half-cocked Fourth Reich conspiracy theory breathlessly reported in the tabloids.

As Kramer had told me yesterday afternoon, the reality which Skorzeny and his new wife had made for themselves in Spain was much more mundane. The SDECE file in the envelope passed to me by Kramer added further details because they weren't going to be made fools of again by the Sûreté and made sure they stayed properly up to date these days.

His first big break in business had been making the appropriate introductions for four West German steel manufacturers to the Spanish state railway company in nineteen fifty-two, earning a one percent commission on a six million dollar contract.

His wife had used the proceeds to start a property empire, including his house in Ireland, a choice of offshore location which was hard to understand unless it had been a long-term speculative purchase. Ireland in nineteen fifty-seven was hardly the new Monaco. If they'd done so to provide a bolt-hole, an insurance policy against the fall of the Franco regime in Spain, then it hadn't worked because his application for residency from nineteen fifty-nine was still in limbo, neither granted nor turned down by the Irish.

I reckoned this last episode could work in my favour if I fed him a convincing story. Assuming his pride was still hurt, and he wanted a way to get back at the Irish, that was.

The atrium of the building was cool after the heat of the street. I took a slow, clanking ride in an open-cage elevator and was finally at the end of my journey.

I knocked and to my surprise it was Skorzeny himself who came to the door and opened up. Despite the greying hair, his beefy frame and the duelling scar down one cheek were instantly recognisable from the photographs in the press. When I saw him standing there in the flesh, Kramer's warning hints came back to me for I was suddenly mesmerised.

It really was him, the hero of Gran Sasso, the man who through strength of will had rescued Mussolini without firing a shot and captured the head of the wavering pro-Axis Hungarian government the same way in a coup the following year in 'forty-four. I stepped inside, so in awe that I only gripped his hand lightly, hardly hearing him ask me if I cared for a drink.

At that moment, I understood all too clearly the seductive power of myth; how normal, rational people could be led astray by a larger-than-life character. And I realised just then that what was true for individuals could also be true for an entire nation too.

He shouted to his secretary in the inner office to bring out coffee, then made me sit with him around a low cane table in the corner of the hallway and lit a cigarette.

I wondered if not being invited into his private office was some kind of physical security precaution, to keep strangers out in the common area. Even if he'd more or less kept his hands clean in the war, as far as anyone could prove, he was still a high-profile representative of the regime and a potential target for all those who might want revenge on the system which had made him. There were confused rumours that he had indeed bought himself some protection with the Mossad through agreeing to deliver them names of Nazi-era engineers working on Egypt's various scientific and weapons programmes. But the truth, as always with Skorzeny, was hard to ascertain.

'So Herr Lenkeit, I understand you wish to talk business. Are you selling or buying?'

When I'd thought about my cover story some more, as the Sabena jet grumbled its way through the night sky, soaring over the Pyrenees while an earlier generation of aircraft would have been clawing up them, I liked Kramer's proposed narrative less and less.

I was to ask Skorzeny for help in finding destinations in the Middle East for milk and butter surpluses from the Common Market. But Skorzeny had never had anything to do with agriculture, as far as I knew. Nor did I, so I decided to dump the idea, just as we wanted to do with the dairy products.

In answer to Skorzeny's question, I placed three of the business cards given to me by Johannes on the table - the ones he'd picked up from East German engineering combines at the Leipzig fair.

'I work for the EEC as a trade adviser, as explained to you by Monsieur Kramer's secretary. But I'm also here on my personal account, to help my private clients sell into the West on the quiet.'

He leaned forward to peer at the names through reading glasses which he unfolded from the top pocket of his jacket.

'Why should I help the enemy?'

'They're still Germans.'

'And these "Germans". What's your connection to them?'

I leant back, sipped my coffee and waved my hand in his direction.

'I'm in export consultancy, just like you. One of my specialist roles at the EEC is to help coordinate the joint efforts of firms from across the Six in developing new external markets, in areas such as machine tools and pharmaceutical manufacturing.'

I had no idea if this kind of thing actually happened, but it was the sort of activity people might expect to take place in a trading bloc.

'Just like any other country, the East Germans have an interest in acquiring advanced technology and equipment to build up their own industries and, from time to time, they come to me for help with selling their products back into the West.'

'You realise it's almost certain that the Stasi know of your little game? That one day they'll come knocking on your door to blackmail you into cooperating with them?'

'The Stasi are no angels. The arrangements work because enough of their people like the sense of well-being that comes from Krugerrands in a Swiss bank vault. After all, what's illegal about helping Zeiss sell a few more binoculars to Dutch birdwatchers?'

'I bet it's not just binoculars. Look, you're young and brash, like I was once. I'm still brash, but I can't help that, it's who I am. But you don't realise the trouble you're storing up for yourself. The Stasi are no one's fools. If they catch their people taking bribes they'll come after you too. A car accident, a heart attack - all of these things can be arranged.'

'It's nothing obvious. In the West it's just business. I get paid a percentage of the sales I direct their way. The managers of the combines are the ones taking the risks by disguising the payments.'

He looked at me over the top of his spectacles, unconvinced.

'What do you think I can do for you then?'

'Just the usual. You have contacts in markets outside Europe. Out of my percentage I'll pay you for introductions which lead to sales.'

'And you've kept your moonlighting secret from your bosses in Brussels? When do you have time for all of this on top of your real EEC job?'

'East Germany has tariff-free access to West Germany, so it has effective tariff-free access to the EEC. It's the unofficial seventh member. Any sales outside the Six which they make through their Luxembourg shell companies count towards the EEC's export statistics. This is my job, as far as I'm concerned.'

'Right. But I don't work that fast. You need to learn the art of persuasion in selling, how to draw in the other side, seduce them, you might say.' He took a drag on his cigarette, washed down by a mouthful of coffee.

'Apart from being linked to the corruption of East German officials in your spare time, are your politics sound?'

'My family were refugees from East Prussia. What do you think?' I looked coldly at him.

He didn't have an immediate answer to my ambiguous response, uncertain of what it could mean. I might hate the Nazis for triggering the war which ended in the loss of the Eastern Territories, or I might be coldly intent on destroying the socialists from East and West who'd tacitly supported the transfer.

'If I was the sort of person who wasn't prepared to leave the past in the past, I wouldn't be here,' I said. 'If I didn't believe in the eventual reunification of Germany, I wouldn't be helping the easterners.'

There was an easier way to improve my nationalist credentials, though.

It was a question I'd wanted to ask ever since Fiedler brought up the idea of seeing the former Sicherheitsdient man. In fact, it was a question I was compelled to ask. As a German, how could I not?

'But before I say more, tell me one thing,' I demanded.

The rest of the room seemed to fall away, and I was left staring down a tunnel with Skorzeny's grey-blue eyes at the far end.

'What was he like?'

Skorzeny raised his eyebrows and nodded. He took a short puff on his cigarette before he answered cautiously, even here in private.

'I remember the first time I met him. He called six candidates to his headquarters in East Prussia to interview us for the job of rescuing Mussolini. Do you know how he chose me for the task, for the mission that changed the course of my life, which would one day take me to presidential palaces all over the world?'

'I need to know.'

I held my breath and he could see the anticipation in my face as I travelled back in time. In my mind's eye I saw a row of commando officers standing to attention in a low-ceilinged concrete command bunker, hidden in the pine forests of what in a few weeks' time would officially recognised by West Germany as Polish territory.

'Tell me,' I said in a harsher voice.

Skorzeny looked at me evenly.

'He said, "What do you know of Italy."'

I'd asked the same sort of question myself to a spotty Stasi lieutenant, only last week.

'So I simply replied, "I'm an Austrian". And then he knew that, just like him, I hadn't forgiven the Italians for annexing South Tyrol either.'

'So he decided, just like that?'

'He had the gift of seeing into people's souls, of immediately understanding what drove them and how to motivate them.'

My school atlas had labelled the areas of Germany chopped off by the Soviets after the war as 'At this time under Polish administration.' When Brandt travelled to Moscow to sign the treaty acknowledging the nineteen forty-five borders, a thousand years of German history in those lands would be over forever. I understood the two Austrians' point of view all too well for myself.

'At that moment, even though I had already been prepared to do so before, I would have walked through any fire, endured any pain to serve that triumphant will. He made us think there was nothing we couldn't do. So we did everything.'

Skorzeny smirked at me, more confident of his audience now. 'We did great things in the war. Despite our fears in the fifties, it's clear to me that we smashed up the Soviet Union so hard, killed so many of their people, that they'll never catch the West now. Losing the Space Race last year should have told people so.'

He warmed to his theme. 'Also, during the war, we suspected the British were burning through their accumulated imperial wealth to keep pace with the American war effort and to buy their seat at the victors' top table. But we had no idea how fast their empire would collapse afterwards, thanks to their bankruptcy. Today they've nothing left. As a percentage of their territory, they've lost far more than we did. That's why everyone who hates the British loves us - from the Indians to the Irish.'

It was like he'd compared notes with Kramer, which in itself gave me a little pause for thought.

'I guess their old power has drained away to such an extent that they want to join the EEC now,' I offered.

He looked blank and pulled on his cigarette again, so I ploughed on.

'And when they do, we and the French will take advantage of their pathetic, naive gratefulness and fleece them for every *pfennig* they still possess.'

The ceiling fan whirled round softly overhead, as the silence lengthened.

'What do you think of the EEC?' I finally asked him. Kramer, Fiedler and their requests could wait a while, I knew it was extremely unlikely I'd ever come back here and have this chance again.

Eventually he replied.

'You tell me. I hope you're looking out for Germany's interests there.'

That was when I realised he had little real idea of what went on in Brussels and the nature of the Project. How could you describe it to someone whose outlook was that of the nineteenth century or even further back, of the Thirty Years' War of religion?

'These are different times now. I flew here in two hours by jet from Brussels. Europe is closer together and even less able these days to escape the gravitational pull of Germany. And it never will.'

He pulled on his cigarette and tipped his head back to blow the smoke up into the draft of the fan, the scar on his cheek glinting in the sunlight as he did so. It marked him out, a man apart from other men.

I tried to keep it easy for him.

'As the EEC grows stronger, Germany grows even stronger inside it. Over time it will become more and more our plaything and less and less that of the French. We'll end up running Europe without firing a shot and without people recognising it - from Ireland in the far west to the Norwegian Arctic Circle. From Gibraltar in the south to the suburbs of Istanbul.'

I wasn't quite sure where the Greek border ended but I think he got the point.

However, if I was being honest with him, I'd have said that I suspected by the time any wider expansion happened, the supranationalists would truly have become that in their own minds. Loyal to their own higher political class first, before any national labels, West German technocrats like Sophie sought to build a Greater Europe, not rebuild a Greater Germany. The irony for Europe being that they were unwittingly bringing about the same thing.

'Just like the EEC, you had all sorts of nationalities working for you during the war, though?'

'Croats, Slovaks, Serbs, Hungarians - even exotic types like Cossacks and a couple of Irishmen. All under German direction, of course,' said the Austrian.

He leant forward and stubbed out his cigarette in the ashtray.

'Let's have a drink. I know somewhere nearby where we can go and won't be disturbed.'

As we got up and went back to the door, this time I saw how Skorzeny had difficulty moving. It wasn't so much of a limp, as only partial control of his legs.

We rode the elevator to the ground floor in silence and he shuffled down the steps from the building out onto the street.

I carefully avoided paying attention to his gait as he shambled down a side street and then down an even narrower alleyway to a small bar.

The establishment was nondescript from the outside but inside it was decorated with black and white unit photos, showing what looked to be a mixture of Spanish and Wehrmacht troops. A framed picture of Franco, its corner wrapped with a red and yellow ribbon took pride of place behind the counter.

Skorzeny clicked his fingers and ordered Scotch for both of us. Whilst we waited on the barman, I looked more closely at one of the snapshots: helmeted soldiers in the snow holding up a Spanish flag to the camera.

Skorzeny noticed my interest.

'Legion Azul on the Eastern Front. Fierce fighters - hated the Communists.'

I hadn't realised the Spanish had joined the party in Russia.

'How many different nationalities fought with us there in the end?'

I knew there had been several foreign units of the Waffen-SS, Balts, Dutch, Norwegians and the French of the SS Charlemagne Division, but there were others I was only vaguely aware of.

'Not enough,' came the brutal answer.

The whisky arrived and with a clink and a '*Prost!*', we drank.

'What's the mood in the Bundeswehr these days? When did you do your service?'

'Nineteen sixty-three to sixty-four. Fifteen months.'

'That wasn't yesterday either. Time passes, even for the young, *nicht wahr*?'

'I can't speak for the attitude of the conscripts going through now, after 'sixty-eight and the time of the student protest nonsense. But when we were under training, as children of the fifties, we still had the strong folk memory of the horror of the Red Army on German soil.'

This was stretching the truth. Growing up, my mother had hardly mentioned anything at all of her early life in East Prussia and certainly nothing of her service in the East as an army nurse with the German Red Cross.

Skorzeny nodded soberly.

'Towards the end, I went on a reconnaissance mission, probing out from the Schwendt bridgehead. We came to a town supposedly under Red Army control, but the Ivans had pulled back for a few hours. As we left, two refugee women came up and begged that we take them and their daughters back with us. We squeezed them onto our Kubelwagen and brought them to Schwendt. But who knows what the Red Army did to them when we had to pull out of there too? What more could we have done?'

Not invading the world's biggest country would have been a good start, I thought. I'd never even heard of Schwendt. So many anonymous little scraps of land fought over at such great cost and suffering.

'How did we manage to hold them off for so long, the world against us?'

He took a long slug before he answered, gazing out of the window of the cafe at a spot on the opposite wall of the alleyway.

'We had six years to get really good at fighting, but some things were true from the start. Determination and the right mental attitude are always the differences between success and failure, all other conditions being equal. They will often even up two forces of unequal strength, as was the situation that we found ourselves in too many times. In the heat of action, any decision is always better than no decision.'

'How did your commandos differ from the enemy's and the Special Forces the Americans have in Vietnam today?'

'Bah. More and more armies want to have these units, but most don't know how to use them. Just because you train a man in peacetime with longer forced marches and a harder obstacle course than your regular troops doesn't make him any more of a soldier. The real question is, does he have the strength of will to look into another man's eye and pull the trigger to end that person's life?'

A chill came over me to the bone. I shuddered as

Skorzeny continued.

'My *Jagdverbände* were required to collect intelligence as well as act on it. I didn't just assault Mussolini's prison. I spent the previous two months finding it. We were expected to be as self-sufficient as possible, especially from our own army.'

He offered me a cigarette and lit one for himself. I borrowed his silver lighter for mine.

'Okay, that's enough chat. What are your guys selling and who do they want to sell to?'

I gave him a run-down of the three firms, thankful for the thoroughness of the Stasi in creating a proper cover story, even for my family. The supposed commercial terms I made up on the spot, though.

'Let me tell you, young man, you're being cheated. Five percent is nowhere near enough for the risks you're taking, and it doesn't leave much for you to pay your own introducers.'

'You know these socialists. They have no real idea of true market values. It's all I could squeeze out of them. Given they started at three percent, I didn't do badly.'

He shook his head.

'You're going about this all wrong. You need to get a sale price from them to you and then you can mark it up to whatever you can get away with. And you also need to find a quiet, out-of-the-way market to start in and learn how to actually sell.'

'How about Ireland. You had dealings there.'

'Yes, but some time ago and less and less these days. I went last year.' Here he shifted his sitting position, rearranging his leg.

'But it was the last trip I intend to make. Frau Skorzeny still goes. She's deciding what to do about our house there.'

I'd come to Madrid just in time, it seemed, whilst Ireland was still on his mind.

'As a place for you to start, it's so-so. We bought at the

bottom of the market in fifty-seven, but since then, the economy's grown along with the rest of Europe. They're still laggards, however. Spain has overtaken them in the past ten years because of planned industrialisation and tourism. Greece and Portugal can't be far behind.'

'Why did you buy there in the first place?'

'My wife had some idea of encouraging other prominent Germans to join us. She thought she could earn real estate fees for introductions on property investments. We know of some Bundeswehr officers who've bought land there as a safe haven for their families in case there's another war.'

'So what else can you tell me of Ireland? Which local businessmen do you recommend I start with?'

'What do you mean? You think there's a list of import agents for East German industrial goods you can just look up in the telephone directory?'

I was getting nowhere fast. All I wanted to do was show him my list of Irish names from Johannes and ask him who he knew.

'Harder than it looks, eh? Old Skorzeny of the Sicherheitsdienst reduced to talking percentages with people not even alive during the war, I'm guessing. You need patience with these things.'

He smiled from the side of his mouth. 'Show me again.'

I laid out the business cards once more on the marble-topped table between us.

He pointed to one, a manufacturer of agricultural machinery.

'You need to get the farmer's association onside with the idea of buying from a Communist country so they'll be happy to recommend these products to their members. The people who run Ireland are very Catholic, sometimes devout, but almost always reactionary.'

'So I would need political sponsorship? How about their intelligence people? Won't they be suspicious of someone introducing East German products? Did they ever chase you?'

'Me? No, they were in love with me when I first went there.'

'Who did you meet from them? Did you know this Captain Kelly who's been arrested for arms trafficking to the IRA?'

'No idea who he is. I haven't really been in favour there since 'sixty-three,' he said more somberly.

'So do you know any names there, in the police and the army intelligence service?'

He frowned and looked at me, askance.

'Why, do you?'

My mind went blank and my mouth went dry. I swallowed, but the seconds stretched out as I desperately tried to think of some plausible riposte.

'Why would I?' I eventually croaked, after I'd spent several long seconds flushing, alternately hot and cold.

He raised an eyebrow.

'I think our conversation has run its course, Herr Lenkeit. Don't you?'

What a disaster. I tried to control my expression.

'As you said, I need to get a better deal from the Easterners before I can do anything else,' I said brokenly.

'That you do, in every way.' He was smirking openly now, plainly enjoying my embarrassment.

But because he'd survived twenty-five years of business and political intrigues since the war, ones played for much higher stakes than today's conversation, he knew to toss a bone to the other side. Because often the sides that people found themselves on changed.

'The nexus of political corruption in Ireland is Charles Haughey. Find out who he really trusts and see where those threads lead you. And watch your back there at all times too. Don't be taken in by their country ways.'

I rose to go, tossing some coins on the table. I didn't insult him by offering to shake hands but gave him an ironic salute as I thanked him and set off back to Brussels.

As our Boeing sat on the taxiway waiting for take-off, I calmed down and attempted a rational assessment of the real damage.

All he had done was catch me fishing for names, but he must surely suspect a link to East Germany? I should have stuck with Kramer's suggested story after all. Unless, of course, he thought that my hints at a connection to the East were itself a camouflage. Round and round we go in this game of bluff and double-bluff and for what real end? I looked critically at my reflection in the porthole as I pondered the question.

Nonetheless, even if he was on speaking terms with West German intelligence, he had no evidence to accuse me with. Not that it would be needed. Despite the contempt which Johannes and Fiedler had for the BND, they'd look at my profile with my East German family background and start to take note of how often I went over there.

I needed to do such a good job in Ireland for the French that all sins would be forgiven by the West.

Chapter Eight

'Well, what do you want to know?'

Willem and I were sitting opposite from Sophie at her desk in Agriculture. We were in what was intended to be a four-person room, but she had obviously arranged things so that she now had it all to herself.

The room was bare and impersonal, no pictures on the wall or plants by the window. Not because she lacked an artistic side or was trying to send some kind of signal to the patriarchy by deliberately avoiding a demonstration of the so-called woman's touch. Simply, I thought, because they were irrelevant to her, focussed as she was entirely on her job.

After my humiliation at the hands of Skorzeny, I was in no mood to take prisoners this morning, even if this was only my second opportunity to speak with her since last year.

'What are the main concerns of the new accession countries over the CAP?' I asked curtly.

'You need to remember firstly that there's no such thing as a new accession country. Britain, Ireland and Denmark first applied in nineteen sixty-one, Norway in 'sixty-two,' she replied, equally cool.

'I understand that they know about the CAP already, but there must be different aspects of it which worry each of them separately.'

'Which of you is looking after which?' She looked from one of us to the other.

'I cover Denmark and Norway. Oskar is responsible

119

for Britain and Ireland.' Willem piped up.

'Denmark - industrial farming, big exporter of bacon, they suck up hundreds of thousands of tonnes of sand eels from the North Sea to provide animal protein to their pig and chicken farms. Not the humble small co-operative farmers they like to make themselves out to be.'

Willem took notes - he was diligent like that. He might have made a nice pen-friend for Petzold under different circumstances.

'Norway. You have a problem there. Halved their agricultural workforce since the war, just like the British.' Here she glanced over to me. 'But it's not the CAP which bothers them. In fact, they will be model EEC members when the Mansholt plan to reorganise agriculture gets going properly.'

She turned to look at me now, tapping the point of her pencil hard on the desktop.

'Ireland - too small to be of relevance. They definitely won't like the Mansholt Plan, though. Around a third of their workforce is in agriculture and a quarter of their farms are under five hectares in size.'

'Is that bad?'

'By comparison, Britain has less than two percent of its workforce in farming. Both the Six and Ireland have a lot of work to do in order to become more efficient. According to Doctor Mansholt, eighty percent of all farms in the EEC are too small to survive.'

'The Irish won't like that figure?' I suggested.

'It's only a ten-year plan, don't forget. Right now, the Irish are desperate to join because Common Market subsidies for almost everything they produce are much, much higher than the market prices they currently earn in Britain and Germany, the two countries where most of their produce goes to. For instance, the minimum support prices paid to EEC producers for beef are sixty percent higher than on the open market.'

Where had the girl in the red cocktail dress gone,

who'd flirted with me at a champagne-fuelled EEC function in 'sixty-nine?

Willem tried to break in again.

'You said that Norway had a different concern than implementing the CAP?'

She kept her eyes fixed on me instead as she answered, pointing up at the ceiling to indicate the atlas on the wall behind her.

'Take a look at the map of Western Europe, Oskar. Even the simplest child can understand why a Common Fisheries Policy was agreed by the Six only a few hours before Great Britain, Ireland and Norway deposited their latest application to join. The annual fishing catch of the Four is double that of the current member states.'

'Really?' we both replied simultaneously.

It was the sort of brazen move that would have been worthy of Sophie herself, but then again, she only reflected the behaviour of those in Brussels she'd learnt from.

If the Four were to put up with this kind of behaviour from the Six, it only proved their desperation to join, boding well for France and Germany's leadership of any future expansions of the EEC, too.

'What have the Four said to that?' asked Willem, determined not to be ignored.

'That's your job, working for Masson, isn't it?' So she did have a shrewd idea, after all, of what it was we really got up to beyond issuing our consolidated EEC most-wanted lists.

That no-one had asked why the Interpol lists weren't already good enough was a sign that Masson was onto a career-winner, building yet another EEC competence to rival that of an existing international organisation. For a second, I panicked that she might be interested in Masson's job herself in a couple of years' time.

She didn't wait on an answer. 'There's something else you need to reflect on too, before you find out what they think about the CFP.'

'What?' asked Willem weakly.

'How did we manage to make fish appear in the European treaties where there hadn't even been the flash of a silvery fin before?'

She was on fire today and despite myself, I found myself realising I'd missed her verve during this past year.

Willem opened and closed his mouth, a little like an expiring fish himself.

'Because we reinterpreted a reference to "fisheries products" in the original Treaty of Rome as implying that the signatories must have intended EEC law to cover the fisheries themselves,' she concluded triumphantly.

'But just to make sure, Agriculture had the farming ministers of the Six agree to an emergency regulation on the very same morning of the accession applications of the Four, making explicit the principle of equal access to each other's fishing grounds.'

Despite my best intentions, my old fascination with her was creeping back.

'And if we can make what's in the sea appear in the treaties, we can eventually do the same to what's under the sea.'

'Gas?' asked Willem. 'We found a big onshore gas field in Groningen ten years ago and some smaller offshore fields in Dutch waters.'

I wondered how they could tell the difference between the two types of terrain in Holland.

She slapped him down for his obtuseness, poor guy. 'Don't be coy, *menheer*. You know the real answer. Hardly more than half a year ago, only last December, the Americans found oil in the Norwegian sector of the North Sea and then they did the same again that very month off Scotland too.'

'But all of this manoeuvring depends on the Four either being very stupid or very desperate - as you said, Sophia, obvious even to a child.'

She darted me a quick look with a touch of venom on

the tip. The pencil was laid on the desk, she folded her arms and leant forwards.

'Britain has been trying to join since nineteen sixty-one. Ten years ago they were the world's fourth-biggest economy. Now they're the sixth. What do you think? Stupid, desperate or both?'

'And the Irish, are they worried about a CFP?'

'Ireland won't care. They're so eager to get someone else to pay their farming subsidies, their fishermen will be forgotten. I doubt they've paid much attention to the CFP, if at all.'

Fishing might be an alternative way of getting myself noticed by the Irish. When it came to warning them of the intentions of Sophie's department in that area, in the words of the ancient Greek philosopher, I would be the one-eyed king in the land of the blind.

'Apart from the Mansholt Plan, what other new developments in the CAP do the new members need to know about?' I asked instead.

'What do you mean, Oskar? We widen our powers and intervene in new markets all the time,' she said, rippling her fingers on the desk.

'If we want to write a memo for our audience on some of the more specific aspects of the CAP - fraud, for instance - what do we put in it?'

She looked at me suspiciously. 'Is that what you're after? So you do need a real favour then? What's in it for us in Agriculture?'

I wondered for a moment, whether I should ditch the CAP fraud idea right away and go to Ireland to talk about halibut instead, rather than be beholden to her, but I ploughed on.

'What areas of the CAP might cause them trouble when they come to implement it? What are the sanctions against countries if we find out they've allowed their farmers to cheat the system?'

'Do you know anything about the CAP, after so many

years here?'

Now she looked sadly disappointed rather than angry, as if a favoured pupil who'd once showed promise had underwhelmed in their exams.

She picked up her pencil and tapped impatiently on the desk again as she made her points.

'We're creating a single, unified market for agricultural produce across the Six and whoever else joins. So no tariffs within the Six. The same minimum guaranteed prices for farm produce and a single pool of subsidies paid out to all farmers in the Community from central funds, all to ensure an even playing field.'

'How is the minimum price calculated?'

'It's agreed each year for the most important product groups, but in every case, set well above the world market price.'

'So how do you stop competition from overseas?'

'That's easy, we just slap punitive levies on any imports to make sure EEC consumers pay the same prices, wherever the produce comes from.'

'The same high prices, you mean,' I countered.

She ignored the statement of the obvious.

'If farmers inside the Six overproduce and drive down the internal market price to below the support level, we intervene to buy up surpluses from food processors like grain mills or dairies, to increase demand and push prices back up again.'

'And if the farmers produce more than we can eat within the EEC?'

'We export the excess.'

'Although our prices are higher than the world prices.'

'So we make up the difference to the farmers between what they earn overseas and the support price with other subsidies. Export subsidies.'

'This is a giant, free market-distorting scam. How is this different to Eastern bloc socialism?' I exclaimed.

She was right, I really should have known all this

already. I did in a way, though. All the terms she'd mentioned were part of the background noise of working at the EEC. I'd just never really connected the dots.

'So who pays for all this? Oh, I was told the answer the other day. From customs tariffs on goods coming into the Six and on levies applied to overseas produce.'

'You complain about socialism but Oskar, think of the alternative. De Gaulle was terrified that if France's farmers were driven off the land, they'd move to the cities to find work, low-paid no doubt, and become easy prey for communism. The Parti Communiste still has a quarter of a million members.'

'But your boss, Mansholt, says most farms in the EEC are too small to survive. So the CAP won't work in the long-term,' I countered.

'It will, because we're giving farmers time to modernise their holdings. The agricultural sector has already considerably raised productivity through increased mechanisation - swapping horses for tractors. And because we've convinced farmers to greatly increase their use of fertilisers, pesticides and herbicides.'

'And what plans have we made, to encourage the maritime nations of north-west Europe to manage their fishing grounds so as to maximise their catches?' I asked.

'You misunderstand once again, Oskar.'

She was shaking her head in disappointment, annoying and frustrating me at the same time. She might be unashamedly confident or arrogant, if you were being unkind, but in honesty, it was starting to attract me again, more than it was putting me off.

'They will be Community fishing grounds from now on. No-one will get to fish there without permits which we will issue in Brussels.

'All of their territorial waters?'

'Everything up to the beach if we can get away with it.'

Willem tried once more to break into our dialogue. 'Who stands to lose the most? It must be the Norwegians and Irish because of their small populations relative to Britain?'

'Norway catches as much as England, Ireland and Denmark put together, and twice as much as the Six,' she said.

The three of us digested this in silence.

'Good luck with selling the CFP to the Norwegians, then,' I said. 'I understand they appreciate direct speaking there, so you should ask Willem for help - he's Dutch to the point of rudeness.'

I closed my notebook. 'If you let us have a briefing on CAP fraud, Willem and I will give you as much early warning as we can of what the accession countries are saying privately about the CFP.'

'Check with your boss first,' she said pointedly, 'and we might have a deal.'

The meeting had been a revelation in more ways than one, aside from my school lesson on agricultural policy. Having seen her twice in one week, whether I liked it or not, I sensed the stirring of the old heartache for her which I had thought was long dead and buried.

The chasm that had opened up between us because of what had happened after Rostock was uncrossable by any rational judgement. But it wouldn't have stopped Skorzeny trying.

And if Skorzeny could find, assault and rescue a hated Italian dictator from a mountaintop prison, maybe I could learn something for her in Ireland to start to build some bridges back in Brussels and see where things went from there. How difficult would it be anyway, to find some people in Ireland to talk with? After all, it was their favourite thing after drinking, or so Heinrich Böll seemed to imply in his book. I guessed I was about to find out.

Chapter Nine

Kramer had been as good as his word about getting things squared away with Masson and called us both to his office to give his final formal instructions for my trip to Ireland. Just under two weeks ago I'd gone to the Normannenstrasse for a similar briefing from my direct Stasi boss and his, and how the same was happening all over again at the Berlaymont.

Unlike Johannes, Masson wasn't quite so calm. Back over the road in our own offices at the Charlemagne building, he was cock of the roost. He'd got through the first year of his leadership of External Investigations without taking many real risks. Producing summaries of the gossip on the diplomatic circuit and in the bars and nightclubs of Brussels about the negotiators from the Four wouldn't stretch him either but would get him in front of the people who mattered at the EEC for the next two years. Much as Masson, I was sure, wanted the EEC to have its own fully-fledged spy agency in the long term, Kramer was now jeopardising Masson's own turbulent-free flightpath to his immediate next job.

The higher you wanted to rise in the organisation, the more you had to lose when moving your chess pieces to get there, and he wasn't even moving me under his own direction. He was probably more worried than I was about me being given an unrealistic tasking from Kramer, even though it was me who'd likely be asked to get close to the IRA.

A lot of people were going to a lot of effort to make

sure General Wolf's conference in Moscow was a success. If the conference was even real, that was, and not something made up to trick us into an investigation of the Irish under pressure of time, as part of an HVA sting.

Kramer had spent too long on manoeuvres not to know what Masson was thinking; he tried hard to make sure Masson believed it was his show, as we'd discussed almost a week ago, last Wednesday.

I watched the master at work, as he made sure Masson got a heart-warming sense of his own self-importance.

'Lenkeit tells me you attended the bilateral meeting with the British last Tuesday. Did you find out anything new for us?'

'It was their main guy, Sir O'Neill, who was there. The same one who's been pathetically hanging around Brussels since 'sixty-seven, grateful for any opportunity to speak to a Commission official.'

'Yes, I remember him. He's Irish too, isn't he?'

'From Northern Ireland, although I imagine he keeps that pretty quiet these days. Not that he needs to try too hard. He sounds exactly the same as the other English.'

'His social class send their children away from home to residential schools. They all end up speaking the same way,' explained Kramer. 'So how does he enjoy being the centre of attention now?'

'You can well guess. Since the thirtieth of June, he's been in his element, finally the bride, no longer the bridesmaid. How would you feel if all the officials who'd given you a good ignoring over the past three years were now forced to listen to your pompous *jacasser*?'

Kramer replied, 'The only downside for him now is having to share the limelight with the Irish, the Danes and the Norwegians. I'd like to see him in action with them around. He probably thinks he should be lead negotiator for the whole lot.'

'Well, if he does, Willem is certain that will make the Norwegians want to cause even more trouble than they're already planning. They were the only ones to ask questions about the CFP, even before we signed it. On the other hand, if the British are thinking that by joining, they can start telling us all what to do, let's see how much of a threat they are by whether they can control even three other applicants.'

'*Alors*, to the task in hand. This is an exciting time for you Masson, getting to send your first man overseas. This is why I asked you to set up External Investigations. And to get to this point in just over a year - well done.'

Kramer should've opened a sugar factory. He was making enough of the stuff to fill a fleet of trucks.

Masson beamed with a false light, for he was no-one's fool either and knew what was going on.

'It's okay, Kramer. It's about time we stretched our wings. But I don't want him doing anything more at this stage than getting to know the key people in the customs service and maybe the police.'

'Indeed, walk before we run.'

If I didn't say something soon, whilst they talked about me in the third person, Masson would get suspicious that I was fully in on Kramer's plan already.

'Don't worry, Philippe. I know to be careful.'

'He does,' said Kramer. 'He does, I have great faith in your man.'

I frowned slightly at Kramer now. He gave me the faintest grin back.

'So, Monsieur Kramer, you provided us with a suggestion of someone to make first contact with. This Mister Doyle?' I asked.

'Well, de Gaulle visited Ireland last year just after he retired. He still needs protection for the rest of his life from any last remnants of the OAS, so I simply went to de Gaulle's former head of presidential security, the Corsican, and asked him who he'd dealt with out there.'

There was a reason why Kramer had got to where he was. You knew he had good connections because he'd had a list of all G2 and Special Branch officers known to both the SDECE and the Sûreté sent to me when I got back from Madrid. About half the names matched the list from Johannes.

'I've done more than that,' Kramer continued. 'Doyle's agreed to take a meeting this Thursday, late afternoon. You need to get yourself on a flight, *rapidement*. Don't worry,' he turned to Masson. 'I had my secretary set up a special expense code so you can charge it to me. Let's not have an overseas trip appear on your books just yet.'

'Great news, all round,' cooed Masson, as he put his document case on the table and took out a neatly ring-bound, double-spaced report entitled *Lessons From the Administration of the CAP 1962-9*.

'This is what we've had prepared to send Lenkeit with, to use as bait,' he said.

Of course, it had been my idea in the first place, and I'd made the effort to get Sophie's help. And it had been Willem and I, who had actually put the document together, from a selection of photostats of Agriculture Directorate memos which Sophie had culled and sent over with commentaries written in her firm, flowing hand.

The brown cardboard-covered file was unassuming from the outside, but it packed a big punch. In fact, it was more dangerous than I believed Masson realised because it was effectively a manual on how to play the system, the distilled knowledge from six countries of a dozen scams and CAP frauds, some more serious than others, all collected together into one place.

Kramer flicked through it and from the way he went very quiet, I sensed he was thinking the same thing.

'No, this is exactly what we need to send Lenkeit with. It will be of interest to just the right people, if used properly, I think. Well done,' he said to Masson.

'Leave it with me for now. I'll send it back to you with Lenkeit. I'd like him to stay for a few minutes to prove to me that he really understands it. There's a lot at stake.'

Irony died.

'Very well. I need to talk with you later about Willem and Norway,' Masson replied, smoothly confident now.

'Call me on my private line once Lenkeit's back over.'

When Masson had gone, Kramer got up to lock the door. When he turned back to face me, the jovial jokiness was gone, which made me feel better, because it meant he was taking the real briefing seriously.

'Okay, did you get anything useful from your Austrian friend in Madrid?'

I drummed my fingers on the table, trying to delay the inevitable.

'No. He's been away from there so long he doesn't know anyone anymore, apart from Charles Haughey, a cabinet minister. Although I imagine most connected people over there do.'

'What went wrong?' he asked, ignoring my misdirection.

'He got suspicious. My story didn't really hold.'

'It was good enough, or should have been. You know Oskar, you never get dealt the perfect hand of cards, but if you're good enough to succeed at the game, you'll find a way to win. So what was the damage?'

'He suspects I'm connected somewhere, perhaps to the Stasi, if he suspects anyone in particular.'

'Well, that's something then. You kept him away from us.'

'He thinks I'm running an export scam for a couple of East German combines.'

Kramer shrugged his shoulders. 'It just changes the cards left on the table that get dealt again in the next round. Work with it.'

'I have another question for you.' My lips were dry. 'Should I take a weapon to Ireland?'

He raised his eyebrows with a dark look. 'Why? Do you have one?'

'I got given one.'

'What? A pistol?'

I nodded back at him.

'That's the very last thing you need. No way are you taking that to Ireland. Why would you even want to?' he asked suspiciously.

'To trade for information, if I come across people who're on the lookout for such things?'

'Save yourself the bother,' he tapped the report. 'This is all you need. Every gang boss and mafioso in Europe would pay well to get hold of this kind of information. Trust me.'

'All of this preparation, visiting Skorzeny, playing tricks on Masson, writing the definitive guide to CAP fraud - it had better be worth it,' I said. 'All to keep me on the right side of the Stasi.'

'No, Oskar. All to keep you on the inside of the Stasi, carrying out personal assignments for Wolf. Nothing in life comes easy, *mon ami*, even to those who make it look that way.'

'And the assignment for France? Why didn't you tell Masson that they wanted the Irish assurances over Kelly checked out?'

Kramer looked at me shrewdly. 'The Irish are desperate to join now, but that wasn't always the case. Wheels have been in motion for decades. You're only getting to watch the last act of the play. Think of yourself as providing one final check as to their current government's intentions. You're giving both the EEC and the Quai d'Orsay an independent view, uncontaminated by any prior contact with Dublin. I don't want Masson trying to second-guess what people want to hear and sanitising any report you might come back with. He won't be able to help himself by doing so. It's in his nature as someone who has learnt his political craft at university, rather than in real life, as I did.'

'Do you trust him with anything?' I asked.

He shrugged. 'Also, work out how to make that contact with the IRA. They must have known haunts. If you get that far, see how much they know about the Bretons. Find out whether Celtic brotherhood still means something in this modern age.'

Chapter Ten

There was no Sabena flight to Dublin, so I was given my first introduction to Ireland by Aer Lingus. It was a slightly disturbing one, from the moment I was greeted at the entrance to the plane.

I didn't know who'd designed the uniforms of the stewardesses. But a poisonous emerald green ensemble, worn with emerald stockings and emerald shoes of exactly the same shade, all topped off with a surreal over-height army-style forage cap, also in emerald of course, should have meant prison time for crimes against fashion. I thought my cousin Karin would concur. The impression was more of a nation trying too hard to prove it was a modern country, rather than one truly at ease with itself in nineteen seventies Western Europe.

My very first sight of Ireland proper, was of two giant chimney stacks off to our left as the plane approached Dublin over the sea, descending through the summer haze for landing. They were still under construction, for a new power station I presumed, so progress of some kind was certainly happening. Maybe the uniform designer's point was valid after all and the country was preparing faster for the new decade than I was giving it credit for. But when your own country had rebuilt itself almost entirely from the ground up and in only twenty-five years, all by its own hard work, then the Irish still had a lot of catching up to do.

On the ground, the impression reversed itself once

more when we reached the white terminal building, glowing bright in the afternoon sun. While it was an attractive, clean-lined Art Deco jewel of the nineteen thirties, that was exactly its problem. The control tower built into the terminal frontage was quaint, but the overall effect was outdated when compared to the brutalist concrete slabs which the airports of most self-respecting capitals boasted.

Once through arrivals and passport control, having got into the taxi for the ride to town, the impression of quaintness was reinforced by the driver sitting on the wrong side of the vehicle. His heavy accent took things a bit too far for the tourists, though. I had to concentrate hard because almost all the English I'd heard to date had either been spoken by a Frenchman or a Dutchman, or else heard at late-night screenings of English-language movies in Brussels cinemas.

'Where to then?'

'The Foreign Ministry, please.'

'Where's that, now?'

'Oh, yes, you call it the "Department of External Affairs" here.'

He muttered something under his breath and swung out into the exit lane from the terminal. As I looked across the car park next to the road, I saw two angular brick buildings sitting back against green fields, with a slim concrete tower rising between them. The tower was horizontally segmented, reminiscent of the watchtowers along the inner German border.

'What's that over there to the left?' I asked.

'The airport church. It opened five years ago. I know a fella who built it.'

'God has his eye on you in Ireland, directly after you land.'

'You're not wrong. Where are you from, fella?'

'West Germany.'

'And what are you doing in Dublin, now?'

135

'I'm with the EEC.'

'For sure. And what are you doing in Ireland for them, now?'

These people were persistent, I'd grant them that. Maybe the vaunted Irish friendliness was simply an insatiable curiosity about other people's business.

Off to the left of the airport road into Dublin, there was a cluster of high-rise apartment blocks in the distance, just as you would see in any other European city. As we drove along, I was beginning to become disappointed again at the increasing ordinariness of it all. Modernity, for all its benefits, couldn't be kept out of any corner of Europe.

As I looked around me, the driver rattled on all the way into the centre. I fed him the usual polite rebuttals, that no, the EEC wasn't going one day to have its own currency or its own army, although I didn't tell him how much some people at the Berlaymont wanted both.

Yes, the EEC had now changed with the retirement of de Gaulle and now welcomed other nations into the club. I didn't give him Kramer's real explanation about the need for France to have had the funding arrangements for the CAP stitched up first.

He pulled up outside what looked like a nobleman's town mansion, complete with pillared portico, facing a park from across a busy street - the kind of government ministry building not seen in Germany since the time of the Kaiser.

I paid the driver and looked suspiciously at my change: a mixture of coins in pence and shillings. I'd had enough of being taken for a fool in Madrid to last me for the rest of the year.

'What are these?' I demanded, holding up a shilling.

'A shilling, same as that five pence coin I gave you too, except that the five pence coin is twelve pence right now until next year when it becomes five.'

'Really? You have the same dumb currency system as the British?'

'Not by choice, but next year is the last of it.'

I mounted the steps and went in. No-one was there. I looked into a couple of small side rooms until I found a secretary in one of them slowly typing out a report. A stack of papers stood next to her machine on the desk. They wouldn't be finished today or tomorrow at her word-per-minute rate.

'I've come to see Mister Doyle.'

'Which Mister Doyle would that be, now?'

'Mister Doyle in Protocol, who worked on the security for de Galle's visit here last year.'

'I don't know of a Doyle who would be involved in that kind of thing. Kathleen!' she shouted through the modern partition wall to the neighbouring office.

Kathleen came out of her rabbit hutch and was equally puzzled.

'This man here says he's looking for a Doyle. What did you say you came for?'

'To give an accession briefing on EEC Agricultural subsidies.'

'You want the Department of Agriculture then,' said Kathleen triumphantly, as if she'd solved a Sherlock Holmes mystery two pages before the end.

'No,' I said stubbornly. 'I was told to meet with a Mister Doyle today at the Department of External Affairs.'

'I'm sorry. If you're here on Agriculture business maybe you've made a mistake. You should go over and see if he works there. They're just on the other side of Saint Stephen's Green from us, somewhere over in the Government Buildings.'

Her description didn't fill me with confidence.

'Does Mister Doyle work at a different office of this Department? How many people do you have?'

'I still don't know which person you mean, and I've worked here twenty years. I know everyone.'

She was getting impatient. Time to show her how Germany expected things to run in the future.

'Well look them all up then. All of the ones who might have dealt with de Gaulle. I'm not leaving here until you do. Please.'

She looked shocked, as if it was the first time in her twenty long years here that anyone had crossed her. With a barely controlled 'humph' she marched back out and closed the door, none too softly either.

'There's a couple of chairs in the inner hall, Mister...' said her friend.

'Lenkeit.'

'Well, you can sit out there then. Out of here, the double doors opposite the entrance.' It was a command rather than a suggestion.

I waited a good forty-five minutes in silence, sitting under an alcove in the wall, being watched disapprovingly by the marble statuary standing on guard there. Mercury, by the looks of him, at least someone was on duty today in Dublin.

I was seeing for myself how their government worked behind the relaxed facade Ireland showed the rest of the world. Too relaxed for their own good so far, I thought. Ready for an intensive course on Sophie's complicated CAP frauds and rest of the highly organised world of the EEC they were not.

As I sat, the odd person came in and out through the open doorway on the other side of the room which led into the main building. Men in dark suits and once a woman in a long navy dress with hair in a beehive, all swept past with scarcely a look. Someone important came out too, with a bald, high-domed head and a strong face, striding across the blue carpet to the exit, followed by a couple of acolytes carrying document cases.

Through the inner doors, I could see a grand staircase in a sky-lit atrium, marble-covered walls and long mirrors.

I carried on waiting as the forty-five minutes threatened to extend to a full sixty. Then, after a longer gap in the traffic, I heard a clip-clip of heels from somewhere up above. I turned my head at the new sound and watched as down the steps came a classical vision of Ireland, of the kind I'd expected to see earlier on the Aer Lingus flight. This one, though, looked like she'd just stepped out of a much better class of airline brochure, one which advertised only to maharajas and oil sheikhs.

The long, tumbling red-gold curls and delicate dusting of freckles over creamy skin would surely have beaten all comers at a Hollywood casting for a nobly virtuous Irish peasant girl, emigrating in hope of a better life in a rough mining town of the old Wild West. Of course, her hair was carefully arranged and her skirt suit in homely tweed looked fitted, but any director would have forgiven her the artifice. I certainly did.

The vision resolved itself into a young woman of about my own age who came up to where I was sitting. She stopped a good metre away and asked if I was 'Mister Lenkeit'.

I got to my feet carefully.

'Yes, guilty,' I replied.

When she spoke, in contrast to the people I'd met so far, her accent did indeed almost sound American and as clear-cut and gently modulated as anything I'd heard at the movies.

'My name is Miss O'Cuacach. I've found your letter of introduction and I've been sent to arrange your meeting with Mister Doyle.'

'I thought something had already been agreed for today?' She wasn't getting away with fobbing me off, just because she looked like the opposite of a sour old office gatekeeper.

'He's only available tomorrow now, but I can arrange a time for whenever you like in the morning.'

'Are you his secretary?'

She flushed slightly and her tone dropped a degree or two in temperature.

'I work for him on the European desk. He doesn't have his own secretary. I'm an executive officer, a translator.'

I pushed her a little, only because I was curious to see what she was really like underneath the smooth skin.

'In Germany we start work at eight,' I said, sidestepping the fact that EEC officials rolled up much later than that to the Berlaymont.

I felt like clicking my heels too. Just for good measure, to make her more uncomfortable than the doubtful look on her face already showed her to be.

'People won't be here at the Department that early. Why don't you come back here at ten o'clock tomorrow morning, but you'll need to call next door, at Number Seventy-Nine, our other office building.'

'Very well,' I said, glancing at my watch. It was still only four o'clock. Is there someone else I can meet here now, though? Another executive officer who works in the domain of international security coordination?'

The confused look came back, the look of someone trying to work out if it was just my clumsy use of English or if there was a deeper meaning to what I was saying.

'I think it's best you start with Mister Doyle,' she said, polite but firm. I had been told the Irish were friendly and the English cold fish by comparison. Miss O'Cuacach wasn't one to be easily charmed, though. She probably got lots of practice from having to rebuff most of the male population of Dublin on a weekly basis.

'Will I get to see you tomorrow?'

'We like to have an interpreter present at meetings which touch on questions of diplomacy. It helps smooth out differences in attitudes, amongst other things. So yes, you will see me again Mister Lenkeit,' she said coolly.

With that, she turned on her stilettos and left.

Hotel it was then, and an early bath before seeing what entertainment was on offer at the hotel bar.

It was the loss of the Irish, if they couldn't be bothered to keep appointments. But I was only due to be here for a week and was worried that I was already a day behind schedule. Still, Kramer had called for patience and given the rate at which I now knew the Irish civil service worked, maybe a week had been optimistic anyway.

When I checked in, I made my preparations for the coming weekend because I reckoned I'd need a distraction after spending a full day tomorrow at the Department of External Affairs. The hotel bar would do for tonight, though.

'Which places do most Germans visit when in Dublin?' I asked the concierge. My plan was to try to avoid them if I could.

'I wouldn't know about Germans especially, sir. Most tourists want to see the places made famous by Yeats and Joyce: Trinity College, the National Library, Abbey Theatre and the pubs they frequented, too.'

'Swift's tomb?' Böll had gone there in his book.

'Yes, it's in Saint Patrick's Cathedral.'

'Nelson's memorial pillar?' He'd mentioned that too.

The concierge ran his tongue over his lips. 'No, that's no longer to be seen. The army had to be called in to demolish it after it became unsafe.'

'How about the German writer Heinrich Böll and the places mentioned in "Irish Journal"? Is there really an armless beggar in the cathedral area?'

The concierge laughed nervously. 'That's not an author I've heard of.'

'What laundry company do you use at this hotel?'

Now he was really unhappy, as if I was deliberately making fun of him.

'The High Park Laundry. Why, are you interested, sir?'

'Oh, no reason, I wanted to know if you used another one which I'd heard of.'

'Bloody Germans,' he said, only partially under his

breath as I made to pick up my bags and go to the room.

I was sorely tempted to reply with a *'What did you say?'* but creating a scene in a public place on my first day here wasn't the smartest move in my line of work.

Despite the concierge's shortness, later that evening the hotel bar proved *gemütlich* enough.

The leather seats arranged around low tables already contained a collection of business travellers of different shapes and sizes. There was an end-of-week feeling, of people still stuck here on a Thursday evening because they had meetings tomorrow which stopped them getting away for the weekend early. Not that I myself was planning to go back to Brussels - we had unlimited budget for travel - but I wanted to make the most of every day I had here, to see what I could sniff out. Besides, I had no-one to go back to.

I asked at the bar for a menu and ordered a beer. The next guy along heard my accent and asked me where I was from.

'West Berlin,' came the reply to my 'Hamburg.'

'What are you doing here?' I asked him, glad to be able to switch to German at the end of a long day.

'Meeting trade unions to negotiate the end of a strike. I'm the company lawyer for a West German manufacturer.'

'Strikes?'

'There's more of them than you might believe. As bad as England, in terms of production days lost.'

'But I thought these guys were desperate for work, that they were still dragging themselves out of poverty?'

'That may be, but they see foreign-owned companies as a soft touch. For some reason they assume that because we've been given government grants to set up business here, that we're under an obligation to stay, regardless of the number of strikes they hit us with.'

My beer arrived and I clinked glasses with him. 'Sounds

like West Berlin, no? Don't you get lots of government grants there too? And no conscription there either?'

'Would you choose to live there, unless you'd been born there?'

'I take your point, but why set up a factory in Ireland in the first place if it's so difficult to do business here?'

'What do you think happens to our West German factory in the first twelve hours of the next war?'

'And you think Ireland will escape that war?'

'It better had, for our company owner's sake. He's bought a thousand acres - that's about four hundred hectares - in the west of Ireland.'

He waved at the barman to get his attention, indicating another beer for himself.

'But you never considered Northern Ireland? They can't be much more of a Soviet target than here?'

'We did briefly. They offered better incentives, but the owner wanted a neutral bolthole.'

'Then Switzerland would have been the logical place to go to?'

'Not on the wages we pay the Irish.'

'So what do they think of us here, apart from being soft touches?' I asked, thinking of the barman's indistinct mutterings.

'You get some hotheads who don't like foreigners coming in and buying up property. There's a German who owns a large farm in County Cork. Last year he had a shoot-out with the IRA who'd come to burn him out. Real cowboys and Indians stuff, like in a Karl May story.'

His drink arrived and we clinked glasses again.

'I want to ask you something about Berlin. I was in the city the other week and heard machine gun fire at two in the morning from the direction of the Wall. Is that usual?'

'They like to make a show of force using the slightest of excuses, but yes, it may well have been an escape attempt.'

'But I didn't hear anything when I tuned into RIAS the

following morning.'

'As I said, it was probably an attempt at escape. How many of those do you imagine are successful? Someone is shot dead about every six months or so.'

'Have the Irish or the British closed the border here, to get a grip of the insurgency?'

'It's just like the border between any other two Western European countries. Less restrictive because there's no passport controls. Although when we went there, we didn't go near a big town. If you're really unlucky coming back from the North through the back country lanes, then there might be a mobile customs check, but not a serious search. Nothing like the Wall, no, not at all.' He laughed to himself at the thought.

'When did you go to the North?'

'Last spring, just before it all started up there. Fishing trip to Lough Erne, right next to the border. It's "Lough", by the way,' he said the word again with a guttural flourish. 'It's pronounced almost the same as the way that the Scots say "loch."'

'What's going to happen to their chances of attracting investment now?'

'They're finished, as far as I can see. If given the choice of investing in Britain or Ireland, why would any industrialist choose the worst of both worlds by setting up shop in Northern Ireland? Ironically, though, if this nonsense carries on and the British have to keep pumping in ever more public subventions to make up for lost wages, they'll make Northern Ireland unaffordable for the Irish to ever take over.'

Every action had an equal and opposite reaction, or so they'd taught me at school.

Chapter Eleven

I turned up at twenty minutes to ten at the red brick annex to the Department of External Affairs, the next door along from the mansion on Saint Stephen's Green. I wanted to make sure the Irish got a taste of German punctuality, which wasn't actually punctuality at all but rather a lack of imagination when it came to changing any agreed arrangement or challenging rules.

The downside of faithful compliance to orders, of course, was that when actual circumstances turned out differently to those envisaged when plans were made, a lack of imagination led to all sorts of trouble.

It was why Johannes went on about my time in the Bundeswehr and how I should always use my initiative, as I'd been shown there. Even if it wasn't his army, he assumed that its officers also kept their instructions focussed on mission objectives rather than details, so as to force junior leaders to think for themselves when the fog of war came down on the battlefield.

On my own in Dublin, already behind schedule on only the second day of my trip, I suspected I'd end up needing all of the initiative I could muster.

Miss O'Cuacach was wise to my little game of trying to pressurise the Irish though, because she arrived only a couple of minutes after me carrying a leather attaché case, diplomat that she was - not a secretary.

But although I was early, she still made me wait in the lobby, coming back shortly before ten to escort me in silence down a long corridor to the back of the building.

When I finally walked in on Doyle, two weeks after being given my first orders in Berlin, I began to understand why de Gaulle's personal security chief and Kramer had thought he might be a suitable entry point to the secret world of the Irish government's confidential agents.

Behind the desk, rising to shake hands, was a middling sort of man, in age, demeanour and appearance. His expression as he eyed me up had a slight fox-like cast to it, giving the impression of someone eager to please a bigger dog, but not altogether trustworthy.

There was no meeting table in his office so we sat rather awkwardly around the desk with Miss O'Cuacach off to one side, just within my range of vision, taking notes on a document pad laid on her lap, feet flat on the floor, legs tight together. I wondered who would type up her jottings afterwards. I'd got away with bullying Kathleen yesterday, but she might resent another Irishwoman telling her what to do even more. Given the speed at which Kathleen worked, though, I wouldn't think any less of Miss O'Cuacach if she typed them herself. Not that I would have anyway, whatever she did.

After the greetings, I let Doyle speak first. Better that he did his own rationalisation for my being here, and convinced himself that my cover story was real.

'I understand you know Mister Kramer of the Commission, is that correct, Mister Lenkeit? And you've been sent by him to explain some of the detailed mechanisms of the CAP to us?'

'Yes, you helped some of his countrymen with de Gaulle's visit last year to... Sneem. Is that how you say it?'

'Yes, yes. It's a village in Kerry.'

'He was given your name by his people in Paris. You liaised between the French presidential security detail and the intelligence agencies here? Because of the threat from the French-Algerian terrorists?'

'How does all that relate to farm subsidies?' he asked,

standoffish now.

Maybe 'terrorists' had been a poor choice of word.

'The topic of my briefing is subsidy fraud, which is what you get whenever large sums of public money are involved but which we at the EEC naturally don't want advertised too widely. We presumed it would be of interest to the Irish law-enforcement bodies, as much as to the Department of Agriculture.'

'I'm sure I don't know what you're talking about, to do with fraud and suchlike.'

Miss O'Cuacach seemed to be writing down in longhand everything that was being said, swiftly crossing and recrossing the pad with her fountain pen. I could almost hear her listening to Doyle's protestation over the scratching of the nib.

'I'm not suggesting it happens here now, but it might in the future,' I said diplomatically. 'What I do want to say, though, is that we don't want this briefing to get into the wrong hands. We don't want to give the wrong people the distilled wisdom from six countries on how to play the CAP system.'

'So you don't mind if the right people get tips from the stable?'

Ah, yes, the famous Irish wit. But whatever worked for him.

'This is deadly serious, Mr. Doyle. Millions of your pounds are at stake.'

'Millions of France and West Germany's pounds,' he muttered quickly, but not quickly enough. Miss O'Cuacach looked at him disapprovingly.

'Who do you have here in Dublin who specialises in agricultural fraud?'

'I'm not sure. We have agents of the Customs Service who watch for smuggling across the border, but I expect Agriculture will tell you that any subsidy fraud here in Ireland would be by people claiming for phantom production - just the same as in the EEC, I'm sure.'

'It's going to be more sophisticated than that in the future. In the EEC, phantom olive groves produce phantom olive oil which is processed into phantom margarine. Plus, each stage can take place in a different country, picking up additional subsidies on the way. Half our battle is getting the national agencies to speak to one another, to trace these scams across borders.'

He was showing a little more interest now.

'So what are the sanctions against countries which don't enforce the rules to the satisfaction of the EEC?'

'Ireland would be guilty of wrecking the system that's been carefully built up over three decades to interlink the Western European economies, ensuring that war amongst us is a thing of the past.'

'We wouldn't want that sort of thing, now.'

No, and you probably wouldn't want to let France and West Germany run your trade, agriculture and fishing from now on, either, but that's the hidden price of your precious farm subsidies.

'So are there any sanctions on the member states, or is it an honesty system?' he asked.

I turned to Miss O'Cuacach, just to make sure. *'Quoi?'*

'Système de l'honnêteté - toutes les parties s'engagent à respecter les règles.'

Doyle looked suitably impressed.

'Yes,' I said. 'It's a system that only works if everyone follows the rules, which means that those who don't get instantly exposed by the others.'

I was vague myself as to what actually did happen to rule-breakers. Sophie would know.

I tapped the edge of the desk with my forefinger. 'So, we need to know that you'll take this seriously at the intergovernmental level. We need your best people on it, people like Colonel Delaney, Commandant O'Brian, Captain Murphy, State Secretary Berry, Superintendent Quinn and Inspector Regan.'

Miss O'Cuacach looked up sharply from her pad.

'Where did you get those names from?'

'They're hardly secrets. Your army intelligence people have got themselves into all sorts of trouble in public recently. People as far afield as Brussels and farther still have been closely watching Dublin with a keen eye these past weeks.'

'Our affairs are our affairs, Mister Lenkeit,' Doyle said. 'We don't take kindly to people telling us what to do here, in case you hadn't noticed.'

'I'm not telling you what to do. I'm trying to give you the highest possible chance of making EEC membership a success, by asking to see the people here who are best equipped to help us.'

'So as Miss O'Cuacach asks, how did you get those names?'

'We know people who know your people. We have our own contacts and our own ability to conduct research.'

'What people are you connected with, then? The sort who would know the names of our people? The British? MI6? Are the British spying on the Department of Agriculture now, the devils?'

The conversation was veering well off-course. I guessed British spies were their national bugbear, the default villain in any story they told themselves, just like French spies had been sixty years ago for us.

'Smuggling of livestock wouldn't be of interest to the big boys in espionage, I imagine. No, I was given some names through a connection who knows the former German commando Herr Otto Skorzeny. He lived here until the mid-sixties, I believe.'

Miss O'Cuacach underlined a word in her notes three times. Now she spoke up.

'I thought you said that breaking the CAP rules jeopardised European peace? What sort of an EEC department are you?'

This was where our versatile name came in handy.

'It's called External Investigations, a sub-department of

Internal Affairs. We support our Agriculture officials when questions of fraud and bribery come up in their international trade discussions. And right now, the accession of Ireland and the others is the most important discussion going on.'

'I told you already, our situation is different. You can't drive a lorry-load of olive, or any other kind of oil, across three different borders here in an afternoon,' replied Doyle again.

'But a ship that leaves here can dock anywhere. All I want to do is to meet with your intelligence people, police, customs, whomever, to brief them on CAP fraud. Then we can include them on the updates our department sends out to the member states. We're prepared to do this even before your accession.'

'You mentioned that earlier, as if it's a done thing,' he countered.

'Germans have learned to be optimistic about the future because pride in the past is closed off to us,' I said loftily.

Miss O'Cuacach's ginger eyebrows shot up and down again.

Doyle twiddled his thumbs for a moment. 'Why don't you show me this briefing or these updates or whatever it is you're talking about and I'll decide where they should go?'

'No, this only works if we know who's getting them. As I said, the information I've brought with me today is highly sensitive.'

I patted my case to show him how well I was guarding the secrets of the Six. 'And anyway, once you've joined, we want intelligence to flow both ways.'

'We don't give access to our intelligence services to the first smooth talker off the plane carrying an EEC business card. How do we even know who he is? That's your job, Miss O'Cuacach.'

'I already called Brussels and spoke with a Monsieur

Masson, who I was directed to by Monsieur Kramer's secretary,' she replied neutrally. I guessed how a conversation with one of the Berlaymont dragons might have gone, having to supplicate them for their jealously-guarded inside knowledge of the organisation's reporting lines.

'Leave your documents with me and I promise I'll see what I can do,' he finally concluded.

'It seems like we're already at an impasse then,' I observed.

He continued, clearly suspicious. 'This is a small country, Mister Lenkeit. Keeping secrets from us is difficult. Sooner or later two people will meet to compare a story and find the gaps. Don't take us for culchies - that's slang for country fools, before Miss O'Cuacach shows off her university degree in smugness again.'

Miss O'Cuacach wasn't much deterred by the insult.

'*Paysans*,' she said contemptuously, with just a hint in her intonation that could have implied she meant the label to apply to Doyle too.

Unless I could think of something quick, my time in Dublin was already over. I pursed my lips, as if about to make a painful concession. I may even have given a shallow sigh.

'As a compromise, if I let you read our fraud briefing here in this office without it leaving my sight, will you get me in front of someone in an intelligence gathering capacity? I don't care what their specific job is, whether they're tracking the local mafia, Yugoslavian guest workers or the IRA. I just need to meet one of the people we'll eventually be working with, to get a sense of what your people might already know.'

Doyle rocked back on his chair and thought for a few seconds.

'Very well. I can probably get you in front of someone but only if we think that what you're going to show us will be of use to those kinds of people. But I doubt now it will be before Tuesday at the earliest.'

For an answer, I reached inside my document case. In an inspired fit of spite, I left the English version in its folder and pulled out the French language copy.

'I presume Miss O'Cuacach can read this?'

She shot me a sneering glance and snapped her fingers for me to hand it over.

I reached back into my case for a copy of the very latest version of the Mansholt Plan, also in French. Just to give her even more opportunity to show off her language skills to Doyle and myself.

She took the fraud manual and Doyle the Mansholt Plan while I sat back on a chair by the door to give them room around the desk.

Doyle obviously knew some French - he worked at the Department of External Affairs, after all. But by the speed his forefinger was tracing each line of the good Dutch doctor's plan, to force elderly farmers off their fields, amalgamating their holdings with those of more energetic, tractor-driving, chemical-spraying younger men, he wasn't ready for the Berlaymont yet. After the first couple of pages he got up and left, rather than carry on being shown up in front of a foreigner and a woman.

From time to time, Miss O'Cuacach asked me a terse question for clarification on the EEC special terms and acronyms but otherwise ignored my presence in the room. I watched her at work for a little while, the copper threads in her amber hair gleaming in the sun as she bent over the desk. Rather than make things awkward while she worked, I dug out my copy of 'Irisches Tagebuch' to finally finish it off, so I could impress her with a few German anecdotes about Ireland at some point in the near future.

At length, she got to her feet with a bundle of papers in her hand and so did I. Positioning myself in front of the door I gently reached out for her notes with a *'S'il vous plaît'*.

In return, she gave me a narrow look with her green

eyes but did hesitantly hand them over. I riffled through the sheets. She had got the gist, the notes getting sparser towards the end as her boredom levels had justifiably increased. But there ought to have been enough bait in what she'd taken down to get them hooked.

'*Excusez-moi.* I need to get these typed up, you need to stay here,' she said, pointing at my chair.

I stepped to one side to let her pass, disappointed that she hadn't suggested that we go for a friendly lunchtime drink instead, now that Friday afternoon was nearly upon us and the civil service working week was surely almost done.

After another hour, just as Böll was getting into his taxi to go to the station and leave Ireland for good, she came back in to tell me that the report had been typed up, but not by whom.

Doyle came in with her, too, looking happier than when he'd left, as if he'd successfully given the Lenkeit problem to someone else.

'As it turns out, Herr Lenkeit, you can come back here on Monday. We may have found someone for you to speak with.'

'Who is it?'

'Someone who works in one of the areas you described earlier. You can brief him about these schemes mentioned in Miss O'Cuacach's translation.'

'And the rest of today?'

'We both have other meetings to attend this afternoon. There are plenty of places around Saint Stephen's Green where you can get some lunch and then you're free for whatever else it is you need to do this afternoon.' He trailed off, hoping I'd take the hint and go.

'Okay.'

Miss O'Cuacach cleared her throat now.

'I mentioned your visit to my father last night. He used to be at the Department of External Affairs too, during the Emergency, *la Deuxième Guerre mondiale*. He knew some of the people at the German embassy back then. He'd like to invite you to lunch with us, at our house, on Sunday after Mass. Here, I've put down the address and directions for you.'

It was the longest speech she'd yet made to me.

She handed over a folded sheet of foolscap. Through the thin paper I could see lines written in a clear, looping hand.

I raised an eyebrow. 'That's very kind of him, and of you, Miss O'Cuacach, to mention me to him. I'd be delighted to accept.'

She looked a little embarrassed as she added, 'When we're at my parent's house, you can call me "Brigid."'

I took my cues from both of them to get out and left.

I wandered out into the sunny street, lost as to what to do with my unexpected free time. Starting the weekend early with Johannes in Berlin was different. That was still work, as far as I was concerned. Truthfully, any hours of enforced idleness weren't great for my state of mind.

I hunted around the streets, getting to know the layout of the city centre a little better.

As I drifted west of Saint Stephen's Green, I came across the cathedral mentioned in Böll's book, Saint Patrick's. For want of a better plan, I thought I might as well make a start on tomorrow's itinerary.

The sign outside said 'Church of Ireland', but it was only when I went inside that I began to realise this meant something different to 'Catholic'. I wandered up and down the aisles, scanning the odd memorial tablet, trying to make sense of inscriptions written in archaic English and found Swift's grave under its brass plaque.

The cathedral really did have regimental flags hanging up, just as Böll had described. But he had neglected to mention that they almost all had a faded British flag in the top left-hand corner. While I understood that the colours dated from before independence, I didn't understand why they were still allowed to be on display. Whatever a change of regime meant in the Germanies, it meant enthusiastic iconoclasm of earlier symbols. That was why some buildings in Hamburg still sported the occasional stylised eagle holding a suspiciously empty wreath in its talons, the Hindu symbol for the sun having been carefully ground down, where it used to be in the centre.

Maybe these flags were somehow inviolable, though, because of the particular blood-sacrifice they represented. In the same way that the monument to the Great War still survived in Hamburg, across from the city hall - '*Vierzigtausend Söhne der Stadt ließen ihr Leben für Euch.*'

There was a different concierge on duty at the hotel when I got back. He gave me the names of a couple of tourist bars, for I'd changed my mind and decided I wasn't quite ready for the full local experience just yet. Besides, part of me wanted to hear what some other foreigners thought of Böll's *redselige Insel* first.

Still, there was one authentic local experience to be had at the pub he directed me to on Baggott Street - my first Guinness. Böll hadn't mentioned the beer by name. In his book it appeared in phrases such as 'endless glasses of dark brown beer,' or 'the dark brown beer flowed'. But he'd referenced it quite often in the text, as it turned out.

The barman poured the deep, dark beer slowly down the side of the glass, then let it stand for what felt like a minute at least, as the thick head formed. The liquid was black in the glass when he handed it over and the head had the consistency of whipped cream as I took my first bite. And 'bite' was the right word in this case. The nutty, caramelised liquid felt so heavy in my mouth it was more like eating than drinking.

I also found this meant that I couldn't gulp it down either. It was a drink for passing the time, for sitting and talking.

The bar was busy, and to make the most of the space, the church pew-like benches were arranged along the walls. I squeezed in next to a late middle-aged couple dressed in smart, casual clothes. The man watched my evident enjoyment and smiled.

'I had my first Guinness here in Ireland, twenty-seven years ago.'

'So long to come back?'

'We're over to see where our folks came from originally.' He extended a hand. 'My name is Kelly and my wife's an O'Dwyer. We're from Chicago, Illinois.'

'Oskar Lenkeit, here on business, from West Germany. When did your families arrive in America?'

My interest seemed to please them.

'The Kellys came just before the Civil War, from Killeedy, Limerick. The O'Dwyers came thirty years later, from Glengariff, Cork.' He looked enquiringly at me, as if I should have recognised the names.

'How old are you, Oskar?' asked Kelly's wife.

'Twenty-five this year.' I replied.

'Same age as our eldest,' she said. 'And what do your folks do in Germany?'

'My mother's a nurse.' They waited but I didn't complete the picture. 'How come you were in Ireland, what, during the war?' I asked instead.

'Not down here. In Northern Ireland. I was in a tank destroyer regiment. We did our training there, before we went to Europe in 'forty-four.'

We smiled politely at one another, dancing a dance, carefully trying to avoid the dangerous topics.

'Where in Germany are your folks from?'

'Originally East Prussia, but my mother ended up in Hamburg.'

Kelly looked at me appraisingly. I could see a new wariness in his eyes, but his wife was oblivious to his look.

'Just like in the States, folks move around all the time,' she said brightly. Kelly shook his head slightly.

'Where did you end up in Germany, Mister Kelly?' I asked.

'Outside Frankfurt-am-Main, Camp Phoenix. It was an old Luftwaffe field which we took over.'

'What did your people do during the war, Oskar? Maybe John met them at some point?'

I smiled politely. 'That's unlikely.'

I thought I saw Kelly jolt his foot against his wife's.

'My mother was in the German Red Cross. She served as an army nurse.'

Kelly looked up as the TV news appeared on a set sitting on top of the bar.

'Look,' he pointed, almost in relief. 'More rioting in Belfast.'

I twisted around so I could see too. There were monochrome images of a white flame flaring up as a Molotov cocktail ignited. There were images of soldiers in drab, unpatterned uniforms advancing behind metal riot shields, a wheeled personnel carrier rolling slowly along behind them.

'It's shocking what's happening there in Belfast,' said Kelly's wife. 'As if there's not enough trouble in the world. They're all Irish. Why can't they get along?'

I had no quick answer, for her or for myself. I strongly suspected the reason many small Germans towns showed the times of both Catholic Mass and Lutheran services on a signpost as you entered was a forgotten legacy of trying to keep the peace after the end of the Thirty Years' War, three hundred years ago. And we were all German, back then, too.

For some light relief, the news report switched to Vietnam. It was a report of the aftermath of a three-week battle by the Airborne Division to hold a hilltop base in one of the border provinces. The North Vietnamese army had infiltrated south, and the Americans had sucked them into a protracted firefight, killing three Communists for every paratrooper who'd fallen.

Kelly's wife sat in silence, transfixed to the screen, her husband lightly gripping her arm. The segment finished and she let out a sigh of relief.

'Our youngest is out there. I have to watch every news report that comes on, in case they mention any casualties by name.'

Kelly explained more. 'He's with the Eleventh Marines, in the artillery. They're somewhere up near the border, towards Da Nang in Quang Nam province.'

He turned to his wife. 'He'll be stationed behind the lines at a fire base. He won't even see the enemy.'

Except that the aerial shots of the American hilltop positions in the TV report had clearly showed discarded artillery ammunition boxes and shell casings around the gun pits - clearly to me anyway.

As he said the exotic names, I caught the scents of the jungle, rotting vegetation and fetid stagnant water, and in the closeness of the pub, I felt the humidity too. I knew that the American troops only served twelve months in theatre, so I asked when he was due back.

'Early in the new year, in six months' time or so, but some of them re-enlist, sign on permanently. And he might get deployed back there again after promotion.'

Kelly's wife looked uncomfortable at this. Her husband remonstrated with her.

'From his letters, he's doing a job you know he loves. Like it or not, some men get a taste for fighting. Trust me, I know,' he said, suddenly far away, probably rolling in his M10, down the main street of a wrecked town somewhere in the Rhineland.

I thought of Skorzeny unsuccessfully offering his services, well into the nineteen-sixties, to train the special forces of various dubious regimes. He was also unable to let go.

'And he's keeping our country safe for your grandchildren, Maureen,' Kelly added, somewhat awkwardly.

'That's the one thing I find difficult about being here,' he confided to me in a lower voice. 'While honest Irish lads are fighting and dying in Vietnam, our own people back here just aren't interested in the blood we're spilling for the defence of the West. It's not honourable for Ireland to sit out the fight against Communism, and when I think back on it these days, against the Nazis too. Not that your folks would have had anything to do with that kind of thing, Mister Lenkeit,' he added hastily.

'There's a reason why the Irish who left Ireland got on and made a success of life in America, and a reason why the ones left behind sit around in bars feeling sorry for themselves,' he concluded.

I guessed he voted Republican.

'Do you have anti-Vietnam protestors in West Germany, Mister Lenkeit?' asked his wife.

'Yes. It's the cause of the day, an easy target for the left-wing,' including for the socialists on the other side of the Berlin Wall too, I could have added.

'How do you feel about them, the anti-war protestors?' I asked her.

'They're getting what they want, aren't they? Nixon said he would bring back the troops and they've started to do so. It was just Vince's fate he came to draft age whilst the war was still going on. Not that he complained about it,' she said, more bitterly now.

My cousin Thomas wasn't the only one keen to pick up a rifle.

I finished my drink, nodding to the couple. We shook hands again and I left to go back to the hotel. As I walked the darkening streets and reflected on the day just past, my latent resentment at the thought of the Irish holding out their hands for West German-funded farm subsidies started to turn to something closer to disgust.

Here they sat, in what they thought was safety, a thousand kilometres away from the AK-47-carrying soldiers I'd seen outside Berlin, trucks upon trucks of them, waiting for the order to come west and force the Irish to finally take part in the twentieth century.

Chapter Twelve

I got up later than usual because today was going to be a slow one. But I was determined to see at least something of Dublin today. I'd felt cheated out of a proper look at East Berlin and Madrid last month.

Having been to the cathedral yesterday, I realised that going through the other places mentioned in Böll's book might be just as exciting, so I quietly put the idea to one side, apart from one particular sight, perhaps.

Back in Chapter Four of 'Irisches Tagebuch', Böll claimed he'd almost been knocked down, if not physically then metaphorically by one of the trucks of the Swastika Laundry, painted in a fetching Nuremberg blood red. If ever there was a sign that the cataclysmic struggle of democracy against fascism had passed the Irish by, the woefully-named Swastika Laundry was it.

Not that I had any intention of actually visiting an industrial laundry. I'd just do what Böll did and wander the streets and see if I spotted a Nazi truck. As it turned out, they were more scarce these days than in nineteen fifty-seven. My full faith in the power of iconoclasm was restored, though, when I asked for Nelson's Pillar and was told it was no more with a 'some of the boys blew it up four years ago.'

I assumed they weren't the army, who presumably had merely finished off the job when the remnants became 'unsafe.'

To be fair, Böll had spent part of his sojourn in Dublin reading letters to the newspaper proposing just that kind

161

of solution.

Wandering for a while, only a little way off the tourist track into the back streets of North Dublin, west of the hotel, the poverty described by Böll was still there to see - crumbling tenements with a scattering of beaten-up cars on the streets outside and children playing in between them. I had assumed that old Heinrich had been using poetic license when he described centuries of dirt in the slums with houses 'no different to those Swift would have seen'. But maybe he hadn't, not now that I was here for myself.

I also took a miss at the slum pubs and their one-man drinking booths where Böll claimed the landlord's customers resigned themselves to private misery. He was big into misery, resignation and hopelessness. I supposed it was because in the mid-fifties, he had been subconsciously hoping to find a country worse off than ourselves, psychologically speaking.

After a while, the novelty of the slums wore off and I gravitated south, back across the Liffey to my reference point, Saint Stephen's Green, wandering with no set objective apart from observing street life like a *flâneur* walking the boulevards of Paris.

As I crossed and recrossed my path, one of my dog-legs took me down a road called Cuffe Street. Something caught my eye outside a public building belonging to the Brick and Stonelayers' Guild, according to the writing across the facade. At street level there was a poster advertising a meeting for later that afternoon, organised by the Communist Party of Ireland, the CPI mentioned by Johannes' boss. The title of the talk was 'Lessons for Ireland from Socialist Liberation Movements Around the World' and a row of socialist world leaders adorned the bottom edge of the flyer, including Johannes' very own Walter Ulbricht.

I wasn't quite sure how an East German socialist

regime qualified as a 'liberation' movement given it was imposed in 'forty-five by the rifles of the Red Army and then kept in place the same way in 'fifty-three, when the workers' revolt of that year was brutally suppressed. Nevertheless, I was intrigued.

I turned over the idea in my mind of going along to hear what they had to say.

I'd had enough of sightseeing anyway, and you never knew which interesting, if not useful, contacts you might make at these things. Johannes' boss had said 'don't get caught', but what could be the harm in meeting the local comrades?

I walked on by a couple of blocks further and found a cafe for lunch, a cheap one for a change. While I sat at the greasy formica table, grabbing a bite, I came to a decision out of growing boredom more than anything else.

Behind the stage of the main hall of the Stonelayers' Guild was the same row of pictures as on the poster. Seeing them for the second time, I realised that the selection and order had been carefully chosen. Fidel Castro and Che Guevara had pride of place, of course, the blown-up photo of the latter draped with a black ribbon. Uncle Ho Chi Minh was there too. I recognised Ngouabi from the former French Congo, Gaddafi from Libya and the puck-like Ulbricht again. I gave old Spitzbart a conspiratorial wink.

The main speaker came on stage wearing a denim jacket with pins of the symbols of different liberation movements down each lapel, from the spear and shield of the ANC to the Palestinian flag of the PLO. He raised his arm in a Black Panther salute to the audience and began.

The actual content of his lecture was less inspiring, to me anyway - potted histories of the socialist revolution each country, apart from East Germany, not to my surprise.

To be fair, he was speaking with the handicap of a poorly-attended talk on a pleasant summer Saturday afternoon. The speaker tried to inject some anti-capitalist passion into his words, delivered at high speed and in a heavy accent which I tried to follow along as best I could in the echoing hall. But only a few rows at the front were even sparsely filled. The sparks of political agitation in Dublin weren't going to burst into the flames of Marxist revolution across the country anytime soon.

After the talk, cups of tea were served at the back and the speaker came and made the point of meeting everyone in turn. He reminded me uncomfortably of a diligent, well-meaning pastor at a church function.

Of course, I didn't escape either and when I told him I was a salesman for agricultural machinery from West Germany but had voted for the Social Democrats, it was like I'd made his day.

He subjected me to a detailed explanation of why the Christian Democrats were Yankee imperialist running dogs. But as he ranted on, I wasn't sure he was that much more enamoured by Brandt's party, probably for not being ideologically pure enough. Though maybe it was simply envy, that West Germany actually possessed a mainstream left-wing party.

According to him, both Fianna Fail, the governing party, and their Fianna Gael rivals were two sides of a single reactionary right-wing coin.

One of his questions, though, brought me up short.

'Do you agree with the actions of the Irish proletariat to socialise the illegally acquired land of German capitalist ranch owners in the west of Ireland?'

It was a lot of jargon to take in at once but thanks to the mention by my West Berlin bar companion from Thursday evening of the attack on the German farmer in Cork, I had a fighting chance of working out his question. I imagined myself as a Prussian, expelled from the former Eastern Territories which were now part of Poland, as I answered with a hard expression.

'The rights of the true citizens of a country to their

people's land overrule any dirty deal for money or influence done with foreign bandits.'

He thought about this for a moment and decided that my ambiguous words could safely be interpreted as a sign of a right-thinking socialist mindset. Rather than that of the other Germans, who'd also made use of a 'socialist' label.

I felt I'd earned the right to ask him a question back.

'Where do most of the Irish stand on the Cold War? Not the true left-wingers, but the Fianna Fail and Fianna Gael voters.'

He sucked his teeth. 'I'd say most simply want to avoid getting caught up in a nuclear war and are happy to use the precedent of the Emergency to allow Ireland to claim neutrality as a kind of unwritten constitutional right.'

It was a moment of clarity in the midst of the rhetoric.

He soon got back on his hobby horse, though, looking slyly at me again as he asked, 'Do you agree with the right of Irish workers to take direct action against foreign factory owners who are removing employment rights and refusing to recognise their employees' trade unions?'

I suspected I was being led into a conversational trap. I put my teacup down on the trestle table and gave the answer my full attention.

'Of course, no progressive person in this decade could think other than to support the oppressed workers. No mercy should be shown to reactionaries.'

'Even if they're German factory owners in Ireland?' he asked triumphantly.

'A true socialist doesn't recognise national boundaries, only class boundaries,' I said, contradicting what I'd just said earlier about the farms.

'Why is it that Germans are the worst of the foreign owners?' he asked more sharply now.

'Who else do you have investing here?'

'A few Dutch but mainly Germans, over here to take our land.'

'I don't really know. There's been an ongoing economic boom for years back home. We have to import factory workers from Italy and Turkey to keep our enlarged economy going. Maybe a factory in Ireland is another way to acquire production capacity that's not available in West Germany?' I surmised.

'A boom built on the exploitation of the working classes, of course,' I added quickly. 'But some of them are buying here because they see it as a safe haven from the next war. Some people still have a real fear of the Red Army, just the other side of the frontier.'

'The partition of Ireland is just as harsh and unfair as that of Germany. We suffer as much as you do.'

I suspected he was wrong and that he deserved a slap on the head for his presumption, but I was the foreigner here, so I kept quiet and let him carry on.

'So do you agree that the existence of Northern Ireland is a gross injustice, a construct whereby the capitalists can divide and control the Irish working class?'

'I can't speak for Ireland, but all Germans on both sides in principle long for the day when there will no longer be any foreign troops in our country and when we can be reunited.'

It was clearly the correct thing to say, and earned me several claps on the back from a couple of the organisers who'd gathered round, as the other lecture attendees drifted off out into the sunshine, postponing the revolution until after the summer holidays.

While I had an audience, I milked it. For what purpose I didn't know yet. I just had a sense that these political activists might lead me somewhere more interesting than Doyle's mystery guest on Monday. In any case, time wasn't on my side in Dublin.

I upped the ante.

'I voted socialist for all the usual reasons but also because I have family in both East and West Germany. I know what separation means. I support Brandt because he's working to erode the border between the Germanies. All nations divided against their will should be reunited.'

Which in my mind didn't necessarily include Northern and Southern Ireland, because as I understood it, most of them had been quite happy to live apart. Not that I was going to say so explicitly here.

'Why didn't you say so earlier? Have you ever been to see your folks in the Democratic Republic?' The speaker was animated again, eyes bright. I wondered if he'd ever actually been to a socialist country.

'I've been to East Germany a few times. But although we're all Germans, even within our family we have very different ideas on how to run society. It's hard to see how the two systems can come together peacefully. One must win and the other fail, hopefully without too much bloodshed in the process. I imagine that's what's happening in Northern Ireland right now?'

One of the organisers was straightening the rows of chairs now, picking up unclaimed photostatted leaflets advertising socialist literature and upcoming meetings, clearly preparing to lock up and shoo us out.

'No, no, that's not the case at all. Only socialism can bring an end to the Troubles, by showing the Irish workers who their true common enemy is.'

The other organisers had also finished their tidying and were ready to leave.

'A few of us are going for a drink at a place we frequent at the top end of Smithfield if you'd like to come and hear some more. The name's Nolan, by the way.'

'I know,' I grinned. 'It was on the leaflet on my seat.'

We piled into a couple of taxis and I listened to the chatter of the other passengers.

'Is Seamus back down from the North, then?'

'Last Wednesday. He was boasting so.'

The speaker received a sharp dig from their neighbour.

Nolan said to me in an over-friendly tone, 'If you hear

talk about some people, about some of the volunteers, we'll ask you to use your discretion and not mention anything to anyone who might ask.'

'The volunteers?'

'The IRA. The real one, not the Provisionals.'

'Will they be there in person?'

'No, no. They tend to drink in different pubs. Keep themselves to themselves, shy wee lambs that they are,' said someone else.

There were sniggers from a couple of the others.

'How can I meet them?' Kramer had asked me to find out how to make contact with the IRA. Johannes' boss had told me not to be in the same room as them. Simply asking my question couldn't hurt, though?

Nolan laughed nervously. 'We're just going for a drink.'

One of Nolan's companions who had shadowed our conversation at Bricklayers' Hall spoke up now for the first time.

'We tend to keep to ourselves for good reasons. The other lot are very suspicious of strangers. Above all, don't ever let them think you're any kind of informant. They have ways of dealing with those types of people.'

Smithfield was back up north across the Liffey again, another downbeat working-class area of Dublin. I wondered how well-off the people were who paid their CPI dues and how often the Party spent money on events held at venues in central Dublin. Although when I thought some more, there was an obvious answer to the question of where their funds might be coming from.

As Nolan went to fetch drinks, I noticed a pile of old United Irishman newspapers left on a shelf by the door.

'What are these?' I asked Nolan's sidekick, a man going only by his first name of Dermot. He didn't have the showy pins in his lapels, but he was also dressed in head-to-toe denim like in some kind of uniform. Sigrid Johannes would have fitted right in.

'Here, have a look.' He peeled one off the top. 'Ach, that's from last year. It's an old one.'

'It's no problem. Here, let me see.' I reached out to take it.

It was an issue from June of last year before the rioting in Northern Ireland had started. The front page article covered the sacking of some striking workers in Dublin and criticism of their trade union for not supporting the strike. On the inside pages, disputes on fishing rights in County Mayo and an IRA action to vandalise fences on a County Galway estate in a land rights dispute. To my understanding of English, the language wasn't particularly extreme and, for me, made some not unreasonable points.

Whoever edited the publication had an awareness of life in the outside world too, as they'd put in a full page on Palestine. I flicked on through. Nolan was waiting on the last of our drinks to be poured at the bar now.

My eye was brought back to the paper again by the headline on page *ocht* - eight I guessed - that read 'New EEC Threat.' So the CPI had clearly anticipated a renewed negotiation a year before Heath won his British election in June of this year, supposedly the event which had kick-started accession again, dragging the other countries along in England's wake.

Nolan arrived back at the table, clutching three pints of red stout.

'Schlanjey,' he said as we began to drink.

'Do you mind?' I asked, indicating the EEC piece on the yellowed page I had spread out on the table.

'No, go ahead. Tell us what you think of their opinions.'

He and Dermot began to talk softly between themselves as I scanned the rest of the article.

It was hot stuff and the writer, whoever he or she was, was nobody's fool. Sophie had mentioned higher Common Market support prices. This article said they were double the open-market price in Ireland. The article mentioned the Mansholt Plan too; while the EEC saw it as a necessary step in modernising agriculture, the United Irishman compared it to forcing farm workers off the land in the nineteenth century to provide cheap labour in the capitalists' factories. However, I wasn't quite sure that the 'EEC industrialists' would force a reversion to a low price policy for agricultural produce once Ireland was sucked in, meting out what the author thought would be a just punishment to greedy, short-sighted Irish farmers for 'sacrificing our independence.'

I turned to Nolan. 'It says here that the Common Market has distorted the price of produce and that the subsidies paid to large producers have led to excessive surpluses. Then later, the writer says that the market should decide prices. Is this a socialist paper?'

Dermot answered for them both. 'It's a debate that's divided the republican movement, how closely and how openly to adopt socialist principles.'

I thought back to Petzold's file and how this same debate had been going on since the mid-thirties.

'But like good, pragmatic socialists, you'll use whichever popular movement is successful, to achieve the goals of the Irish proletariat? Like Lenin in nineteen seventeen?' I asked.

Dermot was on the verge of replying but Nolan had found his second wind.

'Nothing's changed in Ireland since the thirties,' he said. 'From the mid-sixties, the republican movement tried to change the agenda from pure nationalism, to widen it to include social justice. But it was too fast for many of the activists, hence the split at the turn of the year.'

'Was it a bitter one?'

'Any split divides our strength and takes us backwards,' Nolan said. 'I have hopes of a reconciliation but attitudes are hardening. There's a generational difference as well. The Provisionals are younger, much younger on average.

Teenagers and unmarried men of your age. The actual IRA come more from the generation of the border campaign in the fifties and sixties.'

'Given that the rival faction is younger, how do they fund themselves to buy arms?'

Nolan shrugged. 'I don't know them that well.'

Dermot spoke up. 'Why do you ask?' he said smoothly.

I took a sip of the red ale. 'Just curious. Just imagining myself in their shoes.'

I sipped again. 'So which side was Captain Kelly trying to import arms for? I read about the story back home. It was in the papers there.'

Dermot answered. 'It will come out in public if it ever comes to trial.'

I backed off and returned to Nolan. I'd idly leafed forward to 'Housing Action Victory in Dublin' on page *deich*, ten, while Dermot was replying.

'I walked around some of the back streets earlier today before the meeting. I also read a book on Ireland by a German before I came. He mentioned a glut of housing in the late fifties with lots of houses advertised in the newspapers for sale and to let. But what's happening now? I haven't seen any empty houses so far in Dublin,' I asked him.

'I don't know which book you're referring to but there is a crisis, because emigration has slowed down and the population is outgrowing the stock of decent housing available. One man's misery is another's profit, though. In this case, the property speculators who Charlie Haughey surrounds himself with. It's an open secret he takes political donations to Fianna Fail from the developers in exchange for telling them which parts of the Green Belt are to be redesignated for housing.'

'How bad is the crisis? And what's being done about it?'

'Families are living in caravans out the Naas Road. People are putting off getting married because of it. The right-wing politicians are in cahoots with the developers who deliberately drag out the building of new homes to maximise their profits. Development land has quintupled in price since the start of the sixties.'

'Do you think EEC membership will make things better here?' I leafed back to the 'New EEC Threat' article.

Nolan slumped in his chair.

'That very question is exactly what we're trying to fight against. People here just don't see the danger. They think joining the EEC is the same as signing another free trade agreement, like the one we did with the British in nineteen sixty-five. No-one sees that it's the thin end of the wedge, that it will one day mean the surrender of all the freedoms we spent eight hundred years struggling for. The previous generation of politicians understood the danger of foreign entanglements, it's why they made sure we stood apart from the imperialists after the war, as well as during the Emergency too.'

I peered at the article for the last time. 'It says here "the EEC is consistently suppressing the small nationalities, the most notorious case being the Bretons."'

Nolan squinted and followed my finger, reading out loud for himself.

'If ever there was a challenge to Irish culture this is it. It cannot survive defeat this time as it has so many times before.'

Dermot spoke. 'As my comrade said, it's hard to make people see what's coming our way. When the First World War started, a banner was hung outside the headquarters of the Transport and General Workers Union. "We serve neither King nor Kaiser". We can't replace London with Brussels. Not now, after so much sacrifice.'

I offered to buy another round.

'Nonsense, Mister Lenkeit. You're our guest here,' commanded Nolan.

'It's "Oskar", please.'

They'd told me something of their world, so I repaid

the compliment as the afternoon turned into evening. I described my four visits to my family in Wismar, told them of the little things of their lives there, trying to paint a picture of what it was like to grow up in a socialist regime, as best as I understood. And because I felt they'd been honest with me, I told them a rounded story with the negatives as well as the socialist positives. Nolan was entranced all the same; a Communist Party of Great Britain meeting in Manchester had indeed been the extent of his travels on Party business.

The bar began to fill up with a mixed crowd of men and women of all ages as Saturday night got going properly. A fiddle and whistle started up in the corner and I had an introduction to their revolutionary songs such as 'Come out ye Blacks and Tans' and 'Sean South'. I got into the mood and started to sing along once I'd picked up a few of the lines.

As Dermot downed more pints, he became ever more cheerful, clapping and slapping me on the back as I hit the high notes when Sean South went to join his 'gallant band' - in the afterlife, that was. For listened to another way, the song was a cheery lament of the superior reaction time, direction of aim and volume of fire laid down by whomever it was they had been attacking.

'So, Comrade Oskar, Germans always have good songs to drink beer to. What do the revolutionary comrades in East Berlin sing?'

He'd seemed to have forgotten I came from West Germany.

I didn't know about the Volksarmee and the jolly marching tunes they no doubt played, but the Irish, in the middle of their civil war right now, could learn a valuable lesson from the words of the first couplet of the East German national anthem, '*Aus Ruine auferstanden*'. Their clue would have been the word 'ruins.'

Part of me, with malicious intent, thought it would be fun to teach them, '*Wir fahren gegen Engel-land*'. After all, the first verse started off as a drinking song. It would have been fun to see the reaction if the British communists ever paid a return visit to Nolan.

I didn't really know any East German marching songs, of course, but thought they might still sing '*Erika*', given that its lyrics were completely harmless. The Bundeswehr certainly still sung it, which was why I knew all the words.

'Okay, listen carefully now.'

'*Erika*' only had five lines, with shouts of '*Erika!*' and a lot of table thumping in between each one as the singers extolled the virtues of the erika flower, blooming on its heath, surrounded by a hundred thousand bees. I had no idea what the name of the flower was in English.

Erika was also the name of the sweetheart left behind at home, but that came in the second verse, which was a verse too many for a pub full of drunken Irishmen and women.

After they eventually got bored with it, Dermot and I sat back down at our table with yet another pint. I'd lost count of how many we'd downed so far.

Overall, the CPI seemed harmless enough. It was the problem with most of the socialists I'd met, east and west, that whatever bizarre interpretation they put on the world around them, they were generally well-meaning and hard to actively hate. Which worked, I supposed, until the name of the next socialist you glad-handed was Stalin or Mao.

Nolan had gone by this time, probably off to write his next speech, making sure to mention the non-combatant Construction Battalions of the Volksarmee which proved that Ulbricht was as harmless and jolly at heart as his photograph hinted at.

Dermot leaned in towards me confidentially, looking drunk. But then compared to the iron-livered Johannes, everyone did.

'The CPI asked Moscow for arms last year.'

'Really? Who did they ask exactly?'

'Some fella we met on a visit to Moscow a couple of

years back.'

'Nolan wasn't invited?'

Dermot smiled. 'Everyone in the movement has their own strengths. Listen, do you think we'll get them, or should we ask the comrades in East Germany? Who would we go to there?'

'You sound worried. Is the IRA in a race against the breakaway faction to get weapons?' I asked.

'They're always on the lookout for new suppliers. Do you know of anyone in the East?'

I shrugged, turning my palms upwards. 'Talk to the guard at the border or at the airport who checks your papers. Say you have a message for the Ministry of State Security. It will get through. They won't make you wait.'

'The volunteers asked at the Chinese embassy in Paris six years ago. Nothing came of it,' he said, carefully enunciating his words. I strained to hear over the increasing din in the bar from the chatter and the music.

'What do you think of Captain Kelly, then?' I asked him more loudly. 'Did what he do help or hinder the cause? Is he a hero of yours?'

Now I realised just how inebriated Dermot was, for he had to pause before answering, so he could assemble his words in the right order. 'Of course he is. I don't care if he's part of the reactionary military forces. His heart is in the right place.'

I deliberately mirrored Dermot's slight swaying, tried to choose the correct level of assertiveness for the tone of my next question.

'Do you think there was more than just him bringing in the arms?'

'If you're as interested in him as all that, why don't we go and see him now?' he swayed back at me.

'It's one in the morning.'

'He gets visitors from the North at all hours. He's used to it.'

'Isn't he on remand awaiting trial?' I asked, trying not

to show my enthusiasm too much. Another part of my brain was trying to tell me that this was maybe taking my local research too far, too fast.

'No. He was given bail. It's not far.'

He suddenly stood up and shouted to the room, 'Comrade Lenkeit is going to pay his respects to the patriot Captain Kelly.'

Fantastic.

'Give over now, Dermot,' came a few cries back at him. I'd have joined in too, if I could have carried off the accent.

'Come on, Oskar. What are you frightened of?' he said, noticing my hesitation. 'Afraid of who's going to find out?' he asked, suspiciously.

'Of course not. Who's coming with us?' I replied, unconvincingly.

'Finish your pint then. Fergus, will you run us over to Terenure?'

Fergus obliged. His car was freezing in the clear night and its suspension was shot, by the way we swayed on the bridge back over the Liffey and then down into the depths of Dublin's southside suburbs.

Dermot and I piled out in front of a modest house joined on one side only to the neighbouring dwelling, an arrangement which I hadn't seen before. Unsteadily, Dermot went up to the door and banged on it with the exaggerated, calibrated care of someone very much in the later stages of drunkenness. I hadn't felt so far behind him myself, when we left the pub after half a day's drinking. But given twenty or so minutes without a top-up, I told myself I had sobered up, even if my liver didn't work that fast in reality.

After three or four minutes standing in the cold, the door cautiously opened and with a 'Hello sir' from Dermot, we were admitted.

I couldn't believe I was actually here, in front of the

central character of the drama. In the past two weeks I'd met Captain Kelly, Otto Skorzeny and possibly Markus Wolf. Maybe it was the sense of well-being engendered by the alcohol in my system but suddenly I was loving my job.

Kelly was a small man, compactly built, with wary, thoughtful eyes. Strangely, I recognised something more of Kramer in him than Johannes, and definitely nothing of Skorzeny. Maybe I'd been looking at Kramer all wrong so far. I knew he was close to the SDECE but hadn't ever thought that he might be on their books, not officially anyway.

'What is it you want now, Johnston? The children are long in bed and the wife's none too pleased at being woken up. Is it trouble you've brought me?'

Dermot swallowed. He was suddenly sobering up now too.

'I have a friend from Germany, originally from Hamburg like your other fella. He wanted to meet you.'

Kelly looked sceptical. 'Come through out of the hall into the kitchen so as not to disturb the family.'

We sat around a simple wooden table under the kitchen clock, the small hand just shy of two. He looked at me with narrowed eyes. 'What is it you want, Mister...?'

'Lenkeit,' said Dermot helpfully. I could have used one of Kelly's imports on him myself, at that point.

At least the car ride had given me some time to devise a story, and the truth was always the best lie, so to speak.

'I'm sorry to disturb you, Captain Kelly. My friend and I were just talking this evening. I only asked him if the government was really behind the importation.'

I'd chosen that last word carefully.

'That's what the court case will prove, I'm hoping.'

I was determined not to run out of steam like I'd done in Madrid. Despite the warnings of the East Germans to stay clear of the subversives, I was here now so might as well make the most of it.

'Did the government really know what they wanted to

achieve? To an outsider, it seems like they changed their minds half-way through.'

'Where did you say you were from again? And how do you know Mister Dermot Johnston?'

'I'm from Hamburg.'

I felt inside my jacket for my passport and slid it over. He thumbed through the pages, pausing at the East German stamps.

'I met Mister Johnston at a CPI meeting here,' I explained.

'My sister lives in Frankfurt. The dealer we went to in Hamburg was called Schleuter. Ever hear tell of him?'

'I'm sorry, Captain Kelly. Hamburg's a big town. Almost two million people. Being a port, we attract dealers of all sorts.'

'It's not "Captain" Kelly anymore,' he said bitterly. 'I resigned from the Army to have the freedom to fight my case.'

'What do your comrades think of that?' I asked.

'My comrades? Some are for me, some against. Some of my friends in the North haven't taken it well, though. I had to stop a bunch of them from going off to shoot Frank Gibbons, like they offered to. That's how you know who your real friends are, by how much they're prepared to do for you.'

I frowned to myself now. There was no-one for whom I'd go that far. Not outside my family.

'Ach, I have a team of bright lawyers from Fitzpatrick and Co, a smart woman lawyer by the name of Moynihan and a young chap called Peter Sutherland. I'm not overly worried. No jury of loyal Irish citizens will convict us for our actions in the North.'

'What will the government do in Northern Ireland now?' I asked.

'They'll let this blow over, then go back to what they've always done. They won't intervene to help the Northerners but they won't stop them helping themselves either.'

'When will it all come to an end?'

'In my opinion? By not intervening, we lose control of the wild men and so it will go on and on until they've sickened themselves on all sides.'

Something troubled me about what he said but I was too tired to grasp hold of it.

'Who else did you know of in Hamburg, in Schleuter's line of work?' It was clumsily done, but he nibbled the bait.

'It was Blaney's idea to go to Hamburg. He might have got the name from someone in Brussels. Called himself Baron Something-or-other, but we think he was really a Canadian. Rumours were he was an intelligence agent himself but who knows? Brussels is confusing.'

'It's a free market. Money is there to be made. Whatever you need, Hamburg can supply it. We ran guns to the Algerians in the fifties, before the French blew up a ship in the harbour.'

'Did they now? And you, Mister Lenkeit, the German from Brussels. Who do you know out there of interest to our people here?'

Dermot had gone quieter and quieter during the exchange. Now he leaned in towards me, as if he was trying to glue his ear to my head.

'I was a police cadet for a couple of years, but I didn't last and moved to Brussels instead. Whoever needs a name just has to ask Johnston here. He'll get me a message.'

Dermot almost tipped over in surprise. He grinned at me in new-found comradeship and punched my back for the umpteenth time tonight.

'Now lads,' said the former captain. 'If we're done, you'll have to excuse me. It's been a long week.'

Dermot thanked Kelly, and he showed us to the door, closing it firmly behind us as soon as we were over the threshold.

We walked down the road, round the corner and out of sight of Kelly's house. Fergus was waiting for us, tucked away from obvious view down a side street. So not as amateur as they liked to pretend in the pub, then.

Dermot got in the front with Fergus and turned around to face me.

'Did you mean what you said back there?'

'I felt sorry for him. It's not right what they've done to him.'

He raised his eyebrows. 'Well, Comrade Lenkeit, we've both had our eyes opened today. Let's go to The Embankment in Tallaght. They'll still be open on a nod and a wink. It's one of ours too.'

I shook my head. 'Thanks but I need to be in Blackrock tomorrow at twelve.'

'So where are you staying? Let us drop you off at your bed and breakfast.'

'I'm at the Gresham Hotel on O'Connell Street,' I said, embarrassed.

We drove back north in silence, each of us waiting on the other making a proposal.

Finally, as we crossed O'Connell Bridge, almost at the hotel. I came to a decision. I'd gone so far outside Johannes' strict boundaries tonight, I might as well go all the way and really make something of it.

'What if I wanted to meet the IRA for myself?'

'And why would you want to do that?'

'I hinted at it to Kelly. I might know people who can help them with their supply problem. Dealers who pay well for introductions, who pay everyone involved well for introductions.'

'Crooked cop, were you? Is that why you had to get out of Hamburg? I'll talk to some people. If they're interested, we'll call you. But they only work on their own terms, they're very cautious. How else do you think they've survived fifty years in the southern twenty-six counties, under a hostile illegitimate government?'

I'd no idea, but I might get some answers later today.

Chapter Thirteen

Dublin - Sunday, 2nd August 1970

I'd woken up still tipsy from the session in the CPI's pub which had started yesterday and stretched into this morning. Thankfully, as the time approached for finding a taxi to take me to lunch with Miss O'Cuacach's family, a couple of aspirin to clear the last effects of my hangover had done enough. I was now ready to make the mental switch from trying to blend in with the proletariat of North Dublin to charming the elite of the southern suburbs.

I didn't expect to find a florist open on Sunday morning. Instead, I lifted the flowers from the vase in my hotel room, shook them dry and wrapped them in the tissue paper which my shirts had come back from the hotel laundry service in. Not the Swastika Laundry, as I'd ascertained, which ought to have pleased my new comrades, even if they disapproved of the Gresham itself as a haunt of the plutocrat class.

Miss O'Cuacach's parents, or 'Brigid' as I would have to get used to calling her, lived in a large house with generous grounds on what was obviously one of the better streets of the pleasant seaside suburb of Blackrock.

The first thing I noticed, after being admitted by Brigid herself, was the small wall-mounted font for holy water by the front door and the decorative theme continued in the rest of the house. There was at least one picture of Mary or an indeterminate saint in each of the rooms I saw afterwards. God was obviously taken seriously at the

O'Cuacachs, so I'd better be on my best Sunday behaviour after all the drinking and suggestions of arms dealing yesterday.

She took me through to the front parlour where her father rose to greet me. Brigid's mother came in too, to receive her flowers and offer me tea but not coffee.

'You have a beautiful house here, Frau O'Cuacach.' And I meant it. In all the little details, from the stained glass above the door to the tiled floor in the hall and the cornicing on the ceilings, it spoke to the wealth of the people who'd built it. Then again, given that I'd grown up in a small flat in a post-war apartment block in a nondescript suburb of Hamburg, most big houses impressed me.

'We bought it fifteen years ago from some Protestants when the girls were little.'

'What happened to them? The Protestants I mean.'

'Oh, both their children had long gone to England with no intention of ever coming back, so they moved over there to retire. We bought at a good time, well before prices started to rise.'

She excused herself, motioning Brigid to remain seated, and went out to fetch a tray with tea things. She left us again to busy herself with setting the table in the dining room across the hallway. From time to time, through the open doorway, I saw her and two girls, younger than Brigid, going in with plates and dishes.

'Tell me about your job, Mister Lenkeit,' asked Brigid's father.

I gave him the story I'd given Doyle about working with our trade officials to combat CAP subsidy fraud, but left out the part about wanting access to the national police and customs authorities so we could share information more widely.

By now, I'd told the anti-fraud fiction so often that I was starting to believe that I worked in Agriculture myself.

'And what do you do now, Mister O'Cuacach? Brigid

told me you worked with the German embassy during the Emergency.' There, I had remembered the correct term.

'Oh, nothing very dramatic. I looked after the welfare of the German internees, made sure they got their Red Cross parcels, had their allotted number of letters home to Germany, that kind of thing.'

'Internees?'

'Mainly airmen who'd lost their way, ran out of fuel and made forced landings in Ireland.'

'I bet those went up towards the end of the war.'

'No, not as much as you might think.'

'What was the attitude of people here to the whole thing?'

'To be fair, mixed. Some politicians, like Dillon were vehemently opposed to neutrality on moral grounds. They understood something of Hitler when others didn't. But most were happy for us to stay out of it, apart from the Irish deserters. I had some dealings with the Army authorities over those people.'

'How could soldiers desert and run away from the fighting if you weren't at war?'

He looked embarrassed.

'Oh, it was the other way around. People deserted from the Irish Army because we weren't fighting. They went to join the British, to get a taste of it. Foolish people, had their heads turned by the British recruiters and by British shillings.'

He was still uncomfortable, though.

'We didn't escape completely, you know. We had bombs fall on Dublin too. We suffered just like Germany did.' I tried not to stare at him too obviously, wondering if he had seen any photographs of flattened cities back then or read any newspaper reports of what white phosphorous did to human bodies.

I cleared my throat. 'Who bombed you? The British, like they did to us?'

'Oh, it was your lot. A navigational error, although it

was still probably the fault of the British. The story is that they jammed the Luftwaffe's radio navigational aids which led to the mistake. About thirty people were killed but we don't hold it against you.'

Yes, but from the way you told it, I might.

'And after the war, Mister O'Cuacach?'

'I stayed at the Department of External Affairs for a while until I was seconded to the Industrial Development Authority. Then I transferred there permanently seven years ago.'

'So Brigid is following in your footsteps?'

Brigid's father looked across to smile broadly at his daughter. I felt a pang of jealousy at the demonstration of paternal pride.

'I hope she goes as far as she can. She studied languages at Trinity College, the best-known of our universities, outside Ireland. She received special permission to go there.'

'Who from?'

'The Archbishop of Dublin.'

'Why?' I asked, uncertain. 'Because she's a woman?'

'Because she's a Catholic and until June of this year the Church banned only the most exceptional students from attending.'

I was nonplussed and tried to rationalise what I was hearing.

'So only the very smartest high school students get to go to university?'

She didn't seem to mind that description. 'It's a Protestant university. Most Catholics go to UCD,' she explained.

My mother, who was a Lutheran, worked at a Catholic hospital in Hamburg. But the Irish, even down here, obviously took their prejudices much more seriously.

'What did you study there?'

'French. But I did some German at secondary school.'

'As I was saying,' Brigid's father came back to the real

point he'd been trying to make. 'I think there will be great opportunities for her in Brussels if our application is successful.'

A-ha, so that's why I was being given lunch. Truly nothing in life was free.

'So what do you think? Do you see any obstacles on our path to admittance into the Common Market?' he asked, not eagerly but not far off either.

'I'm only a junior member in the team assisting Ireland. Can you explain to me why Ireland is so desperate to join?' It never hurt to hear things twice, or even three times over.

'Germany is what we aspire to become. The economy of every other OECD country has grown by fifty percent in the past decade, Britain excepted. Even Greece and Portugal have overtaken us.'

So Skorzeny hadn't been far off the mark. He had a better head for business than people gave the old SS man credit for.

'And now that Britain is joining the EEC we have to as well. They, and West Germany, take the bulk of our agricultural exports. If we don't join, we'll be outside a new tariff wall. Furthermore, the Irish taxpayer has come to believe it will no longer be them, but the rich EEC countries paying to support farm gate prices. Adding all that together, you can understand why we've come to believe it's a question of not only future prosperity but national survival.'

'So you'll agree to any accession conditions, however onerous?'

'I'll let you into a secret, Mister Lenkeit. Something which particularly concerns my superior at the Industrial Development Authority. Since nineteen sixty-six, all of Ireland's industrial strategy and planning exercises have been suspended, abandoned to the exclusive focus of getting us into the EEC. The Authority can't start to properly compete for inward investment again until after we've joined and understand better the constraints the

EEC will place on our activities. Any offers of incentives we make to foreign businesses today can't easily be guaranteed for the long-term, post-accession.'

'The word at the Berlaymont is that Heath will agree to anything too. He wants his place in history. More than that, I'm not qualified to say.'

I turned to Brigid. 'What would you like to do in Brussels?'

'I don't really know yet what might be on offer. I suppose translators are always in demand. If Agriculture is such a growth area, maybe I might apply for a position there.'

'God forbid, Brigid. You would be wasted counting sheep and issuing export permits,' said her father. Agriculture seemed to give Sophie enough power and status though. I wondered how she and Brigid would get on if they ever met.

'Tell me something else Mister O'Cuacach. Your family name - is it Irish?'

'You mean Gaelic? Yes, our old family name was Cooke, but my father had me christened as O'Cuacach when I was born in nineteen eighteen. He wanted to make a break with the past.'

'It sounds a bit like "Cooke" when you say it.'

'But we only had girls, so the name will die out when I'm gone. Not that I'm complaining. We have been blessed with four beautiful daughters.' Brigid blushed at this. 'Each one more beautiful than the last.'

Brigid, sitting on an upright chair next to her father's leather armchair, tapped him lightly on the shoulder. 'Daddy! You told us you had no favourites.'

He hadn't said that he did.

'It's caused Brigid some problems, though. People look at the name and assume we're a republican family.'

'What's meant by that term?'

'Historically, someone who was against the terms of the treaty signed with the British in nineteen twenty-one which gave us independence. Someone who believes that the reunification of Ireland should take place by any means necessary - think Malcolm X. A "nationalist" is someone who also believes in the reunification of Ireland but only through political means, if possible.'

'How did it cause Brigid problems?'

Seeing her in action at the Department of External Affairs, she didn't give the impression that any prejudices would bother her very much.

'It's subtle. As the decades have passed since the War of Independence, the old fervour has faded, for the language as well as for forcing the issue of reunification on the North. Fianna Fail came out of the republican movement, but these days they're just another Christian Democratic party, much like every other one of their kind in Western Europe.'

'So republicans are seen by some as being a little too fierce for the modern world?' I could have added a world where governments were ever more worried about terrorism from all kinds of people. The French sponsored terrorists in Quebec and they got Breton terrorists in return.

'Roughly about that, especially amongst those politicians and establishment figures trying to ensure accession is successful.'

'I see. So what's really going on behind the scenes with this gun-running case that's to come to trial?'

Brigid's father didn't break stride as he answered.

'Exactly what I just said about how important it is for us that we join the EEC. Why do you think Haughey, Blaney and Captain Kelly were thrown to the wolves? Why do you think they were only too happy to charge a former Belgian Nazi alongside them? Maybe to smear them by implication? Why do you think they were arrested and charged, fortuitously, as it turned out, only a few days before we and the British lodged our new accession applications? It was a message to the EEC that we had our house in order. The northern nationalists will just have to take their chances with the British Army.'

But in the pub yesterday, the United Irishman article from June last year showed that accession was scarcely unexpected. If the Lynch government was really as worried about ensuring a successful application as Brigid's father seemed to believe, why would they have even started down the path of arming the terrorists? Unless they had been swept along by the sudden events of the summer of that year but taken stock later on, when the immediate crisis of the rioting in the northern cities had passed. Still, I wasn't ready to admit my reading around the subject to Brigid and her father. Not yet anyway.

'Sorry, who are "Haughey" and "Blaney"?' I asked instead, once again knowing part of the answer.

Haughey had been mentioned by Skorzeny as a suggested entry point for bribing the Irish government, and an obvious target for every other foreign intelligence service too. Blaney had only been mentioned in passing by Captain Kelly last night. He was the other cabinet conspirator alongside Haughey.

'Charles Haughey is, was, the Minister for Finance. Married to the daughter of the previous Taoiseach - that's "Prime Minister" - to Lynch.'

'I know,' I replied. 'And "Tanaiste" is his deputy.'

I remembered it from Petzold's file in Berlin. What he wouldn't have given to have been here now, even if Brigid hadn't been sitting with us, looking smart in the knee-length dress she'd worn to Sunday Mass earlier, coolly observing her father educate me. I realised I was getting a possible insight into how she viewed these things too.

'Very clever man, complex. But his weakness is that he's a part-time politician, part-time property speculator, as some might say. Kept himself very much on the nationalist side of Fianna Fail until now. On the surface his involvement in an arms smuggling ring to republicans was completely against his previous record.'

'But under the surface?'

'My view, and it's only mine, is that he was trying to arrange things so as to deliberately cause a crisis to unseat Lynch and buy support from Blaney and his republican wing at the same time. For a fresh leadership bid, no doubt. Blaney was his rival in the last campaign in 'sixty-six to replace Haughey's father-in-law. In the end, Jack Lynch was chosen as the compromise candidate between the two wings of the party.'

'Blaney and Haughey in something together should have rung all sorts of alarm bells.'

'It's easy being wise after the event.'

'I'm German. We have good experience of that. So the Irish government found it out and stopped it? Or did the government tacitly bless it until it became public knowledge and then they had to be seen to do something?'

'Remember what I said. Both strands of Irish politics want this country reunited. As I'm sure you'll understand.'

'So work it out for yourself is that what you're saying, Mister O'Cuacach?' I grinned.

Brigid looked pleased, too, at my apparent warming to her father. But I gave him a caution as well.

'There's more historic German territory than just East and West Germany. But we've given up on the parts now lying in Poland and Russia. Sometimes you have to accept things can't be the way you want them.'

'Ministers in Lynch's government, perhaps Lynch himself, thought they would help the northern republicans and nationalists on the quiet. Just because that avenue is closed off to protect the more important and immediate EEC accession process doesn't mean the end of a strategy for the North.'

'How do you mean, Mister O'Cuacach?'

'Do you know who a charcoal burner is?'

I mouthed the words silently.

'*Holzkohlebrenner*, perhaps. What does he do?' I looked at Brigid for help.

'Makes charcoal from wood in the forest. *"Charbonnier"*, I think,' she said.

'Ah, okay. We call him a *"Köhler"* - coaler, I guess.'

Brigid's father returned to his theme, sipping his tea.

'For fifty years, the North has represented a rival system in Ireland, just like East Germany does to you. Most of its people are not our people, so the time isn't right for immediate annexation, much as people here rightly feel for their fellow Catholics.'

He sounded smooth and reasonable, sitting at ease in his house, legs crossed, saucer balanced on his knee.

'So we let them destroy themselves. The charcoal burner sets the wood alight but controls the fire sealed inside the mound of earth heaped over it. He slowly drags out the burning, taking his time until the heartwood is fully consumed. All we have to do in the North is just enough to keep the fire going, a little extra oxygen here. Some more fuel as needed there. We simply ensure the fire doesn't spread out of control into our own woods.'

He replaced his empty cup on the tea tray, teaspoon laid neatly on the saucer. The sight troubled me somehow, more than just hearing the words he said.

'I have another personal reason too. Despite our head-start in the early sixties, until last year the North had done better than us in attracting foreign investment. They started earlier and offered deeper tax concessions. All that will come to an end now,' he added smugly. 'Why would foreign investors looking for low-cost labour go up there now, in the current circumstances?'

The doorbell rang, and Brigid's father excused himself to go and answer it. We heard an earthy guffaw at the door and he brought through a heavy-set man in a dark suit with moist, meaty hands delivering a crushing grip.

'This is my friend from the Legion of Mary, Seamus Mullen of the Garda. I think you were looking to meet some policemen, Brigid was saying?'

Yes, but I didn't want it broadcast to the world. Then again, as Doyle had warned, this was a small country.

Brigid's mother popped her head around the door.

'Will you take some tea, Guard Mullen, while you wait? The heat is fierce. You'll need a drop before lunch for it will be another minute or two yet.'

There was another guffaw.

'Listen to you, Mary. I haven't been a proper Guard since nineteen forty-four.'

'Mister Lenkeit has brought the good weather with him,' she replied, before turning to me to explain. 'The temperature has been in the sixties all week, and set to continue.'

I raised my eyebrows, for while sunny, I was sure it hadn't got above twenty. She must have meant Fahrenheit.

She left the room to put the finishing touches to lunch. I tried to join into her private joke with Mullen but then wished I hadn't.

'Isn't "Guard" also an English word?' I asked innocently.

'It's the colloquial term used to respectfully address members of *An Garda Síochána*, generally when wearing their uniform and going about their public duties. And what are you doing here in Ireland anyway?' he asked, looking at me coldly.

'I'm from the EEC, working with Miss O'Cuacach on Ireland's entry into the Common Market,' I replied evenly.

'Is that all you get up to here?' he said curtly.

Brigid's father cleared his throat.

'Maybe some questions for later. I believe Mary's almost ready for us now.'

Brigid's mother called us into the dining room on cue and fussed her guests into the seats around the table, just the way she wanted.

'You sit there, Mister Lenkeit, between Brigid and her father.'

She shooed her husband to the head of the table. Down our side of the table, after me and then Brigid, came her youngest sister. I sat directly opposite Mullen and next to him, Brigid's mother and then her younger sister.

'Did you go to Mass on Saturday night, Mister Lenkeit?' asked Brigid's mother.

I considered this quickly and made the judgement that it would be better to be an agnostic than a Protestant.

'No, Frau O'Cuacach. I've only ever been a couple of times to a German church.'

As soon as I'd said it, it felt wrong, not least because in my mind's eye I could see my aunt's pastor, tutting and shaking his head. For the reality was that in the past year, I had been a few more times to church, but still only when accompanying my mother on my visits back home to her in Hamburg.

I would sit and listen to her minister's platitudes, hearing the inoffensive words, but choosing to not understand what they meant, telling myself that feigned ignorance was innocence.

'And your family, Frau O'Cuacach?' Brigid's younger sister, at the bottom of the table, tittered at my use of the German term of address, but her mother seemed taken with the novelty.

'We go in Blackrock, to Saint John the Baptist. Father Molloy still says the Latin Mass in the proper way.'

Brigid's father carved the beef, serving Mullen and myself before passing the platter down the table.

'Thank you for the flowers, Mister Lenkeit. Look girls, at how pretty they are,' said their mother.

Mullen smirked at me from across the table as if I was the sort of dainty young man he'd have collared down by the docks in his earlier days, propositioning sailors.

'What does your family do, Mister Lenkeit?' asked Brigid's mother.

'My mother is a nurse. She's also called Mary, in a sense. 'Maria' is how we say it in German. I never knew my father.'

The suggestion of illegitimacy had different effects on the diners.

Brigid's mother went suddenly silent before offering more vegetables in a flustered way. But Brigid's younger sister looked suitably scandalised, if not a little bright-eyed, I thought, at the idea of forbidden sex gone wrong.

Her youngest sister, though, was oblivious to the coded message. As the last of four children, she would turn out either to be very quiet or very boisterous in later life. Whichever it was going to be, she took her chance now with the pause in the conversation.

'How many sisters do you have?' she asked. It came out, though, as more of a vain hope that there might be somebody worse off than herself.

'None, unfortunately.' From the look on her face, the youngest didn't agree. 'But I do have a cousin, of about your age I think. She's called Karin.'

I could sense Brigid's mother trying to work out how that might have come about.

'And you, Frau O'Cuacach? I thought Mister O'Cuacach said you have four daughters?'

'Our eldest, Frances, lives in Westmeath now, where my family came from. Married to a farmer with a herd of two hundred Charolais.'

Whether these were cows, sheep or pigs, I had no idea, but I did realise I was meant to be suitably impressed, even though this was the twentieth century, not the eighteenth.

'How many Charolais will it take to win Brigid?' I asked lightly.

Her younger sister interjected. 'She's spoken for, I expect, after she went to the summer ball at the Curragh last month with that Army captain.'

Brigid's sister was sitting opposite us, but one place down from Brigid. Otherwise, I was sure she'd have got a kick under the table.

'Yes,' said Brigid's mother hastily. 'But soldiers in

Ireland don't have many career prospects. Not unless you count getting shot at by the Turks in Cyprus.'

Strictly speaking, I was sure the bullets came from the Greek side, too.

'Have you always been at the EEC, Mister Lenkeit?' asked Brigid's younger sister again, clearly determined to press home her temporary advantage. She gave the impression of a sibling keen to make the most of every opportunity to compete with her rival.

'I was in the police for a couple of years between leaving the army and going to Brussels to work for the EEC.'

Uniforms might not impress Brigid's mother, but her sister right now was giving me a look which suggested that if we went to a bar and I bought her a couple of drinks, she'd be mine for the taking.

Mullen cocked an ear at my disclosure though. 'What branch of the police were you in, Lenkeit?'

'I was an ordinary policeman. Street patrol. But we sometimes worked alongside the *Kriminalpolizei*. You call it the "Special Branch" here I think?'

I knew from Petzold's briefing file they didn't.

If Brigid's younger sister was impressed, Mullen wasn't.

'That can't be right,' he said, sharply, 'Our Special Branch is for combating the illegal organisations.'

I wondered why Mullen didn't just say 'IRA'.

'You mean like the Irish mafia?' I asked, to needle him a little.

Brigid's father chuckled.

Brigid spoke up briefly. '*Kriminalpolizei* are the detective branch of the police, their remit is wider than that of the Special Branch,' she said, then went silent again.

'Did you ever have any exciting cases, Mister Lenkeit,' asked Brigid's younger sister over-brightly.

'Nothing worth a story,' I replied politely. I saw Brigid's father give her a warning glance now, to rein herself in.

'Yes, Lenkeit, tell us about your time on the beat on the

Reeperbahn. You must have seen a sight or two there,' said Mullen nastily.

From Frau O'Cuacach's blank expression, I was sure she had no idea that the Reeperbahn was the centre of Hamburg's entertainment industry, a definition which stretched to include four thousand unregistered prostitutes. On top of the fifteen hundred or so the police knew about officially, that was.

'Well, the most out-of-place thing we would see there was the Holy Army banging their drums and playing their trumpets.'

'The Holy Army?' asked Frau O'Cuacach, suddenly interested again.

'Yes, they wear uniforms and play hymn tunes. They also collect money for their practical work helping the less fortunate, so to speak.'

'Are they a Protestant thing then?' She sniffed disapprovingly.

Brigid's father snapped his fingers. 'He means the Salvation Army, of course.'

I tried the direct German translation of the original English name on my tongue. '*Rettungsarmee*, I suppose.' They were figures of fun in Hamburg's red-light district but to their credit, they kept at their work.

Even if Brigid's mother was unaware as to the Reeperbahn's reputation, her younger sister had heard of its other claim to fame. 'Did you ever see the Beatles play, when they were in Hamburg?'

'I was still at school back then. But when I joined the police, I met the constable who claimed to have been the one to arrest Paul in nineteen sixty, before his deportation from West Germany.'

One of several who'd made the same claim, of course.

'He's my favourite,' said Brigid's mother chirpily, to what I was sure was Brigid's mortification by the way she took a tighter grip on her knife and fork. 'Such a lovely Irish lad and such a shame at their all falling out with one another the other month.'

'Do you have any interesting stories, sir?' I asked Mullen. He looked at me darkly for an instant, but then launched into an anecdote to the whole table about a racehorse which had been dyed a different colour to fool the bookmakers. The scam would have worked, except that the stable hand forgot to apply the colour under the harness. And I didn't believe much of his tale at all. It was just the sort of embellished story a policeman in, say, Special Branch, might keep in hand for times when he had no intention of letting his listeners know what it was he actually did.

We'd sat through most of lunch so far, but only now towards the end did Brigid ask her own question.

'Did you serve in a special regiment when you were in the army?'

I laughed, thinking of Skorzeny jumping out of his glider on the rocky landing strip of Gran Sasso mountain, MP 40 held at the alert.

'No. We were just regular infantry, *Kanonenfutter*. You have to understand that the NATO armies can't stop the Soviets from invading Western Europe. We soldiers were, are just an expendable tripwire, to give the West enough warning time for the Americans to launch a nuclear counterattack.'

I took a quick scan of the table, but the implications didn't seem to have registered with any of them, of what would happen if the Americans wavered and didn't risk hitting the red button for the sake of Europe. I wondered if the Irish would remain in denial, right up until the unloading ramps of the Soviet Navy's assault ships hit the Dublin quays. I'd be alright, though. Fiedler might even send me back to help the KGB set up shop here. Or I might be back anyway, in ten years' time, to do the same for whatever EEC External Investigations had mutated into.

Brigid didn't reply or explain her army question and on

that cheery note, lunch came to an end.

Brigid's father, Mullen and I were ushered outside into the sunshine to smoke, whilst Brigid's mother and all three daughters cleared away.

We sat at the bottom of the garden on a couple of wooden benches, facing the house and out of easy earshot.

The jovial mask of the *raconteur* slipped and Mullen launched into me.

'What were you doing attending a Communist Party meeting yesterday afternoon? Are you a secret Red?'

Brigid's father was clearly in on this too. Setting up guests for police interrogation was obviously one of his party tricks. He sat and watched as Mullen worried at his new bone.

'How do you know that?'

'Brigid's father here has links to the CIB. Some of their people saw you coming out of Bricklayer's Hall.'

'CIB? What's that, the Irish branch of the CIA?'

'Catholic Information Bureau. John McQuaid's church organisation which monitors socialist threats to Ireland,' Brigid's father replied.

'Who's John McQuaid again?'

'Archbishop of Dublin, Primate of Ireland and unofficial Tanaiste since nineteen forty,' answered Mullen. 'We monitor all threats to the Church and her flock. Abortionists, hippies, pornographers, Protestant missionaries and Communists. We pay especial attention to the godless socialists. We've made them so distasteful to decent folk in Ireland that even the illegal organisations had enough of their leadership taking them in that direction, and they split over it last year.'

'If Ireland is so anti-communist, why aren't you in NATO?'

'Now don't get us wrong, Mister Lenkeit,' said Brigid's father emolliently. 'We're just as keen to prove our Free World credentials as the bigger countries but because of our neutrality principles we have to try harder than other places.'

Well, they could have fooled me. The pair of them hadn't done endless exercises and route marches for a year round and round the Munster Training Area, preparing for the onslaught of the Soviet juggernaut, as I had done.

I decided to play along with Mullen for a while.

'I'd seen all the tourist places mentioned in my book by yesterday lunchtime. I got bored, came across an advertisement for a meeting and was surprised because I had no idea the Communists had any active presence in Ireland at all. Like you, I wanted to check them out.'

'Check out who? People you knew already in Ireland? You know some Reds from back home, given that half your country is Communist?'

Mullen just wouldn't let go.

I simply didn't believe the Catholic Church would go to that much trouble to monitor Communists these days. Maybe in the forties and early fifties, when Europe had been in turmoil, when the eastern states like Czechoslovakia and Poland had just fallen like dominoes to the socialist parties. But surely not still in the seventies. That was the job of the secular authorities, like Mullen's actual employer.

'I only just arrived on Thursday. How would I know people here?'

I'd bet there had been a police informer at the pub. The description of the Catholic Information Bureau had to be almost entirely made up, like his racehorse story. I'd got someone's attention in the Garda, but not in the right way.

'How long are you planning to hang around Dublin for, trying to meet the wrong sort of people?' he persisted.

'I'm due to leave next Sunday,' I replied neutrally.

'Which exact police force were you with in Germany? No tricks now, because I will check you out. If you're here for any other purpose than you claim to be, well, you've seen with Captain Kelly how fast we move. We're putting that other Kraut on trial along with Kelly too, the Nazi fella, Albert Luykx, and we'll do the same to you.'

I looked at him coolly as he tried to provoke me by confusing the Belgian, Luykx, for a German.

'I was in the Hamburg *Landespolizei,* from nineteen sixty-five to sixty-six. However, I think you have the wrong idea. I was curious about your Communist Party and went to their talk to hear what they had to say for themselves. If you had been visiting West Germany, you might have done the same.' Except he couldn't, because we'd banned our Communist Party outright in nineteen fifty-six.

He didn't reply, finally satisfied that he'd got the information he wanted, I expected. Good luck with checking my record though. I didn't expect him to get very far, not anywhere fast, anyway. If Kelly's questions about Hamburg early this morning were anything to go by, none of them had much of a clue about the Continent. Bringing them inside information on the CAP was saving some poor junior at the Department of External Affairs or at Agriculture, weeks, or more likely months, of work.

Brigid's mother came down the garden. 'Any more tea, Chief Superintendent Mullen?'

'No thank you, Mary. It's time I was going.'

'I need to make my excuses as well, Frau O'Cuacach,' I said, taking my opportunity to get away too.

'Why doesn't Brigid show you the way back to the station? You can take the path through Blackrock Park by the shore,' she said, somewhat encouragingly.

I'd obviously impressed someone at Brigid's house today. As she and I left, though, her younger sister flashed Brigid a look that you only got when sucking on bitter lemons.

'Frigid Brigid about to claim another victim,' she muttered under her breath by the door, as I took my leave of the family.

As we walked along, not saying much, it dawned on me that she might be shyer than I realised. It was sometimes the way with girls like her. They would have men hanging on their every word if only they realised it and opened their mouths. Then again, maybe she knew it all too well and didn't appreciate being manoeuvred into artificial social situations by her mother.

I'd been invited on Friday afternoon to come today for lunch, presumably for Brigid's benefit, to make contacts for her possible future in Brussels. And for her father to get an inside track on accession to impress his boss at the Industrial Development Authority. Based on Mullen's little performance, though, inviting him must have been a last-minute decision, just like my meeting with the CPI.

'Do you really want to work in Brussels?' I asked.

'What's it like being there?'

I paused because the EEC was a world of its own in so many ways, hard to quickly describe to an outsider.

'There's nothing which I can easily relate it to. It operates on a whole different timetable to any government department you've ever come across, in any country. Take monetary union for example, targeted for nineteen eighty under the Werner Plan. But Werner's been advocating that since the early sixties, and perhaps even earlier than that still, as I've been told.'

She looked at me with renewed interest.

'Think of how those plans are nurtured, made and remade, passed down from superior to up-and-coming subordinate. They have to be, because they take decades to come to pass. What other organisation in the Western World operates on those timescales? That's why it's a place apart. If you were to join, unquestioning loyalty to the Project is the only way to thrive there.'

'Why shouldn't I give it a go? If the six countries of the EEC become ten I would have thought that would make it a different place to what you describe. Anyway, if I were ever to get married whilst working for the Irish civil service, I'd have to leave my job.'

While an interesting observation, it was also my excuse to test that particular ground.

'What does your boyfriend do in the Army?'

'I never said I had a boyfriend.'

'Someone as pretty as you must have one.'

I had nothing to lose. I was out of here in a week, unless Kramer told me to stay on.

She blushed red to the roots of her red hair. 'How about you?'

'Girlfriends? I could never keep them.'

Strictly speaking, that wasn't quite true. My first serious girlfriend in Brussels turned out to be an obsessive, following me around everywhere and was only dumped with difficulty. With a start, I realised that she'd been called Brigid too, or 'Brigitte' in French.

What I'd said much have sounded a little louche, for she walked slightly further apart from me as we turned into a small park cut off from the beach by a railway line running along a sea-wall.

As we walked along, I could see a diving platform beyond the railway, further out towards the sea, with boys and girls queuing up along rust-streaked ladders, waiting their turn to jump.

'What's that?' I pointed.

'Blackrock Baths. It's an outdoor sea pool. Popular in the summer, in the winter not so much.'

'Did you ever dive from the top platform?'

'Why, do you think I would have been scared?'

Although her words were assertive, her eyes gave little of that away. It was unsettling, but in a way, fascinating too.

'I don't know what to think, it seems you steer your own course, Miss O'Cuacach.'

The station was another little Georgian-style jewel with a miniature portico, just like the main building of the Department of External Affairs.

'Here we are, Mister Lenkeit. You want the nearside platform for the Dublin train.'

I went up to the timetable board to work out the next departure. But when I came back to say 'Until tomorrow', she had already turned on her low-slung court shoes and was walking quickly away, without so much as a shake of the hands.

I waited for the train, sitting on a bench, watching the children jump from the diving platform into the water accompanied by shouts and screams from their friends. As I sat there, the thing which had troubled me earlier, when Brigid's father had told me his analogy of the charcoal burner stoking the fire in Northern Ireland, came back to me, clearer now.

Someone reporting on the trial of Adolf Eichmann by the Israelis in nineteen sixty-one had used the phrase the 'banality of evil' to describe the balding bureaucrat who'd taken the minutes of the Wannsee conference. Mister O'Cuacach had sat relaxed in his armchair in his neat suburban house, stirring a spoon in his patterned china cup and talking of disposing of the fates of individuals too, less dramatically of course, but still, as if he were God Himself.

Chapter Fourteen

A new working week dawned bright and warm as Brigid's mother had predicted. As I walked from the hotel down the street, on my way across the Liffey to Saint Stephen's Green, I heard the odd English and American voice as tourists pointed out the monument to O'Connell at the bottom. He stood marooned on an island surrounded by traffic. Presumably he was the person who the street and the bridge across the river had been named after, although the Irish surnames got repeated so often you couldn't always be sure.

I wondered how many Irish went in the opposite direction, away from Dublin, and if Skorzeny was hearing Irish voices on the Gran Via in Madrid right now. Maybe they just went on package holidays to the coast along with all the others: Germans, Dutch and English.

Brigid was waiting for me in the lobby. I greeted her cheerfully enough, but she was still in her shell and gave me the cool, silent treatment again on the way back to Doyle's room.

Doyle, however, was more human despite it being a Monday. Whatever he'd got up to at the weekend, a round of golf or listening to a mellifluous Latin mass, he was in a good mood today as he rose from his desk.

He led us down the corridor outside his office, almost to the very back of the building, to a larger room than his own, but even more sparsely furnished, although it did have a proper wooden meeting table and chairs.

On one of these chairs, tipped back against the wall, with his feet up on the table and smoking, sat a new man, somewhere in his thirties I guessed. With his wide collar, broad paisley tie and soft brown corduroy trousers, he didn't give the impression that a government office was his natural habitat.

When the door opened, he jumped up, stubbed out his cigarette and let Doyle make the introductions while he eyed up both Brigid and I, but mainly Brigid.

'This is Mister Sweeney from the Department of Agriculture. He works together with the Customs Service as a preventive officer, stopping pig smuggling across the border.'

I'd bet the special pig unit wasn't what General Fiedler had in mind when he sent me to penetrate the Irish security organs.

'Mister Lenkeit is with the EEC and is keen to talk to someone in your area about agricultural subsidy fraud.'

'Sure he is, now,' said Sweeney, looking anything but sure. 'And who is this vision of loveliness?' He was a lot more sure about what Brigid might have to offer.

Doyle clicked his tongue in disapproval.

'This is Miss O'Cuacach. She's to be given full cooperation from the Department of Agriculture too.' As if Sweeney needed telling.

'Good day to you now.'

Doyle left us to it and Sweeney slumped back in his chair again, while we took our seats on the opposite side of the table.

'Jaysus, what did they stick us in here for, on such a roasting hot day?' was his opening line. I ignored this and carefully laid my report of CAP fraud on the table, along with that old standby from Friday, the Mansholt Plan, always useful for extra padding in a meeting.

I could tell Brigid was disgusted that they were both in English and that her translation efforts on Friday had been for nothing, but I'd had to make obtaining the documents require that little extra effort, to make them seem of value. Plus, putting the Irish to trouble helped them learn their lesson of who was boss in the new Europe.

I tapped the report and looked him in the eye. 'Fraud in agriculture is a serious problem across Europe and the EEC, as you know from your own job.'

He looked noncommittally at me.

'I'm here to help you and to get across the message that even before you join the EEC, you in Ireland need to bring the focus of all of your intelligence agencies to bear on this problem.'

'I think you'll find that we have a few other things to focus on right now on this island. And anyway, no-one outside Ireland tells us what to do. Not since nineteen sixteen,' he retorted.

'Fraud knows no borders. Animals don't carry passports,' I told him.

Brigid nodded approvingly, her specially-permitted Trinity College education had taught her to appreciate solid German logic like that.

'Well, aren't you the clever one. Why do you think I spend all those nights up to my ankles in fresh pig muck, looking around farms that were meant to have been abandoned twenty years ago?' He glanced briefly at Brigid, as if nervous she could still smell something on his clothes.

Skorzeny too, as well as Kramer, had told me to be patient when it came to selling, so I tried again from the beginning.

'Perhaps you can explain to me what your job as a smuggling prevention officer involves, Mister Sweeney?'

'Ach, enough of that. You can call me "Jim."'

'Who are your main customers in the frontier zone?'

'Frontier zone? What do you think Ireland is? East and West Germany, divided by the Iron Curtain? The locals come and go as they please - farmers, smugglers, pigs and all. Four thousand a week get brought south.'

'What's the cash incentive?'

'The price per pig in the South is four pounds higher than in the North. Sometimes they move up to a hundred at a time.' At thirteen French francs to the pound sterling, four hundred pounds for a night work was just over five thousand francs. Madame Kramer could buy a couple of carpets with that, if she economised.

'All that will come to an end once you join the EEC. Internal tariffs were eliminated two years ago.'

'So you're coming to put me out of a job, is it now?' he asked mockingly.

'Don't worry. We'll bring you a whole load of new, different things to work on.'

'God be praised.'

He was starting to really annoy me now. I flicked a glance at Brigid for some inspiration to be the worthier man.

'What Mister Lenkeit is saying is that fraud will become more complex. Instead of it just being our government putting up customs tariffs against Northern produce to protect our farmers, you'll have two different administrations handing out subsidies, right next to each other.'

I picked up the baton. 'These support prices are not inconsiderable. You can see how a pig might be taken back and forth across the border, spending half of its short life in the North and half in the South and earning subsidies in both places.'

'Okay, then. Tell me some more,' he said, mollified. 'I was told you've brought me something to read?'

'May I?' I came round to his side of the table, pulled up a chair beside him and laid the report down between us. Brigid came to stand behind us, hovering to help with my explanations as I took him through the basics of the manual.

I was pleased to see that her time spent taking notes from the French text on Friday hadn't been wasted, for after a while she sat down on the other side of him and took over, as my own efforts to explain the concepts in English flagged.

This he didn't seem to mind at all, and she definitely had fewer quips and clever comments thrown back at her than I did.

The morning drew on, and eventually we were done. I got up to open a window, overlooking the lawn behind the Department of External Affairs main building. In the closeness of the room, it was now getting as hot for me, as Sweeney had been complaining about to himself earlier.

'Leave that now,' said Sweeney to me. 'We're finished here.'

Brigid collected up the report and slipped it into her case without asking. She didn't hide what she was doing, just appropriated it as if she didn't trust Sweeney not to do the same. He didn't seem bothered in the least, even if he had noticed it, for he had other plans.

'Let's get out of here, I have a special expenses account we can use.'

I knew a bit about those from my first EEC job, in Internal Affairs.

'I'll take you both to O'Connell Bridge House for lunch.'

As with the eldest O'Cuacach sister's herd of Charolais, I was obviously meant to be impressed but didn't know why.

'It was the tallest building in central Dublin when completed,' Brigid explained. 'It's still one of the tallest. There's a fine view over the Liffey from the rooftop restaurant.'

Well, if she thought it was fine, I wasn't going to object.

We made our way across Saint Stephen's Green, retracing my footsteps from this morning all the way back up to the river.

O'Connell Bridge House stood at the corner of the

bridge and the southern quay. We stopped for a drink at the bar of the ground floor Carlisle Grill while we waited for a table at the top.

'Lair of the mohairs,' Brigid said cryptically as she sipped her wine, perched up on a high stool by the bar while Sweeney and I stood guard on either side of her.

This time, Sweeney did the explaining.

'Haughey's crowd, well, his crowd up until May of this year when he got arrested. Not that that bothers his sort for long. He'll bounce back somehow, just you see.'

'Who are his crowd? The property developers?'

Sweeney grinned. 'You're standing in one of those people's buildings now. Belongs to a friend of Haughey's called John Byrne. Miraculously, he got planning permission for this place without having to lose any office rental space in the design to a garage for car parking. That's what is normally required by Dublin Corporation for any new development, or so the newspapers say.'

It was the most animated I'd seen Sweeney so far. I watched him over my Harp lager beer, as his tone became bitter.

'But it gets cosier. The architect that Byrne contracted for the design was the son of a former Minister for External Affairs and the brother of Garrett Fitzgerald, the Fianna Gael politician who was an old friend of Haughey's from their student days together.'

Sweeney stopped to light a cigarette and give me time to catch up. He carried on between puffs.

'Garrett was the one Haughey originally tried to tempt into joining Fianna Fail, when Fitzgerald was deciding which party to throw his lot in with, before he entered politics. Still, although they ended up on opposite sides, it can't hurt Haughey to have friends everywhere - especially now, in his time of trouble.'

'Are things really as interconnected here, as Jim says they are?' I asked Brigid, allowing myself to test the use of Sweeney's first name, as we were out of the office.

'Mister Doyle told you so on Friday.'

'So is all this development easing the housing crisis?' I asked, showing off to her my newly-acquired knowledge of local current affairs.

Her brow furrowed slightly before she replied.

'It's destroying Dublin, that's what it's doing.'

But an explanation was going to have to wait because we were called for our table.

We rode the lift to the top floor and were seated at a table towards the back, away from the wide window overlooking the quayside. Sweeney and I faced Brigid.

We both watched with bated breath, waiting to see how far forward she would lean, as she shrugged off her light linen jacket. Underneath, she was wearing a sleeveless dress which exposed her pale arms to the weak Irish summer sunshine making its way into the room.

I gulped and asked my next question.

'How do you mean "destroying Dublin"? I haven't seen what you're talking about.'

'I'll show you later, Oskar.' Sweeney pricked up his ears at the use of my first name now.

'Look for the concrete blocks in the middle of Georgian terraces,' she said.

'Sorry? So far, Dublin looks like any other city to me but only lightly war-damaged. Neat, though, without any bomb sites.'

She shook her head, unable to make me understand. On the other hand, neither could she, although all she had to do was look around the centre of any large town in Germany and see how few buildings had survived. Even Königsberg, all the way over on the far side of East Prussia, hadn't escaped.

'Do you even know anything about our building at the Department? Did you wonder how old it is or how we acquired it?'

'I never asked.'

She pursed her lips at my disinterest and bent over her menu instead of enlightening me.

As we waited on our food arriving, I looked round the other tables while Sweeney tried to discover whether he knew anyone in common with Brigid.

The other diners reminded me of Reeperbahn club owners, squeezed into smart suits for dinner in the commercial centre of Hamburg. For all Brigid's distress at what the mohair-wearing men here were doing to old Dublin, there was a vibrancy and energy as they snapped fingers for drinks, spoke faster than I could easily follow and clapped people on the shoulders as they walked past the tables of apparent strangers.

I wished I could have taken Fiedler here to show him. Whilst he was poring over his next move in the chess game that was international espionage, the Volkspolizei were running around arresting illegal taxi drivers. In its paranoia, the police state was stifling exactly the kind of entrepreneurial wealth-creating spirit that his country needed for any hope of economic prosperity or even, in the long term, its very survival.

Sweeney, though, was happy to take his cue from our surroundings and make the most of his personal opportunities at lunch. Despite having failed to establish any likely mutual acquaintance with Brigid, he'd obviously made enough effort to get her talking more freely with him as we ate. I wasn't quite sure she had the same interest in horses and what he called 'showbands', but she was giving him more attentiveness after half-a-day than to me, who apparently was her ticket out of Dublin to the architectural delights of the Berlaymont.

I followed the conversation of the pair of them well enough. By now, my ear was properly tuned into the accents around me, as long as people spoke slowly. As we were finishing our meal, I suddenly overheard clearly some other words being spoken at the table behind us, and so did Brigid.

'I bought a factory in Shannon from a German fella last month. Daft Kraut thought he'd be getting a grant for equipment, said it was the only reason he'd invested in the first place.'

'What happened?'

'He didn't realise the grant was dependent on creating thirty jobs. Then got all hoity-toity when it didn't come through. Said he'd been lied to and would rather sell up than be cheated, as he put it. More money than sense.'

'There'll be more of their money coming our way soon if Lynch pulls it off.'

They went off onto another story but I'd heard enough and so had Brigid, for she looked thoroughly embarrassed.

We finished eating and as Sweeney waited on the bill, she relented at ignoring me throughout lunch and perhaps for letting me overhear what had been said at the next table.

'Let me show you what I meant earlier, Oskar.'

She led me to the window of the restaurant facing north over the Liffey and stood beside me, pointing out the sights.

'There's O'Connell Street which your hotel is on. Half-way up it is the General Post Office, the GPO, headquarters of the Irish Volunteers during the Easter Rising against the British in nineteen sixteen. You used to be able to look down on Nelson's Pillar when this building was first opened but that's gone now. Look along the river to the right - that's Liberty Hall.'

Another concrete tower block stood proud of the quay, completely out of scale next to the buildings around it. I began to see what she meant.

'Who does that building belong to?' I asked, meaning to which property developer.

'It's a trade union building. The Transport and General Workers,' she said.

I remembered what Dermot had said in the CPI pub about the banner that hung during the First World War outside what must have been the trade union's previous headquarters building.

'Neither King nor Kaiser,' I muttered to myself.

'What did you say?' she asked.

'Nothing.'

'And at street level it's worse. Once one old building in a terrace is replaced with a concrete block, the whole effect is ruined and the planners decide the rest isn't worth saving.'

As I followed her back to our table, I heard another of the over-loud diners comment to his lunch companion as we walked past.

'Isn't that the O'Cuacach girl?'

'Who's she here with today?'

When I saw her face again, the O'Cuacach girl gave no indication that she'd overheard them, but by now I knew how good she was at masking her emotions.

We got back to our room at the Department of External Affairs at half past two, whereupon Sweeney announced he was done for the day. I felt my timetable slipping away again, for having reached a pig smuggling prevention officer, I was still only at the bottom layer of the hierarchy of Irish intelligence agents, if I even had a foot on the right pyramid at all.

I stood there, frustrated, weighing up what I could tell him to get the right sort of attention and undo my false step with the Garda, thanks to my drinking bout with the CPI.

'What's your plans for tonight, Oskar?' he asked, surprising me. 'If you like, I'll take you to an authentic working-class Irish pub. Nothing too republican for you. No rebel songs.'

'Okay, I'd like that. Very good of you.'

I glanced at Brigid before asking him. 'Just you and me, Jim?'

'I have some work to catch up on,' said Brigid.

'Who else can I meet today?' I quizzed her. 'How about Finance, or Customs, or your intelligence people?'

She bit her lip. 'It all depends what Mister Doyle and Mister Sweeney decide. I can't make other departments meet with you.'

'What's that?' asked Sweeney. 'You want to meet with other people who deal with the North?'

'I was told by my bosses to talk to as many people as possible over here to make sure everyone is aware of the fraud problem. We found a few names through our own contacts, like Captain Fleming and Captain Browne in the Irish Army.'

Brigid was trying to be extra inscrutable now. But the longer we spent together, the better I was learning to read her.

'I'll ask around,' said Sweeney. 'We can talk about it some more tonight, if you like.'

It was better than nothing, but at this rate, by the end of the week there was no way I would have anything much to tell the people at the Berlaymont, let alone elsewhere. I couldn't afford that.

'When do you want to meet?' I asked.

He gave me the time and place. The three of us walked back down together to the lobby.

Whistling to himself, Sweeney went out into the sunshine, crossing the road to go through the park and back to the Department of Agriculture in Government Buildings, just to the north-east of Saint Stephen's Green.

I turned to Brigid. 'If you want to keep the fraud report for the rest of the day, Miss O'Cuacach, that's fine. But I'll need to get it back from you tomorrow.'

She answered impassively. 'Come back here same time tomorrow. I'll have it for you then.'

She was a *verdammt* cool type. Not a gramme of embarrassment at having appropriated it earlier without asking first.

Well, I could be cool too. I trotted off into Saint Stephen's Green, waited five minutes on a bench overlooking the ponds, then came back to Number Seventy-Nine and went in bold as brass, straight up to Doyle's office.

I gave a single knock and entered without waiting on an invitation. He was at his desk scribbling away and looked up in surprise, to my satisfaction.

'I met with Sweeney this morning but this won't do at all. He's way too junior for what I need.'

Doyle gripped his pencil at both ends. 'And what would please the man from the Commission?' he asked grimly.

I went up and rapped on his desk with my knuckles. 'Don't be clever with us, Doyle. You've too much at stake. If you don't get me in front of the real intelligence people here, I'm going round the various police and army headquarters buildings in Phoenix Park until I get what I want.'

'You cheeky wee pup. So this is what joining the Community means? We're trying to be communal but you're not making it easy for us.'

'Neither King nor Kaiser, but it's your choice in the end.'

'You've a mouth on you today. Can't handle your lunchtime pint? Or did they only serve you half a one?'

'I've given you a warning. Give me something worthwhile that I can report back to my people.'

'I'll see you tomorrow too,' he shouted after me as I left.

It was a shame I'd had to annoy Brigid's boss and upset the departmental applecart but duty called, much as I'd have liked to have taken my time in Ireland to see how far I might get with her. Despite the army officer friend lurking in the background.

What better place was there to make an international call to Kramer than the historic GPO, the head office of the Irish postal service?

The atrium was light and airy, marble floor and marble-covered counters. It was possibly the smartest and nicest post office I'd ever been in. The Irish hadn't stinted themselves, in the past at least, when it came to providing grand public buildings for their capital.

I found an empty international phone booth and weighed up my options as to whether to call Kramer or Masson. I had a better chance of getting hold of Masson but I suspected he'd want me back next week to remind everyone of who was in charge of the department. I wondered if he was already having second thoughts about Kramer's assignment, growing unhappy at him for sending me overseas in the first place. However, if I did make decent progress in the next few days, I wouldn't be surprised if he came out to Dublin himself next week for a final meeting or two, just to make sure any credit attached more to him than to me.

But if I went over Masson's head to get Kramer's blessing to extend the trip, which I was sure he would give, well that would definitely displease my immediate boss.

I made my decision and the international operator connected me to Kramer's outer office.

I switched back to French.

'This is Lenkeit from Internal Affairs. May I speak with Monsieur Kramer?'

'He's in conference right now. He's not to be disturbed.'

'When will he next be available again?'

'Let me check his diary, *un moment* … You can try again tomorrow at this time, if it's urgent.'

I thought about it for a second or two. 'Very well. Please tell him I'll call him then and that I may need to be out of town for longer than I thought.'

That would have to do until tomorrow. At least the

GPO was handy to the hotel. And the Garda couldn't tap every phone in Dublin.

Sweeney had given me the name of a pub on the northern bank of the Liffey. It sat at the corner of North Wall and a side street running down to the river, parallel to a canal which joined the river by way of a lock. A lifting bridge carried North Wall over the canal. A rusty tramp steamer wearing the Dutch flag was moored alongside the quay, in front of the windows of the pub. The building was nothing special to look at from the outside, but inside was pleasant enough. The early evening clientele of dock workers were nowhere near as loud as those at the CPI's place.

Sweeney was already at the bar, smoking and exchanging a few desultory words with the barman while he waited. He nodded to me as I walked in and ordered me a Guinness.

'Schlanjey,' he said, after the long wait for the head to settle. I clinked glasses in return.

'*Prost!*'

'Enjoying your stay in Dublin so far?'

'Sure, my first time in Ireland. But I'll be sad to leave the beer when I go back to Brussels.'

I'd obviously said the right thing, going by his grin.

'What beer do you have in Germany?' he asked.

'All kinds. Pilsner, lager, wheat beer, even heavy ales like your stout. The Belgians have almost as many, it seems, even for such a small country.'

'And does Ireland seem small to a German too?'

'It holds a certain fascination for us,' I said, speaking on behalf of Böll and his million or so fans. 'One of the few neutral countries in what you call the Emergency, so not a country which has strong opinions of us either, we imagine. Please forgive me when I say this next thing, I'm only telling you how Germans see Ireland. For us, it's like a kind of benign, smaller version of England but without the imperial rivalry.'

'Do you hate the Brits then?'

'They killed my grandfather in an air-raid and bombed my home town to hell.'

As I said this, I realised it needed more explanation.

'They were separate events. My grandfather was working in a factory near Danzig. At least my aunt told me it was the English.'

I remembered now what Johannes had said about Böll's English U-boat story, and wondered how she knew the nationality of a plane flying five kilometres up in the air. But I was on surer ground when it came to the firestorm.

'When I was in the police in Hamburg, sometimes at the end of a long night shift in the small hours of the morning, the older men would occasionally point out some of the places we passed by on our beat that had been especially badly bombed during the war.'

'The so-and-so building used to stand there, blown apart by a two-tonne bomb, or, there was an air-raid shelter in the cellar of this building where one hundred children died of asphyxiation. But the worst were the tales from the firestorm. Twenty-seventh of July, nineteen forty-three, a date Hamburg will never forget. The city had already been bombed the previous four nights, so all the conditions were right for what came next.'

'What were they, then?'

'Broken fire mains from the previous raids, firemen diverted to other cities under attack, continuing dry weather and strong winds. That night, the fire grew and grew, into a kind of cyclone, eight hundred degrees of heat, two hundred kilometres per hour wind speed.'

I watched as his lips moved silently, doing the conversion into miles.

'People were picked up by the gusts and tossed aside like leaves, trees were bent double by the force of the hurricane. The heat was so intense that it melted the surface of the roads in places. But people couldn't tell this from looking in the half light. So they fled from falling buildings, out into the street and got stuck in the asphalt as their feet burned. Then they would fall down or topple over in the wind. People watched helpless at others on their hands and knees, trapped in superheated tar.'

'Jaysus.' Sweeney sucked solemnly at his pint.

With a deep sigh I continued. 'But the worst, the absolute worst place, was a canal by the Inner Alster lake. A phosphorus incendiary bomb had showered a group of people who'd just escaped from a collapsing building. They jumped into the nearby canal to try to put out the burning jelly sticking to their heads and faces. The problem was that phosphorus instantly reignites when exposed again to air, as it did whenever they came back up to take a breath. So they had a choice - death by drowning or death by fire.'

Sweeney's eyes went to a faraway place as he played out an image for himself of desperate people, squirming in agony in the water.

'After I was told the story, I could never pass that place again, looking down at the black water without wondering what those people were thinking in their last moments.'

'Jaysus.'

'Indeed. So yes, I hate the Brits. But do you know why I really, really hate them?'

He shook his head dumbly.

'After the war, we found out the operational name for their bombing raid, them being the Allies, because the Americans took part as well. It was "Operation Gomorrah."'

I waited expectantly on his reaction.

'Operation what?'

'"Gomorrah", like in the Bible, you know, when God allowed *schwefel* and fire to rain on the city of Gomorrah.'

'I don't know that story. It must be in the Protestant bible. But sure, it's just what you'd expect of the Brits.'

The story had lost its momentum in translation. I

wanted to explain to him how the German industrial cities were the most socialist and most anti-Nazi areas of pre-war Germany, and that their working-class civilian populations had least deserved a biblical punishment, a holocaust of the pre-atomic era, but it would have been too difficult. As would trying to explain that I hated Sophie's social class, who had been largely ambivalent towards the Nazis, almost as much as I hated the British too.

'We're not allowed to talk about this in Germany. It's a closed subject, like so many others.'

I sucked at my pint now. There was nothing much more to say so we finished that round in silence. I bought the next one and we took it over to drink at a table with a view of the tramp steamer's ochre-painted superstructure.

'So what do you think of Brigid?' he asked, trying to move the evening's conversation onto a more cheerful topic. 'I don't mind doing any number of EEC assignments, if she's part of the package.'

'Do you really think she's for the likes of you or me?'

'How do you mean?' he asked.

'Went to university, her father seems to be high up in some Catholic lay order, they all live in a big house in Blackrock,' I suggested.

'How do you know I didn't go to university? Or that I can't charm her off her high horse?' he asked with a grin.

'People with degrees don't choose to drink in Byrne & Sons' pub in the Dublin docks. Not unless they're policemen meeting an informant.'

'Ha ha. Is that the sort of thing you did in Hamburg?'

No, it wasn't, Jim. And unless I'd missed Brigid telling you over lunch that I was ex-police, why didn't you stop me at the start of my Hamburg story? But I didn't say that.

'You must be joking. I was a probationer cadet, don't know what you would call that here. I quit for the EEC before I finished training.'

'Are there jobs for policemen there, then?'

'Not really. I went into Internal Affairs, we checked out excessive lunch expenses, bribery, thefts of handbags from cloakrooms. The idea was to wash all our dirty laundry ourselves.'

'Sure now, doesn't everyone do that?'

'How about you, how did you end up in Agriculture?'

'I paid attention to my lessons at school when I was present, that was. Got enough marks in my Leaving Certificate to get a job as a civil servant.'

'So how do the police work here? What do you call the different ranks?'

He seemed uncertain as how to answer.

'What's a Chief Superintendent? I saw it mentioned in a newspaper article.'

'Oh, that's high up.'

'What's the equivalent army rank? Lieutenant Colonel?'

'Maybe higher,' he suggested.

A full colonel in the army was the same as a *Polizeidirektor* in West Germany, or in the case of the Stasi, a full colonel. They kept the hierarchy easy to understand like that in the East, just so that no-one had any excuses for not knowing their place.

'I see.'

An old man came into the bar, wearing a grubby jacket worn through at the elbows. He looked around the room, searching for someone. The publican stopped polishing the glass in his hand, putting it down and laying both his hands on the counter.

'Now then, Frank. What are you doing here? Didn't your daughter say to leave off the drink now?'

Sweeney glanced up, worried. 'Sorry, Oskar. He's an old friend. I need to get him home,' he said distractedly. 'I'll see you tomorrow. Just you go straight back along the quay and you'll hit O'Connell Street.'

He gathered up his packet of cigarettes and got to his feet gulping down the last of his beer. I watched as he walked over to the old man Frank and put his arm around him. I wondered how fresh the new visitor smelled.

'Mister Byrne here is right. You've had a drop or two already tonight, haven't you, Frank?' asked Sweeney in a solicitous voice.

'Ach, you know how the craving takes me sore sometimes,' said the man.

'Now, now and what would your wife, God rest her soul, say if she could see you? Come away and I'll see you home before you get yourself into trouble.'

With a backward glance at me and a toss of his head, he steered the old man out into the deepening twilight.

I finished my drink in my own good time and was tempted to have another, despite the warning of Frank's threadbare coat. I was troubled by the retelling of my Hamburg stories and didn't know why. My mother had arrived there, to a shell of a city in 'forty-five, two years after the firestorm, a refugee herself from the east. But none of our family had been through the particular horror of what the city had experienced.

As I walked back along the bank of the Liffey, lost in thought, the city lights reflected off the water's surface. Each one a little fire burning hot, hot in the darkness.

Chapter Fifteen

I made my way to the Department of External Affairs offices the following morning, wondering whether what I'd said to Doyle yesterday would have had any effect. I'd woken up deciding that unless they gave me an indication by the middle of the week that I would get to meet more serious players than the jovial Sweeney, I was going to have to try a direct approach to the IRA. Just as I'd thought I might have to, back at the Normannenstrasse.

I was also wondering if the Irish authorities even had a clear short-term strategy for engaging with the northern insurgents. I suspected that it was rather the active players, like Haughey and Kelly, who were making the running, dragging the Irish government along behind them, in reaction to events.

By the time I arrived at Saint Stephen's Green, my opinion had hardened further and I resolved that unless nothing changed by the end of this day, I would get back in touch with Dermot at the CPI somehow. I'd go back to their pub to find him, ask for a meeting with the IRA and get straight to the point.

I'd offer to broker my own arms deal for them with the French and try to find out who in the Irish government they thought might tacitly support them. Someone who might permit an arms transfer in the middle of the Celtic Sea, far from shore in international waters.

Kramer wouldn't have to follow through, but he might. He might want to take the initiative in Ireland himself and lead the SDECE down a path of his own choosing.

Brigid was waiting for me in the lobby again and took me straight to Doyle's office. Today, the sly fox look was gone and he greeted me coldly.

'You mentioned yesterday, once again, that you wanted to meet more of our intelligence people.'

'Yes, that's right. To make sure I hit everyone important.'

'You also said you wanted to know that we took the combatting of fraud and other criminal activities by the illegal organisations seriously.'

'Yes, I did.'

'So, we're getting you out of Dublin for a couple of days, taking you up country to see some of the work we're doing in that line.'

It was one way to stop me camping outside the headquarters of the Garda in Phoenix Park.

'Okay, thank you. It sounds intriguing. Who am I seeing up there?'

'Mister Sweeney will drive you to the north west tomorrow. Miss O'Cuacach has kindly agreed to go along as a translator too, if needed. Sweeney will explain more. In a minute, Miss O'Cuacach will take you to him.'

So, they weren't wasting any time either, getting me out of their hair and perhaps trying to prevent me fraternising any further with the comrades at the CPI. What was it that Skorzeny had said, not to be fooled by their 'country ways'?

'I don't know what to say. Thank you for laying this on. The more I know, the more I can help you in different ways.'

'Perhaps. Let's see better where we all stand before getting any friendlier,' he replied.

But no new names, for the time being. It was progress of a kind, though, I supposed. Dermot at the CPI would have to wait a little longer before I could buy him his next pint.

Disappointingly, we didn't go from Doyle's office up to the Government Buildings to meet Sweeney at Agriculture and see where all the action in the world of beef export subsidies and animal health happened. Instead, Brigid took me back down the same corridor to the rear of the building and to the same room we'd met together in yesterday. It was almost as if they were embarrassed by me and wanted to hide me away. Or maybe it was because Sweeney was as unknown to the Department of Agriculture as I was.

Such doubts didn't assail him, though. When we walked in, Sweeney looked all fired up, as if he'd been let off the leash with a license to cause mischief.

'So we're taking you on a tour of Ireland, Oskar,' he said cheerfully. 'I've been told to show you just how much we know about the illegal organisations and what they get up to around the border.'

'And how much is that?'

'I'll show you some of the places they use, known to us and the police, because even in the most obscure corners of Ireland, everyone's into their neighbours' business. We'll take you to see an army unit that watches over the border too.'

'Any army intelligence people attached to them up there?' I ventured.

'Oh, I don't know about that. I don't know where that lot are based exactly. Still, once we're out of Dublin, we'll be freer to discuss anything you might want to know, about what we're doing up there. You can ask me any questions you like once we get to Donegal,' he suggested.

'Is that where we're going? The county that's almost entirely cut off from the rest of Ireland by the Six Counties?'

Because just like dropping in the word 'Chekists' when speaking with Johannes' boss, winning over the other side by using their own nomenclature cost nothing, words were free. It pleased Sweeney, anyway.

'Yes, that's right. It's about a five-hour drive, but we're aiming to return to Dublin by Friday. You should be back in Brussels by Sunday at the latest, depending on what further arrangements we might come to. I'll pick you up tomorrow morning at your hotel at half past eight.'

He was now being as elliptical as Kramer had been at his briefing to me in Brussels when he'd turned the air conditioning up high. It sounded, unless I was imagining it, like he was trailing some bait for me, making me an offer of some kind. I hadn't set out last night to tell a tale of British bombing and what I thought of their air force, but maybe it had somehow worked in my favour.

Using up the rest of the week for his tour of the wilder parts of Ireland would take more time than I was happy with, but I had no real choice, not if I wanted to find out who was really on the other end of the fishing line.

'When we get there, we'll be outside in rough country for some time. It gets wet in Donegal, all year round. You'll need to buy some outdoor things here in Dublin today. Brigid can show you where to go. I'm sure she won't pass up the chance to go shopping,' he said, grinning cheekily at her.

With Sweeney's endorsement ringing in her ears, which even to me sounded a touch patronising, Brigid escorted me downstairs and we walked out into the street together.

'Listen, Brigid. I can buy for myself. Just point me in the right direction. I passed a department store on Grafton Street on Saturday and there's always Clery's on O'Connell Street.'

She glanced at her watch.

'No, I'll come with you for a bit. Irish rain is especially heavy. You'll need expert advice,' she said, somewhat clumsily.

But instead of heading north from Saint Stephen's Green we rolled south, down Harcourt Street, passing a couple of stores I thought were promising. It wasn't my city, so I wasn't going to tell her where to go, but she was acting oddly.

'How about here?' I asked at the third menswear shop we came to.

She shook her head, smiling quietly to herself. Just when things were about to get really awkward and it seemed we were about to leave the commercial centre entirely, we hit a taxi rank. She looked at her watch again and came to a decision.

'There's someone else I'd like you to meet before we travel north.'

The taxi took us to a bar in Ballsbridge in the south of the city. She strode in through the doors, getting a couple of not so under-the-breath comments from the late morning drinkers nursing their pints. She quickly glanced around the bar and went straight over to a cubicle at the back. Its only occupant was a short, wiry man in a green twill jacket with a half-drunk Guinness in front of him. He looked up with eyes only for Brigid, but no smile.

She closed the lower three-quarter-height door and sat opposite him, hands clasped before her, resting on the table top.

With a half-glance at me she said, 'Mister Lenkeit, I'd like you to meet Captain Fleming of the Irish Army, and formerly,' here she lowered her voice, 'with G2.'

We shook hands quickly. His grip was firm and his eyes were cold. I matched him look for look.

'Miss O'Cuacach tells me you're headed for the north west and could use a conversation with a serving officer.'

I looked at Brigid in feigned surprise at finally meeting one of the people on my list, or so was being suggested. 'Why, thank you. That would help.'

'First things first, who are you, really?' he asked with narrowed eyes.

'How about you? How long were you in G2? What do

you do in the Army now?'

Brigid intervened before a real stand-off ensued.

'Padraig left that particular department a year ago to go to America and attend the US Ranger course. The Irish Army has recently established its own Ranger unit.'

'When was that?' I asked.

'Nineteen sixty-eight,' he snapped. 'And now your story.'

So a year before the riots really kicked off in Northern Ireland.

'I work for a division at the EEC which goes around fixing political problems that don't fit neatly under any other department.'

I felt I owed Brigid something approximating the truth, now that she'd got me in front of one of the people on my list who I'd wanted to meet.

I turned to her. 'But that's only for you to know, back at the Department.'

She was impassive, as usual.

'I'm interested to know what people in the Army think of Captain Kelly,' I asked, turning back to him. This was the real deal. I wasn't going to waste exposing myself to someone like Sweeney.

'What do you already know then, of the world of subversive organisations and of my world?' asked Fleming.

Maybe the trip to meet Skorzeny in Madrid hadn't been wasted after all.

'I've already explained to Miss O'Cuacach that I was born in Hamburg and was in the police there. Among other things, it's West Germany's biggest port and a centre for the European illegal arms trade. I was in the infantry for a year too, so I know about small arms and basic demolition techniques. In the course of my work I've also spent time with Otto Skorzeny, the famous Nazi commando, hearing what he has to say about unconventional warfare.' It wasn't much of a list, though.

'Are you a patriot, Mister Lenkeit?'

'I'm a German. I have to be a patriot because no-one else likes us.'

'What would you be prepared to do to reunite your country?'

I wanted to ask him the same question, but judged that the time hadn't come.

'What can any German do? We're occupied by foreign troops from NATO in the West and troops from the Warsaw Pact in the East. And that's not to forget the bits of Germany which have been lost to Poland and Russia. Not that anyone cares.' I muttered the last part under my breath.

'That's why I can't imagine that there would have been anyone in the Irish Army opposed to what Kelly was doing,' I continued, hoping he'd say more.

Fleming stared at me with wary eyes.

'Are you a big man at the EEC, then?'

'Within our special department, I'm responsible for making sure that there's no obstacles to Britain and Ireland getting into the EEC.'

It was no worse an exaggeration than how I'd described External Investigations a minute ago. It seemed to be the answer Fleming was hoping for.

'And are you known to the British? Have you had any dealings with them yet?'

I still couldn't work out yet where his questions were headed.

'I haven't but my boss has met the British negotiator, Sir O'Neill, who's from Northern Ireland.'

The captain practically spat on the ground.

'If he's a British knight, then he's a traitor to the name of O'Neill.'

Out of the side of my eyes, I was relieved to see that Brigid was gently pursing her lips in disapproval. It was getting a little too medieval for my liking as well.

'Why the hatred? Because he's working for the British or because he's working for the EEC?'

Fleming frowned at me. I tried to explain.

'He's in love with the EEC. He'll do anything to make sure England signs away its trade and treasure to Brussels. I'd have thought you would approve of that?'

'I don't trust any of them, which is why we shouldn't have any entangling alliances.'

I tried to tease him out a bit more, hoping to eventually hear if he wanted to buy arms for the IRA, now that Captain Kelly was tied up on bail.

'So what do the Irish Rangers do?'

'You'll find that out on Friday. Miss O'Cuacach has organised a visit for you to one of our bases.'

'Okay then. What were the US Rangers like?'

He relaxed a little, back on safer ground. 'They're tough enough. When I was at Fort Benning, they were being rushed through training, to cycle them out to Vietnam.'

Something didn't feel right about the way he'd just said that last statement. I realised at that moment too, the extent of my annoyance that Brigid really did have a boyfriend, after all.

'Didn't you want to go out there with them?'

The clouds came over his face again.

'What are you trying to say?'

The slow anger, that had been building up inside me for a few days now came to a head. I hadn't really been aware before now of how strong it had grown.

'I served my time in the struggle of our age, discouraging the Soviets from getting any idea of rolling West. You Irish sit here behind your ditch, doing nothing.'

I didn't know if 'ditch' was the right English word but he seemed to understand my meaning well enough.

'You have no right to say that. You don't understand our special situation with the Brits,' he said brusquely. His fingers gripped his pint glass tightly.

'I and everyone else in Western Europe understand it well enough. You're scared of standing up to be counted.'

He looked at me shrewdly. 'Are you saying I'm scared

to fight? Me personally? Fuck you. I'm a special-forces-trained soldier.'

I made myself calm down. 'No, I didn't say that directly.' However, my self-control didn't last long. 'But if you've passed the US Ranger course, you could ask to join the US Army on secondment - do a tour on attachment to their Rangers in Vietnam. You must know some people who could get you out there, if you really wanted to. What's the point of being trained with the special forces if you never get to fight?'

He looked at me stony-faced now, like he'd suddenly moved beyond anger to its far side.

Still, I was sure of my position too.

'It wouldn't be the first time Irish soldiers have passed judgement on the morals of their politicians and taken themselves off to fight for a cause they believed in.'

'What on earth are you talking about, you strange Kraut bastard?'

'He means the deserters during the Emergency, I think. My father told him about them.' Fleming raised an eyebrow. 'On Sunday at lunch,' she added unhappily, speaking in a quieter voice.

'They were traitors to their flag, back then too,' he retorted.

But now my patience was also at its end.

'You're sitting here in a pub, while Irish soldiers are dying in the jungles of Vietnam,' I said matter-of-factly, echoing the first Kelly I'd met in Dublin.

His hard-man control started to strain. I caught a glimpse in his eyes of a furnace deep within, glowing cherry-red.

He finished his pint. 'I'm sorry you have to put up with all this, Brigid. He'd better be worth our time.'

Then, without a backwards glance, he stalked off.

Well, that couldn't have gone any worse. What a waste of my first chance to get within touching distance of G2.

I simmered down myself and apologised to Brigid.

'I'm sorry about that. I don't know what happened.'

'No, no,' she said calmly. 'He gets like that from time to time. I think maybe you're just too similar in character.'

'I'm sorry, once more.'

She smiled uncertainly.

'I know him. Come Friday he'll have forgotten it.'

I rather wished she didn't know him that well.

I offered to buy us lunch back in town but she declined with a shake of her head. We called a cab and rode back in silence to the centre. As we headed north, I saw what I'd been looking for since Thursday.

Unlike what Böll had said, it was more white than red with only the bottom third of the truck painted that colour. Bang in the middle of the back doors was a white swastika on a black disc. They hadn't even bothered to reverse its direction. If the vehicle had been red overall, the Swastika Laundry would have been driving trucks painted almost exactly like the German national flag from 'thirty-three to 'forty-five.

Despite my earlier apology, I was still on a short fuse after the encounter with Fleming. But now I really lost it, with Brigid unfairly bearing the brunt of my frustration.

'*Was zum Teufel* … I read about this, but I still never really expected to see it. What the hell are your authorities thinking? You think it's funny to shamelessly parade the Nazi flag in your capital, just to remind everyone of your moral ambiguity twenty-five years ago?'

I didn't raise my voice but she got the message clearly enough. Now it was her turn to flush, but with embarrassment rather than anger.

'You have to understand the context. We were and are next door to a dominant neighbour. People here are loath to conform in everything to what the British do and give up our independence of action.'

There was so much I could say to that.

'Is that why you welcomed Skorzeny and other Nazis

into your home after the war then?'

She looked straight back at me, saying quite calmly, 'Yes, I think so. The right to determine who can and cannot come into your country is one of the marks of nationhood. They had committed no crime here, but if it had been proven they had committed a crime elsewhere they would have been no longer welcome.'

'That's sophistry, that's legalism, it's just not a morally good judgement.'

To her point, though, Skorzeny never had been given his residency for the war crimes rumour mill about his time in the SS had started up again in the mid-sixties.

'I'm sorry, it's just that if Ireland is to join West Germany inside the EEC, you can't be independent in the same way in the future. You need to respect our views too. And make a decision about which side of the Cold War you're on. You can't take our money for your farmers and expect a free ride in other areas.'

She nodded quietly, whether in agreement or just to avoid prolonging my rant I had no idea.

'And that damn laundry needs to be closed down.'

We got out at the Department of External Affairs. She slung her handbag over her shoulder and stood quietly before me, watching to satisfy herself that I was ready to face the Irish public again.

'I'll see you at half past eight tomorrow morning, then,' she said, somewhat flatly.

My own disappointment caught me by surprise. Despite what had happened during the last sixty minutes, I'd unconsciously hoped she'd want to shepherd me around Dublin some more.

'Fine. How far is it again?'

'About six or seven hours, I think. We'll stop along the way.'

'Where will we be staying?'

'There's a hotel booked in Bundoran for all of us.'

She looked at me coolly. Many thoughts flashed through my head, but none I could speak out loud.

I kicked around the centre for a while, bought a waxed shooting jacket and a leather grip on expenses, then made my way back to the GPO for my pre-booked call with Kramer.

'*Hein*, how are things in Ireland?' he asked.

'Slow. I've met a couple of people now in the right areas but not the actual people we need.'

'So when will you meet those men?'

I could always spin a story out of my encounters with Chief Superintendent Mullen and Captain Fleming if I had to. I could even namedrop Captain Kelly too, at a stretch.

'Your contact has arranged a trip for me to possibly meet some of them privately. I'm going tomorrow and I should be back here on Friday. But I might need to stay until next week. When should I let Masson know?'

I couldn't hear it over the static but I imagined him tapping his teeth.

'Can you call him during your trip, from wherever you're going to? No later than Friday.'

I wondered whether and how I could broach the idea of some freelance arms dealing on behalf of the SDECE.

'Can I give any special incentives to the *Québécois*?'

'It's your decision and you'll stand or fall by it on your own. Still, I should be able to eventually sell that kind of idea in the Hexagon, despite what I said to you the other week. As long as you don't overpromise.'

So that was that. What chance did the British have now in the north, with everyone out to get them: the French, East and West Germans, as well as the Irish?

Chapter Sixteen

At twenty past eight in the morning Sweeney pulled up at the entrance to the Gresham in a black Ford Cortina with Brigid already in the back. She'd probably realised I'd already be outside with my bag and wanted to convince me that Ireland could hit any standards of punctuality its new masters might demand.

Sweeney jumped out to open the boot with an enthusiastic grin, pleased with himself for his extreme punctuality, extreme for Ireland anyway.

I stowed the grip I'd bought yesterday in Grafton Street in the boot, alongside his own, and two cases of Brigid's.

'Sit in the back with Brigid,' he said. I wondered what his game was. He probably wanted to relegate me to being an admiring spectator of his driving skills. For confirmation, he virtually spun the wheels as he set off into the morning traffic and did nothing to avoid the impression of a racing car driver thereafter. Presumably he had some kind of pass or identity card that gave him immunity from the traffic cops, not that I'd seen many so far.

The day's conversation started in the same vein. 'What sort of car do you drive in Germany?' he asked, forgetting that I lived in Brussels. 'A Porsche, a Mercedes-Benz?'

'A Volkswagen Type Three.'

'A boring Type for a boring type.' The pun even worked in German.

'Boring is cheap and reliable.' And anonymously

discreet, I might have added, but didn't. Though I could have said that that most people in East Germany would be desperate to own any kind of car.

'You can tell what a man is like with the ladies from the car he drives,' he said, as he tweaked the end of his moustache. Brigid stared straight ahead, expressionless in the morning sun. He might have been helping confused old men find their way back home on Monday evening from the pub, but behind the wheel on Wednesday morning, with an attractive girl in the back, compelled to listen to him for the next five hours, he was ticking all the stereotypical boxes.

'Is this your car?' I asked. 'Why do you have a two-way radio in the front?'

The factory-fitted radio had been removed and a customised set with a hand-held microphone-transmitter was hooked onto the fascia.

'I use it for work. The Cortina is the most popular car in Ireland and black is a good colour when parked up along hedgerows near the border. The radio is so I can hear what's happening on the police channels.'

We left Dublin and I waited for us to join the autobahn, or 'motorway' as the English called it, but I was to be disappointed.

Instead, as the road to Navan twisted and turned, Sweeney whipped the steering wheel back and forth, keeping a tight line. Brigid suddenly laid her forehead on Sweeney's seat in front of her and closed her eyes.

'There was no driving test in this country until nineteen sixty-four and sometimes it shows,' she murmured queasily.

'Slow down a bit, please. I don't feel so good,' I told Sweeney.

He tutted and said, 'I thought you'd be used to this speed, coming from Germany. Is it true that there's no speed limits on the autobahns?'

'Yes, it's why Jochen Rindt is leading this year's Grand Prix.'

'I thought he was Austrian?'

'Born in Germany, parents were killed in an air-raid on Hamburg, grew up with grandparents in Austria.'

'The raid you told me about?'

'Don't know,' I replied. 'There were a few.'

Brigid yawned, either from boredom, a reaction to subsiding nausea or both. After another little while she started checking her watch repeatedly, asking Sweeney if we were 'there' yet.

Sweeney was impatient. 'It'll add half-an-hour to our journey or however long you decide to waste there.'

'But we're passing by the foot of the hill, and after Navan we've only got another four or so hours to go.'

He was torn between wanting to comply with her wishes and trying to set a new Irish speed record for driving from Dublin to Bundoran.

We turned off the main road up a lane and past a handful of parked cars along the verges. Sweeney ignored these and turned off the public highway, climbing up a long drive to stop by a church overshadowed by trees. He said he'd stay with the car and promptly lit up, one elbow hanging out of the rolled-down window.

I turned to Brigid with a questioning look as we got out.

'Just past here,' she said, somewhat shyly. 'We have something to show you at the top of the hill.'

'Where is this?'

'It's the Hill of Tara, where the High Kings of Ireland were proclaimed. It's as old as Stonehenge.'

'Why's that important?'

'Stonehenge is in England. It's a circle of standing stones.'

'So what do the Irish have to prove?'

We walked up a gentle incline along a sheep track, past

the open mouth of a passageway which led into a grassy mound.

'What's that?'

'The Hill of the Hostages. A burial mound for several hundred people.'

The name didn't inspire me with confidence. The Ancient Irish obviously subscribed to the Russian school of prisoner of war treatment.

'Hostages or human sacrifices?' I asked.

'Depends on which stories you listen to,' she said.

I felt a cold frisson as we walked on by, up over the concentric rings of earthworks around the summit.

On the flat top I saw an upright stone and a grave marker. Brigid made her way over to the former, her eyes coming alive as she approached it.

'This is the Stone of Destiny,' she said. 'It called out when touched by the rightful king of Ireland. It was also said to have the power of rejuvenation and to grant a long reign. Here, Oskar, place your hand on the Stone. Do you feel its power?'

Sweeney had decided that looking at old stones would be unmanly in front of Brigid, and I wasn't that keen myself on touching an erect symbol of Irish royal potency.

But he didn't know what he was missing as I watched her laying her long fingers down along the mottled stone, hair gently waving in the breeze.

'Try it,' she commanded. 'Maybe you're the long-lost king of Ireland, come from over the water to save us all,' she teased.

'If it grants me a long reign, I will,' I said, placing my hand near hers. 'How many times did de Valera visit it then?' She rewarded me with a toss of her head and a '*Touché.*'

I stepped back. 'What's this one, then?' I asked, walking the few metres over to the headstone, just across from the Stone of Destiny. 'What happened in seventeen ninety-eight? Who were the "United Irishmen"?'

'There was a revolt that year by Catholics and Presbyterians acting together. Presbyterians are like the Lutherans in Germany. No, that's not right.' She paused and restarted. 'It was a revolt against the ruling class who were in the official state church - Lutherans if you will, by Catholics and the other Protestant sects which the Anglicans, the Church of Ireland, were repressing.'

I was confused, so I asked the obvious question. 'Who won?'

'Oh, the Anglo-Irish. There was a battle on this very hill. Both these stones mark the mass grave of the rebels.'

I refrained from any quips about how if the victors were Anglo-Irish then you could say that both sides had won.

'How far can you see from here?'

'They say that thirteen of the thirty-two counties of Ireland are visible from the Stone. Even the mountains of Mourne in the North. But not today.' There was a haze in the air and unlike Moses, I wasn't able to look down upon the Promised Land.

I wanted to prolong the stop for as long as possible and spend as much time with Brigid on her own, as she started to warm up and become more human now that we had left Dublin behind.

'What else happened here?'

Her face fell. She was usually reserved but now she was now truly solemn.

'It was the last great meeting held by the…,' she searched for a phrase, 'the human rights campaigner Daniel O'Connell in eighteen forty-three. No-one knows for sure, but several hundred thousand people are said to have attended. The crowd stretched all the way down the slope to the road.'

I took a look down to the bottom for myself and tried to imagine the empty greensward covered with jostling, bewhiskered Victorians.

'What was he famous for? Ah, he's the one with the

statue by the bridge.'

'He agitated for the repeal of the laws discriminating against Catholics and Presbyterians, preventing them taking their seats in the British Parliament. Then he agitated for the repeal of the Act of Union, the law uniting Ireland to Great Britain - but by peaceful means only. He was the Gandhi of his time.'

'Did it work?'

'No. The next meeting after Tara was to have been even bigger, at Clontarf, just outside Dublin. But it was stopped by the militia. Then two years later came the Famine.'

'More misery?'

'A million perished, a million emigrated. Population reduction on the scale of...' Her voice trailed off, but I knew what she had been about to say.

When we got back down to the car, I asked Sweeney if I could drive.

'Let me have a go. I've never driven a right-hand-drive car before.'

I discovered that the backwardness of Irish and British driving conventions was kind to left-handers. Using the right hand to work the gear stick seemed much more natural to me.

For Brigid's sake as well as my own in the first few minutes, I deliberately took it slow through the bends. Sweeney was contemptuous, though.

'You drive like a woman,' he said, hurriedly adding, 'present company excepted.'

'*Doch, die Deutschen sind Weicheier*,' I muttered under my breath. There was a snort from the back. She had obviously remembered more German from school than she gave herself credit for.

I waited to see if she would translate for me, but nothing was forthcoming. With a toss of his head, he asked me to explain.

'The Germans are nothing but soft eggs.'

'Soft eggs?'

'Like when you cook them.'

'What? Scrambled, fried?'

'No, when you put them in a pan of water and cook them. *Gekochtes Eier*.'

I half-turned to say it for Brigid's benefit, hoping she'd help me out. She didn't, but Sweeney had already worked it out for himself.

'Oh, you mean boiled eggs. "Soft-boiled eggs". You Germans have a strange way of speaking.'

I drove us to Cavan, where we stopped for lunch and liquid refreshment.

As Sweeney sipped his Guinness on the bench to the side of the door into the pub, he became expansive.

'I can't wait to go back to sea tomorrow. My Da is a fisherman. I used to love going out with him and my eldest brother for mackerel.'

'What do you mean, "to sea"?'

'We've got something to show you on one of the islands off the west coast of Donegal.'

'Where are you from then, that your father was a fisherman?'

'We're from Westport. It's in County Mayo.'

'Mayo, God help us,' I replied.

There was a peal of laughter from Brigid.

'Where on earth did you learn that phrase from?'

'Have a guess.'

'Not from that old book again?' she asked.

'Everything I know about Ireland comes from it.' Everything that was, apart from what I'd learnt from the file on Ireland, which the East German foreign intelligence service had put together for me.

'Anyway, to change the topic. How do you stay so fluent in French?' I asked.

'I practice with a French journalist at his flat in Dublin.'

Both Sweeney and I carefully said nothing to this.

'Do you practice with any Germans?' I asked in all innocence.

'I haven't found any good-looking ones yet, or any who're such good teachers as Yves.'

I was surprised. Flirtatiousness wasn't her style at all. Not from the couple of days we'd spent together so far. But I could have told her that as far as Sweeney was concerned, she'd just hung out the red lantern for tonight.

As he got back into the car, Sweeney deliberately let his jacket swing open so that Brigid got a good look at his shoulder holster and what I thought looked like a revolver.

'What are you carrying?' I asked with interest.

'Smith & Wesson Police Special.'

He took it out and spun the chamber.

'You want to take a look?' he said, offering it hopefully to Brigid.

Whoever Sweeney worked for, it couldn't be the Department of Agriculture. The Customs Service maybe. I didn't know what the Irish Army issued to its officers as a sidearm, but like most Western armies, it was probably the Browning Hi-Power. However, as the name suggested, Sweeney's model of Smith & Wesson had been marketed for sale to police forces. The reason the police preferred revolvers was their supposed greater reliability in close-quarters situations. Still, who knew what other special undercover units the Irish had? Maybe the Agriculture boys really were worried about cattle rustlers.

We drove half-an-hour out of Cavan and hit a town where we crossed a fair-sized river. As Sweeney took us over the narrow bridge, he made a strange announcement.

'Do you watch Western movies, Oskar?'

'Sure. Everyone likes Clint Eastwood.'

'In the Civil War, one of the IRA was shot whilst holding up a shop here, trying to get supplies for their camp in the hills. So the volunteers came back a month later to get revenge. They sealed off the town, both road and rail access, and went hunting for the people they believed had killed their gang member. But they had no idea who they were after, so they just shot the owner of the shop which the first fella had held up and then the shopkeeper's employee. After that, they went on the rampage, burning and shooting up the town before the National Army arrived.'

That was a lot of information to take in at once.

'What civil war?' I asked in bewilderment. Whatever the black hats had done back then, the town didn't look too much the worse for wear now.

'Nineteen twenty-two to -three, after the Free State came into being,' answered Brigid.

'What was that one about?' I asked incredulously.

I couldn't believe it hadn't been in Petzold's file on Ireland. I blamed Johannes and his eagerness to go out for a beer, in case it had been there all along and I'd missed it.

'No, it was between those who supported the Provisional Government and the Treaty they signed with the British, and those who were against it. The Anti-Treaty forces my father mentioned on Sunday.'

'He didn't say they'd come to blows over it.'

'The old IRA basically split into two factions. The Anti-Treaty side thought the Treaty didn't go far enough in giving Ireland independence.'

'I still don't understand. Wasn't it like a colony in Africa, once the European flag is hauled down, it's down?'

'It's more complicated than that…' her voice faded, as if it was going to be much more difficult for her to explain than she'd realised.

Well, I was sure now that none of this had been in Petzold's file. If things went wrong here, I could always blame the failure of the mission on him and his ignorance of nineteen-twenties Irish politics. To be fair, though, the first couple of years of the Weimar Republic in Germany were a tangled story of putsch and counter-putsch too.

But now Brigid rallied her forces, determined to plough on and enlighten me, patiently answering my questions. She told me how Ireland had been given an intermediate status, part of the British Commonwealth and with the English king still as the head of state, thus requiring deputies to the Irish parliament to take an oath of allegiance. I tried pointing out that the English royal family were actually German, but the joke fell flat. Sweeney piped up too, with a story about the eight Anti-Treaty rebels who the forces of the new Government had tied to a landmine, alive, and then blown up.

'That was devilishly cruel,' I said. 'Like something the Russians would have done on the Eastern Front. Imagine knowing what was going to happen as you were being roped together?'

Brigid spoke up again. It was a story they had both heard of.

'It was done to simulate them having been killed clearing other mines - Irish violence always has a purpose. They say that as the ropes were being tied, they just quietly said their goodbyes and asked for time to pray. There was a ninth man, but, miraculously, he survived.'

'That certainly was his lucky day. I wonder how he felt, the rest of his life, about having have survived, when the others didn't?' I asked.

Sweeney called out from the front, 'He must have prayed harder than the rest.'

'What would you pray for, if you knew you were about to face your Maker?' asked Brigid. I wasn't sure who she meant out of Sweeney and myself.

'I'm not sure that's how it works,' I said, lost in my own thoughts now. 'I don't think God rewards you for doing more good deeds for him than the next person. It's what they call "grace" - you get mercy even when you don't deserve it.'

'That's not the impression our Church gives,' said

Sweeney. 'The Jesuits who taught me at school weren't overgenerous with their mercy. What's the catch in your church? There's always a catch with these priests.'

I reddened with embarrassment. 'You're expected to say sorry for your sins.'

'And have you?' asked Brigid.

My heart hardened. 'We don't go to confession in our religion.'

And that was enough theological discussion for the time being.

We drove on and Sweeney returned to the topic of the Civil War.

'Which side were the O'Cuacachs on?' asked Sweeney. He asked in a genuinely casual way, as if it was of historical curiosity only. 'The Sweeneys had people on both sides. We have aunts who still won't talk to each other.'

Brigid was uncharacteristically slow to answer.

'My grandfather fought for the Anti-Treaty side. He was caught up in the early romance of the Rising and he changed our family name back to the Irish version when my father was born. At the very start, he thought that de Valera was God's gift to Ireland, but eventually felt betrayed when he formed a political party and ran for office in what Grandad saw as an illegitimate state. And he's still angry at my father for taking a job from Lemass, because he was the leader of Fianna Fail, Dev's party.'

'How's he going to feel about you if you take a job at the EEC, working to reunite Ireland with England and eight other countries?' I asked.

'Is that what it's about, then?' asked Sweeney sharply. 'When we met on Monday, I thought it was all about agricultural subsidies?'

I was surprised because I'd assumed the implications were obvious but then again, I'd assumed the same when speaking with Skorzeny, too - neither of them had spent four years immersed in the organisation like I had.

'Well, not immediately of course. But that's always been the intention,' I replied.

Sweeney became agitated, wobbling the steering wheel. He was taking this surprisingly badly. 'And did you know about this too, Brigid?'

I tried to distract him and save her from having to answer. 'If your father's a fisherman, then you've got something else to worry about now, rather than what might happen a few years' time.'

'What do you mean?'

'Your government needs to watch out for the Common Fisheries Policy in the accession negotiations, Brigid, as well as for the CAP,' I said, now diverting back to her.

'What's that thing then, subsidies for fishermen?' he asked.

'I'll tell you more later,' I said, realising it might be an even more delicate topic than the history of the Civil War.

Finally, we arrived at Bundoran in the early afternoon, a small seaside resort town towards the eastern end of Donegal Bay.

We were to stay in a large hotel on a promontory. Once Sweeney had parked and we had got out to take a closer look, it was clear the place had seen better days.

'I have to drive on up the coast to Burtonport to make arrangements to get us out to Gola Island tomorrow,' he said, as we waited at the reception desk to check in.

'Do you want to drive up with me and see some more of Donegal?' he asked, looking at Brigid now.

'Whatever Oskar wants to do,' she replied.

After meeting Captain Fleming in Ballsbridge, I'd more or less given up on her, unless I got a signal, any signal truthfully, of some kind. But I hadn't bargained on getting in the way of Sweeney's attempts to charm Brigid off her high horse, as he'd put it on Monday night.

'I'm happy to go with you and Jim, if you really want me to come along.' I tried to say it in the most favourable way for him.

Not surprisingly, he looked put out all the same, when she nodded in agreement. Maybe I'd be able to have a quiet word with him on his own later.

'Okay, be back here in ten minutes. I have to leave on the dot, with or without you.'

Brigid was wise to his attempt to ditch me, because she made us both wait a full five minutes after the agreed time before she reappeared downstairs. Grumpily, Sweeney drove in silence almost another hour and a half up the coast to a small village past a lake, facing an inlet dotted with rocky islands.

He parked by a pub and stumped off down to the harbour to find whoever it was he needed to speak with.

The pub was tiny. Even though it was still only late afternoon, there were a couple of older men nursing pints. Brigid chose a table near the bar, watching me as I went up to order.

Behind the counter was a black and white photograph of four bearded men around a table next to an open door. I looked around and saw a back door leading to a garden at the rear of the pub and the same table next to it, as in the photo. The men stared at the camera with far-away eyes set in pale skin, their beards of differing lengths and thicknesses. All were youngish, wearing a variety of fishermen's jerseys, none of which were too clean either.

As the publican poured, I asked him about the picture. 'Some special people?'

He looked at me neutrally. 'Who's asking?'

'This is Mister Lenkeit, from West Germany.' Brigid had appeared next to me at the counter.

He rattled off something to her in a language I didn't recognise. Irish, presumably. She answered in the same tongue, but in a halting and hesitant manner.

'Let's hear some German, then,' he said, turning back to me.

'Ich heiße Oskar Lenkeit. Ich komme aus Hamburg, und ich mag irische Mädchen.'

Brigid lightly punched me on the arm.

'Well then, because your young lady spoke so graciously, I can tell you that they were countrymen of yours, came ashore to have a pint as a dare.'

'Because the beer here was so bad?'

'Because they came off a U-boat during the Emergency.'

'Really?'

'Yes, really.' He looked at me evenly, challenging me to contradict him.

The story was too bizarre not to want to dig into further. I didn't want him to clam up, so started with some easy questions.

'When was this, nineteen forty?' It was a guess, based on the assumption that as the war progressed, such a prank would have been less and less likely - if it had actually happened.

'Forty-one. You can still see the leading marks out between Inishinny and Lahon Island where they brought their submarine into the inlet.'

'What are "leading marks"? Sorry - I'm not a sailor.'

'If you take yourself down there, you'll find a concrete pillar low down by the water and another up the hill. When the two are in line, a boat can find a safe way through the channel. There's German writing on the one up the hill. Some people from Dublin arranged for it to be put there.'

'Are you sure this isn't a yarn for the tourists?' I asked smiling, as if Irish assistance to the Kriegsmarine during the *Atlantikschlacht* was all just a big joke. But the barman wasn't smiling back. Go over to Inishinny Island way and take a look for yourself. It was my mother's cousin who brought them here. Wearing their uniforms, they were.'

I pointed to the nondescript fishermen's gear they had on in the picture.

'They covered them up for the photograph. They had

dark gear on underneath, one had a German eagle on his. My ma's cousin had instructions from Dublin to take them supplies. Four bags of potatoes, four bags of cabbages and a whole pig cut up into pieces. They picked it all up by rowboat, then the four in the picture came up over the hill to find the nearest pub and walked in here.

'Ach Paddy, not that old story again,' called out one of the regulars.

'You didn't see it for yourself, though?' I insisted.

'Look at the picture. There's your proof,' he said impatiently now. It certainly had pride of place here.

'What did people back then feel about Germans coming here, in that way?'

'Anybody fighting the British was welcome, even though a couple of the lads in the village fought for the Brits.'

This story was already too weird for me, but I kept on.

'Why would they have done that, fought for the British I mean?' I pointedly asked Brigid, guessing the other men in the pub would be only too happy to help her out.

Her brow furrowed and she shrugged her shoulders, preferring to keep her counsel.

The other of the two regulars present answered for her.

'Davey G had always fancied having a go at flying, saw an advertisement for the Royal Air Force and joined up as an air-gunner. Got shot down over Berlin for his trouble and sent his ma to an early grave, God rest her soul. Big Tommy joined the infantry, the Inniskillings, fought his way through Burma, but was court-martialled here after the war because it was the Irish Army he'd deserted from, so as to join the British one.'

'That wasn't the whole story about Tommy Finnegan,' said his drinking companion. 'The nuns had taken his children in the meantime and he couldn't get them back.'

I didn't know what to make of that, so I ignored it.

'So the Irish just like fighting, they don't mind who for or who against - that's the explanation?'

This time I got a smile from the barman.

'Take yourself over there, see if you can make any sense of the words on the ould post.'

That was going on the itinerary for tomorrow, for sure. Even if I had to promise Sweeney, I'd listen to his horseracing stories from Monday lunchtime again.

The barman gave me a final caution, topping off one of the strangest stories I'd heard for some time.

'But if you do go there up to the higher post, don't damage the fairy tree at the top. I reckon digging at its roots to have the sea mark put in is why those boys never made it back here after the war, as they promised they'd do.'

We took our drinks out to the garden, sitting side by side on a long wooden bench overlooking the sea.

'Schlanjey,' I waved my glass at her. 'What did you make of the story, Brigid?'

'There's a few of those which go around.'

'So your father helped round up the deserters then? And why did the nuns take that man's children?'

'Maybe he wasn't married to the mother, maybe she couldn't cope on her own and gave them up to a church orphanage.'

'My mother brought me up on her own. She was twenty and she wasn't married,' I countered.

'I thought that might have been the case, when you said what you did at lunch on Sunday.' Her eyes softened in what looked suspiciously like a quiet pity.

But I wasn't going to let Brigid into my family history, not for anything, and definitely not to get sympathy, or even to get more than sympathy from her.

On impulse I asked her, 'If we have time tomorrow, shall we go and check out the barman's story? Search for the leading marks?'

'I don't know how long the trip to Gola will be, but we can ask Jim. Here he comes.'

Sweeney indeed appeared in the doorway, a pint in his hand.

'What are you pair talking about?'

'I was just telling Oskar that it's not "Schlan-jey", but "Slan-tchuh". I'll write it out for you later and explain it,' she said to me, as cool as anything.

'After whatever we see on Gola tomorrow, do we have time to look around the coast here a bit more? I asked Sweeney.

He shrugged. 'Take yourself where you like. You can have the use of the car if you want. I have to see a fella over the border in the afternoon.'

He shifted his pint to the other hand so he could check his watch.

'Let me finish this and we'll go back to eat at the hotel.'

We reconvened for dinner, and I scanned the menu to see what was on offer. The prices on the page had been altered upwards at least once and in some cases two times. I supposed inflation went hand in hand with a property boom, and that rising prices had even reached as far as Donegal.

Sweeney saw me looking and made to reassure me.

'Have whatever you like. I still have my special expenses account.'

Sweeney was in an expansive mood again. I guessed he was going to try his luck with Brigid tonight, and I didn't plan to stop him.

He regaled her with stories of the injuries he'd inflicted on other players during the hurling matches from his time as an active player. He reminded her that he had no time for that now because he had to keep a watch on the border for the UVF - Protestant terrorists from the North, apparently.

I sensed he was struggling to make headway, though, and he proved his desperation with a different plan of attack. One which involved reminding everyone of why they hated Germans and liked each other instead, presumably with the added bonus of encouraging me to clear off to my room.

'When you think about it, the way the Orangemen force the Catholics to live in ghettos and then burn them out is just what the Nazis would have done. You should know all about that sort of thing, Oskar, coming from Germany.'

'Who are "Orangemen"?'

Brigid helped me out again. 'It's what we sometimes call the people who run the northern state.'

'And what is their crime, exactly, up there over the border?' I knew for myself there was some kind of parallel with the black civil rights movement in America, but not the details.

But Brigid didn't try to take me through those. It had been a long enough day.

'Let's say it another way. The English left the Unionists alone for fifty years to do as they pleased. They had their chance to build a society that was fair to everyone living there, and maybe even to persuade the northern Catholics of the benefits of the arrangement they have with Britain. But who knows? They wasted it.'

Sweeney butted back in, having already forgotten his new plan of attack.

'We should have done what you lot did. During the Emergency, when the Brits were distracted elsewhere, we should have invaded and sent the Protestants back to Scotland.'

Böll had described disabusing the rural Irish of Nazi sympathies as like drawing teeth. He did it in a gentle, friendly way, between the fifth and the sixth pints. I decided on my own approach.

'But that presumes that Germany would have won the war. Is that what you really would have wanted? Hitler didn't hate the English especially. He admired their colonial ruling class, saw them as a model for the administrators of the new Greater Germany.'

He was silent, I suspected feeling embarrassed now. And his rash words weren't really in his character, from the little I'd already got to know him. I wondered what else Brigid could drive men to do.

'I met one of his top men once, Otto Skorzeny, who led their commando force. He told me that he set up a training school on the border between Croatia and Serbia to ensure his students saw action, because that lot were always at each other's throats.'

He hadn't said so actually, not to me anyway. I'd read it in Kramer's SDECE file on him. I tossed in another fact I dredged up from somewhere else, trying to make my point.

'Why do you think Ukrainians were used by both sides against the Poles, at different times in the war? Keeping nationalist tendencies in check by setting non-Germans against one another was a standard method of control. What do you think we would have done here?'

He said nothing, so I carried on.

'If Germany had won, another possibility is that Britain would have had its original nineteen twenty-two territory restored and had Ireland given back to them. All to toss them a bone and make defeat more palatable.'

'Which would have given them an almighty rebellion on their hands down here.'

'Which would have kept the British Army busy for the first ten years of German rule of the New European Order, keeping them quiet whilst we consolidated other parts of Greater Germany. And when the fighting got too vicious even for the British, who would they have used in the South? Their Protestant auxiliaries from the North, of course.'

Sweeney looked chastened now, and dangerous.

'Germany would not have been the friend you imagined it would be.' I could have added that it still wasn't.

On that note, I made my excuses and left because I still

had to get Sweeney to tell me who it was he was acting for in G2 or the Special Branch, who it was who wanted to play freedom fighters in the North. I supposed I'd see tomorrow how successful he'd been on his personal mission in Donegal, by the way he and Brigid treated each other at breakfast.

Chapter Seventeen

In the morning in the hotel restaurant overlooking the bay, Brigid and Sweeney indeed maintained a cautious neutrality when speaking with one another. They didn't come across as a pair who'd hooked up, spent the night together and were now trying to avoid drawing attention to it by being unnaturally reserved. I suspected the spark had gone from Sweeney because he'd been rebuffed yesterday evening after I left. I hoped for all our sakes today that Brigid had tried to let him down gently, if she had.

But given what I knew of Sweeney so far, he didn't strike me as the sort of person to be kept down for long, and the light came back into his eye when he started to tell us about our upcoming trip to Gola Island.

'It's going to be fresh this morning on the way over but the weather's meant to settle down later on. Make sure you have a big breakfast for plenty of ballast.'

He looked the part of a fisherman in his yellow PVC cagoule over a thick woollen shirt.

Brigid, by contrast, was wearing a high-buttoned tweed riding jacket, slacks and sensible flat-heeled shoes, as if she was a non-participating attendee at a gymkhana, rather than about to go to sea.

For myself, despite growing up in Hamburg, I'd never even been around the harbour on a tourist cruise. The only time I'd been to sea for real was a familiarisation day put on for army conscripts by the Bundesmarine at the Kiel naval base. We had spent most of the day being given lectures in a draughty shed while they took us in batches of twenty, out on a fast attack boat down to the mouth of the fjord for some high-speed S-turns and then back in again.

I'd asked to drive from Bundoran to Burtonport, to help me memorise the route for the way back later. Sweeney had told us at breakfast he'd arranged to be picked up there by his border contact after our trip across to Gola, and said he'd get dropped off in Bundoran again after he was done.

Depending on how early we got back from the boat journey to Gola, I would try to persuade Brigid to commit to coming with me to find the leading mark the barman had mentioned further round the coast.

Once we were past Donegal Town, apart from Sweeney giving me the odd direction now and then, he and Brigid didn't speak much for the rest of the journey and I settled down to concentrate on the road. As it twisted and turned, dipping up and down again, I would catch glimpses of the grey sea through the folds in the hills. And as Sweeney had predicted, there were indeed flecks of white on the caps of the long Atlantic rollers.

I parked by the quayside at Burtonport and we got out of the car into a stiff breeze. The boats alongside the harbour wall were bobbing gently up and down, even this far into the inlet. I saw Brigid hesitate and an uncertain expression come over her face, as she carried on down to the far end of the breakwater and the fishing boat there which Sweeney had indicated to us.

Sweeney leapt down onto the wooden deck and turned round to reach up and help Brigid. She took his hands and jumped down. Whatever had happened last night, she wasn't refusing physical contact this morning. Or maybe I had misjudged them at breakfast and he had been successful after all, despite my scepticism.

He went into the wheelhouse to exchange words with the owner. Through the glass, I saw several red-coloured notes peeled off the top of a wad of cash and handed over. The diesel engine coughed into life, and the skipper's mate, who was sitting on a bollard up on the quayside, flicked his cigarette into the water. Casting off the lines, he jumped down into the boat at what seemed the last possible second, as it was pulling away from the wall.

Brigid leaned on the rail and looked out at the sides of the channel as we chugged into the steepening waves. From sea level, Donegal took on a new aspect. Black and brown rocks slick with the wash of the surf. The green grass of the machair, running down almost into the sea. And sheep tracks too, hugging corners directly over frothing water that even Rindt would have found impossible to take, with or without four-wheel drive.

We left the inlet and headed out across a bay towards an island three or four kilometres away. Brigid was keeping a firm grip on the handrail, still not communicating. I went to find Sweeney instead, in through a door to a compartment at the back of the wheelhouse and then on through another door in the forward bulkhead to the bridge, I supposed it would be called.

Sweeney was rolling gently on the balls of his feet as the boat met the waves. With a sigh, he sucked in the briny air, his eyes glittering in the reflected light off the water as he looked to the horizon. Maybe he was thinking about the future he could have had if he'd stayed in Mayo, wrestling with the sea week in and week out, constantly renewing himself with the satisfaction of a hard day's work done well. I wondered if the sea had the same effect on Johannes, if it secretly called to him sometimes too.

That day, running out from Kiel had been a rough day too, and half of the infantrymen I was with were sick - but not me, thankfully. One of the matelots had told us that when you stood still in one place on the deck, the rocking of the boat tricked your brain into thinking you were moving across it, with the nausea which resulted. The answer for some, was to fix your eyes on the horizon, which didn't move. But that only worked above decks, of course. Back in the present when I now glanced back aft out of the side window, I could see Brigid was still standing there by the rail, feet apart and head bowed.

Sweeney snapped out of his reverie and started to ask me about the Common Fisheries Policy.

'So what's this EEC fishing policy thing again?' he asked. 'What will it mean for my Da and for Mister MacNamara here?'

'It's brand new. It was signed only a few hours before the Ireland and the other three countries lodged their accession applications on the thirtieth of June.

Sweeney and the skipper looked at each other. They weren't anyone's fools and obviously suspected underhand dealings.

'So what does it mean, the EEC will subsidise fishermen and protect our fishing grounds from the Scots and the French?'

'No. Under the CFP, all the fishing grounds of the member states are to be managed as one, with each nation being given an allocation from Brussels, even to fish in their own national waters.' There was no point in sweetening the pill, I thought.

'How does that work? We've always fished here. What rights do these other countries have?'

'Whatever rights and quotas the EEC decides to give them. And the new countries have to accept whatever arrangements were already in place when they applied to join, even if those arrangements were only a few hours old.'

Sweeney looked disgusted. MacNamara glowered.

'It's part of the plan by the French to extract as much wealth from the new member states as possible, which means Britain and Norway, when it comes to fishing. Ireland is just being swept along with the stitch-up of the others. In Ireland's favour, though, when it comes to agriculture, the British and Germans will effectively be the ones paying subsidies into the bank accounts of Irish farmers.'

'That doesn't help us here in Donegal,' said MacNamara. 'Typical Dubliners, jackeens the lot of them.'

'Neil Blaney is a Donegal TD. He's part of this back-stabbing too,' said Sweeney.

'He's not part of anything anymore. Not after his arrest - or so I would assume,' I said.

'Can't Ireland negotiate a different deal? After all, we're so small compared to the big countries,' asked MacNamara.

'Look at the Atlantic chart. Scotland and Norway are fishing super-powers. The French want a share of that and the Dutch too.'

Sometimes you had to be cruel to be kind.

'But that's not the worst. Franco over in Spain won't live forever. If the Spanish join the EEC at some later date, they'll really make a dent in your catch.'

Sweeney looked grim. 'Then what the feck are we joining the EEC for - to keep the Midlands farmers happy?' He spat out of the open side window of the wheelhouse to the lee, away from the direction of the wind.

'You might get a derogation. It's what the EEC calls a delay for new members in adopting the rules,' I offered.

'I reckon my Da will stop fishing in ten years' time. Maybe he'll be okay. What was the point of nineteen sixteen, if we end up being ruled by a different set of foreigners?' he asked bitterly. 'I've been going out to fish with him all my life, off and on, even during the Emergency. One of my earliest memories is watching the German planes flying up the west coast, on their way to bomb the Brits in Atlantic. Great big ones with four engines, out every day they were so.'

The boat chugged on. The skipper threaded us between the first island I'd seen and the mainland, then pointed us across the next bay, finally heading directly for Gola.

Sweeney took the wheel for a while, standing legs apart, nudging the steering from time to time to correct the boat's course for the effect of the current. Looking astern at the straight wake behind us, I saw he hadn't lost his sailor's touch as he aimed for the far side of the island.

I wondered where Brigid had got to because she was no longer clenching onto the rail. Going back into the aft compartment of the wheelhouse I found her, curled along the bench seat against the rear bulkhead, looking up at me with wary eyes. Her slick skin was deathly pale against her tousled red-gold hair, making her look even more Irish than usual. She tried to get up, swinging her long legs onto the deck, but was immediately sick next to her feet. In her eyes I saw defeat and my heart went out to her.

The after-cabin had a tiny galley area with a sink. I bent down and scraped her returned breakfast, as best I could, onto a dirty plate with a knife, which I found in the slops basin. I went out to toss the contents over the leeward side and came back to find her lying back down again, a picture of misery. There was a filthy mop in a bucket of dark grey water standing in one corner of the space and I did the best I could with the rest of the mess, washing away the signs of her shame into the bilge grating by the door. She looked at me gratefully as I laid my hand on her sweaty brow. 'Stay there. I'll call you once we're at the island.'

She nodded, lips tightly pursed, looking once more like death warmed up.

Thankfully, for her sake, it was only a few minutes more until we arrived at the jetty on Gola. Weeds grew through the cracks in the concrete, rags of nets and ropes flapped in the wind, caught on rusty barbed wire.

The skipper's mate did his thing with the ropes again, but Brigid wasn't for moving, fearful that getting up would trigger her nausea again, even in the comparative shelter of the little harbour.

Sweeney and I climbed up the unmade road towards the centre of the island.

'What are we looking for?' I asked.

'Those,' he said, pointing to an empty oil drum in a field off to the left, torn ragged by what looked like aimed shots, rather than fully automatic fire.

We went up to the rust-eaten drum to take a closer look, then walked up the range, in the direction the shots had come from, as indicated by the orientation of the exit blooms of peeled-back metal.

After a couple of hundred metres we came upon the firing point, a raised area of flattened grass, surrounded by discarded brass cartridges.

'Untidy, aren't they?'

'They're not regular soldiers,' he replied, in a defensive tone of voice.

'So here we are, Jim, at the edge of the world with no Brigid to get between us. Now we can be honest with each other, can't we? "Ask any question you like" isn't that what you said in Dublin? As we say in German, now we're finally speaking "under four eyes."'

I picked up a spent cartridge and tossed it from hand to hand.

'The Department of Agriculture don't pack pistols. So, what's your brief, to watch the guy from Brussels who's asking to meet with everyone here? Are you worried Haughey and Kelly have some last trick up their sleeves, trying to find someone to entrap and smear to get themselves off the hook?'

His clear grey eyes held mine.

'Or are you secretly hoping I'm not just here to offer help on understanding CAP fraud, but might instead be wanting to find the parts of the Irish government who're still in the market for assistance in the North? You have to jump one way or another now.'

'Do you really hate the British?'

'Do you think I made up those stories about the Royal Air Force and Hamburg?'

'No, I don't.' He weighed up his words and came to a decision. 'So, if you were offering help, what kind would it be?'

'What does the Irish government really hope to achieve up here, on the other side of the border? And which part of the IRA are they using to do it with?'

'But what are you offering, Oskar Lenkeit? Whoever it is you work for, are they open to helping those people you just mentioned, directly, without involving us?'

I shook my head. 'I don't jump that fast. Above all, selling is the art of persuasion, of learning how to draw in the other side,' I said, paraphrasing Skorzeny.

'But certain of the countries at the EEC might be interested in keeping the insurgency alive, to weaken England for various reasons of their own, such as making sure they really do feel the need to join the EEC.'

He picked up a spent cartridge of his own to fidget with, trying to buy time.

'Let me make it easy for you, Jim. If you tell me who within the factions of the IRA it is that the government wants to help unofficially, I'll find out for you if there's any interest on the Continent. However, no names of my principals yet.'

'After we get back to Burtonport, I'm leaving you to go across the border this afternoon, as I told you yesterday. I'll have an answer for you in the next couple of days.'

'Fair enough.' I really wanted to ask who he was working for within the government, but I needed to listen to my own advice and take my time. If he didn't eventually come up with a name, I already had a few of my own which I could suggest in my report for the Stasi. It was only a report after all, and one that the East Germans would never be able to check up on.

'So the IRA came here for some shooting practice, and some mortar practice too, it appears?' I pointed to some blackened patches of grass off to the side of the range.

'More likely they were getting rid of unstable home-made explosives. The volunteers have been raiding gelignite stores at quarries up and down Ireland the past year, alongside armed robberies on banks, but it's not enough. If they're to sustain an effective bombing campaign, they need reliable sources of explosives. Their own home-grown efforts, so far, have sometimes proven to be as dangerous to themselves as to the Brits.'

'So what is a sustainable bombing campaign? How often do they need to set off a bomb to keep the pot stirring and Irishmen at each other's throats?' I thought back to Brigid father's analogy about charcoal burners, keeping the fire contained under a mound of earth, secretly burning out the heart of the wood.

Sweeney looked uncertain. He lit a cigarette to give himself more time to think.

'Gola is an uninhabited island. The last farmers left five or so years ago. But nothing goes on in the State without our people knowing. It doesn't matter how many guns the IRA are able to import from Hamburg or Boston or elsewhere. Guns lying in a crate on the docks are just that. Without somewhere to conduct weapons training and to make their bombs, to get medical treatment and find safe houses to lie up in, their campaign in the North will be as successful as their last one, in the fifties. The one that no-one outside Ireland has heard of.'

He flicked his cigarette to get rid of the ash.

'So they need us which means that anyone from the outside who wants to help them has to go through us first.'

'And where do the Irish Rangers stand? The ones that we're seeing tomorrow, if you get my meaning?'

'They're just soldiers. They follow the orders they're given.'

He dropped his cigarette on the grass and ground it out. He turned over the cartridge he'd been fidgeting with, looking at the headstamp.

'Three-oh-threes. They're practicing with the Lee-Enfield rifles our Army used back at the time of the Emergency.'

We made our way back to the boat to find Brigid much more cheerful. She'd got up and off the boat whilst we'd been away for our wander and was now sitting on the slipway, up at the landward end, swinging her legs over the edge. She didn't seem bothered that we'd left her, or interested to know what we'd found.

'I felt like I wanted to die earlier, on the way over here. I would have given anything to have been whisked off that boat and put back on dry land.'

'And now?'

She looked sheepish. 'Immediately after I was sick, I suddenly felt better. For the next half-a-minute I felt like a million dollars, on top of the world, able to do anything - but it didn't last.'

'Never mind, it will be calmer on the way back.'

'Good, because I've nothing left to bring up.'

The skipper put the engines astern, angled out and away from the broken-down quay, and steered his craft around back into the bay.

On the return leg I asked the skipper to point out Inishinny Island and asked if he had ever seen the leading marks the barman had mentioned.

'Here, take a look for yourself,' he said, handing me a pair of ancient Zeiss binoculars with a knotted cord for a neck strap. The island was fringed with innumerable isolated rocks, making its actual edge hard to see. I scanned the coastline between it and a kilometre-long inlet up to a wide strand, just before we turned the corner again, to head down to Burtonport.

Just before the turn, down by the water's edge, I was sure there was a cairn of stones. It wasn't a pillar, but it was something at least.

'Ever seen that before?' I pointed. But I was too late, for the angle was rapidly changing as he wheeled over, and it was gone before he found it.

'Could you bring a boat up the inlet we just passed?'

'To Cloughglass Strand?'

'I guess so,'

'With care, yes. You people have some strange notions.'

'He's after Nazi submarines,' said Sweeney.

I reddened. 'We heard a story yesterday in a pub in Burtonport.'

'Och aye, there's a few of those, right enough. Doesn't mean they're all blether though.'

We got back to Burtonport and Sweeney said his thanks to the skipper. I watched them get ready to turn around and go out again. If they'd noticed my cleaning job on the deckhouse floor, they didn't mention it.

Sweeney reached down to help Brigid up onto the quay, but she brushed his hand away this time, in her impatience to get off the boat. If he was put out, he didn't show it. Glancing at his watch a couple of times, he checked with me that I knew the road back and said he was off to the pub to meet his contact.

'Off you go now. Don't get thirsty and come nosing in after me. I'll get myself dropped back at Bundoran in time for dinner at the hotel.'

That suited me just fine. Off he went and I asked Brigid if she was still interested in an explore.

'Why not? It's still dry and it's only one o'clock.' She declined the offer of lunch, not that I would have known where to buy it for her if she hadn't, and off we went on a wild goose chase.

To my surprise, the beach I'd seen from the boat was easy enough to find. I took the only road north and we were there in ten minutes. Still, if someone had come ashore there, they'd have had to have been picked up in a vehicle to make it to the publican's bar quickly, if they didn't want to hang around on land too long. I wasn't believing the story any better, the more I tested the details.

We left our coats in the car and walked down to the strand, but there was nothing to see at first. There were some rocks at the side of the inlet that I might have mistaken from the boat for a cairn, but nothing obvious. I wandered with Brigid up that way anyway, in the absence of another plan.

'Why are you so keen to check out this story?' she finally asked.

'I don't know, maybe looking for needles in haystacks is to be the theme of my visit.'

I scrambled up the hill, and she followed at her own pace. Then I did see something. An actual cairn on up a little further, and indeed next to a stunted tree in a hollow. The cairn was right out on the lip of the hollow, a steep drop down the seaward side of the slope.

I turned round in triumph to Brigid. 'You see? Not just an old story.'

I handed my way around the cairn, eager to find the 'German writing' the barman had mentioned. As I pulled on the stones, they were solid under my grip. I took a closer look, reaching between the gaps with my fingers, trying to feel what was underneath. I heaved up and down on one of the rocks which protruded out more than the rest, eventually pulling it away completely, revealing a concrete pillar underneath, around which the cairn had been built.

Facing out to sea, I found what the men in the pub had been talking about, a heavily corroded metal plate, engraved with what once had been some initials and a couple of lines of text, neither of them legible anymore.

It could have been anything, a memorial to a particular person or event, or a poem marking some artist's favourite spot on the coast. I could see how local lore might have turned the writing into Nazi code, but there was nothing really to be seen. I supposed a dry stone cairn wouldn't have survived for long, balancing on the edge of the slope, which was why it was built with a concrete core.

'All this way for nothing,' I called out to Brigid, as she hauled herself up to reach where I was standing.

I moved away from the metal plate and she drew near to take a closer look, tracing the indentations with her finger, trying to decipher the letters. I was desperately tempted to place my right hand on the small of her back to keep her from falling, or so I told myself. I reached out, hovering for an instant over her blouse, the warmth of her body flowing through the material. But the moment passed, and I withdrew my hand again.

With a sigh of frustration, I made a show of looking at the tree growing next to the cairn.

'So are there any Irish legends about these trees? If you kiss a girl under one do you get good luck? Or lots of children?'

She smiled and said, 'Oh don't joke, the locals swear by them and the priests out in the country have to make a show of respect too.'

'You mean if you don't kiss the girl, you definitely get bad luck?' She didn't offer to do the right thing by the fairies.

We stood side by side, looking out to sea. If you let your eye unfocus, the cairn was in line with one of the prominent rocks, thrusting jaggedly out of the water. It was as good as it was going to get.

An hour and a half later, we were back in Bundoran and it was then that I realised I'd better call Masson while I still had the chance. At reception, as I asked the hotel to put me through to Brussels from my room, Brigid turned to say she'd take a walk down the beach towards the town.

After some grumbling the hotel agreed. I went upstairs, got connected and heard Masson faintly at the end of the line.

'*Allo?*'

'It's Oskar. Listen, I almost certainly need to stay on until next week. I'll try to be back by next Thursday, in a week's time.' I reckoned I shouldn't test him by trying for more than the full seven days.

'Will you have secured a full set of contacts by then?' It was difficult to make out what he was asking, so faint was the line.

I mentally made a list of people I could quote if I had to - Chief Superintendent Mullen, Captain Fleming, Sweeney, Dermot Johnston of the CPI.

'I have enough so far to justify coming back out here again, if needs be.'

I thought I heard him say 'okay' before the line went dead. It would do for now.

I peered out of the window of my room overlooking the beach and saw Brigid walking towards the end of some rocks jutting out into the sea.

'Why not?' I thought to myself.

I made my way down the path from the hotel to the sand but as I walked towards her, she jumped off the boulders and came back up the beach towards me.

Just as we met, a crowd of children burst out from the low dunes, surging past us on their way to the waterline, shrieking and crying out to each other excitedly. A harassed nun followed along behind, trying to keep up.

'You have a handful there, Sister,' said Brigid.

'There from over the border, staying away from Derry for a few weeks because of all the trouble there. They've been put up in the Army camp in Finner.'

They didn't look particularly traumatised to me, as they splashed through the shallows, but I supposed that might sometimes be the way with children.

A small girl of about five or six had been left behind by the others and came up to where Brigid was speaking with the nun. She slipped her hand into Brigid's and said, 'Miss,

Miss, give us a swing, round and around over the sand.'

Brigid looked across at me with a disconcerting smile on her face. Before I could think of a suitable remark, she pushed the child in my direction, promising her an even faster swing from me. Looking like a fool, I gripped the kid by its sweaty little wrists and swirled it around, feet flying through the air, just a couple of times for Brigid's sake.

'You're a natural,' she said to me, grinning strangely again.

When we got back to the hotel for dinner, she went up to bathe, saying she needed to wash her hair after having been sick. When she arrived back down, she had changed too, back into the same dress she'd worn at the restaurant on top of O'Connell Bridge House.

As we ate, she opened up, talking more about her family I'd met on Sunday and her older sister who was married to the farmer - 'Charolais' were a recently-introduced breed of beef cattle to Ireland, it appeared. But even though she spoke with affection about her parents and sisters, I had the sense that it really was Brigid who was her father's favourite, the only one of the daughters to be educated at university, now that her youngest sister had decided against it.

The evening sun faded, as we finished dinner and went to the bar to wait, for a while anyway, on Sweeney's return.

We must have been there for nearly an hour. Just as conversation started to flag and our wait was about to get awkward, he rolled in, already partly the worse for wear. If the people he'd been meeting with were anything like the CPI on Saturday night, I wouldn't have been surprised at the state he was in.

Whatever he'd been up to this afternoon, he was in that frame of mind now where he had to keep drinking. For some reason, probably to show Brigid I could look after a friend, I decided to keep him sweet by matching him drink for drink. She made the mistake of not immediately leaving us to it, and was swept along too, to a lesser degree - although she was better at disguising a slower pace than I could carry off.

He quizzed us about our afternoon and started to complain at having to run around Donegal as a tour guide for Krauts, as the drink took an even stronger hold of him.

He started slamming his drinks away, moving to neat whiskey downed in one or two gulps, as his mood failed to improve. Then he got onto the Common Fisheries Policy again, of all things, indignant at the piracy planned by the buccaneers of the Berlaymont.

Finally, my patience was exhausted. I was becoming distressed in a way too, at seeing his kindly, happy-go-lucky personality being driven out by the drink.

He went to relieve himself and when he came back, he found Brigid and I speaking in French as we conferred on what to do with him next, on how to persuade him to stop.

'What are you pair saying? *Voulez-vous couchez avec moi?*' he sneered. Brigid flashed him an angry look, to which he responded with an even more poisonous one of his own.

'That's enough, Mister Sweeney. Pull yourself together. Remember where you're going to tomorrow,' she said. 'I'm off to bed, as it happens. But you're welcome to stay here, in fact, please do so. And don't you even think of following me upstairs.'

I hazily wondered, if that was what had happened last night after I'd left, and if the warning to Sweeney could be taken as a request to me to escort her back to her room. Just to protect her from unwanted attention.

I did know that no good would come of it if I stayed in the bar with him in his cups. It had been a mistake to keep him company and match his consumption. All I had achieved was to prove that Sweeney was a depressive, rather than a cheerful drunk.

'I'm going up as well, Jim. I'm a bit blue too,' I said, translating the German slang for being drunk word for word because my mind was no longer the sharpest, either.

Brigid and I left the bar together and went up the shallow, creaking stairs to the first-floor landing.

I was a few steps beneath her as she climbed. I averted my eyes from her hips, but the sight of her slender fingers gently stroking the smooth handrail of the bannister on the way up was just as difficult to avoid in my tipsy state.

I walked down the corridor with her, away from my own room, not meaning anything else by it apart from knowing for some reason in my befuddlement that I had to see her safe back.

'This is my room,' she said with a faint smile and a shake of her head as she stopped outside her door to fish the key from her handbag. 'Your room is back there, Oskar,' she pointed down the corridor again.

'*Sehr gut Fräulein*. See you in the morning.' With a half-salute, I turned and went back to my own room. She took her time with the lock on the door, because I didn't hear it close behind her until I was almost back at the staircase.

I opened the window a crack, lay back on the bed and lit a cigarette. Sometimes, when I'd been in a smoke-filled bar for a while and had consumed a certain amount of drink, I just had to have one.

I puffed down its length, tapping the ash onto the floor without caring. My mind wandered back through the events of the day, trying to work out how Sweeney's excursion over the border fitted in, and I felt myself in danger of drifting off with a lit cigarette in my hand.

With a vigorous shake to clear my head, I swung my feet back onto the floor. Just as I was stubbing out my cigarette on the bedside ashtray, there was a knock at the door. I went over and pulled it open with a raised eyebrow. Brigid stood there, a hand on one hip, her chest pushed out and showing obvious signs of anticipation. Either that or she had got particularly cold standing in the corridor.

Later, as we rocked gently back and forth, she closed her eyes, as if she was trying to make the memory last for as long as she could, to save it up for some future period of drought. Or maybe she was imagining I was someone else.

I wondered what it would be like to have sex with someone you truly loved, instead of the casual girlfriends I'd known to date. Perhaps with someone like Sophie. But Sophie was even more out of reach than Brigid, good Catholic girl that she was supposed to be.

Chapter Eighteen

In the pale grey light at six, I watched Brigid as she stalked across the room on her pale alabaster legs to the bathroom and heard the gurgle of the taps as the hot water started to flow.

After a little while, I went in and she quickly crossed her arms over her chest to protect her modesty. A bit late for that, I thought.

'I needed to bathe again,' she said, embarrassed.

In answer, I gave her a chaste kiss on the top of her head and told her to come down to breakfast at least ten minutes after me.

I had little hope that the ruse would fool Sweeney, but it was worth a try. I loaded up my plate at the buffet and made my way over to where he was sitting, or rather slumped, stretched out on his chair.

'So,' said Sweeney nastily. 'Did you *couchez avec moi* last night? Her Irish boyfriend won't be very happy if he finds out and if you piss me off any more today, I just might make sure he does.'

My own temper flared. I had already reached the end of my own patience with him last night.

Although I was the one who needed his cooperation, perhaps more than he did mine, I couldn't help myself.

'Even if she did, think of it as a metaphor for Ireland ending her isolation and seeking the protection of a more powerful sponsor in the EEC.'

He gave me a sour look.

'Fuck you, you're just as arrogant as the Brits you claim to hate.' He shook his head heavily, still drunk from last night.

When Brigid came down, she flushed pink when she saw us glowering at one another, and we ate in tense silence. Sweeney made a couple of curt comments about our visit to the Irish Army today and some loaded hints as to how they were ready to take on anyone who threatened Ireland from outside its borders.

Fort Dunree was a good two hours' drive away, despite it being in the same county. Sweeney took things slow to begin with, driving faster as he sobered up.

We took forever, skirting around Lough Swilly, a long inlet of the sea running deep into Donegal. I remembered the West Berlin lawyer I'd met the day I arrived, over a week ago now, telling me that the word for 'lake' wasn't spelt in the Scottish way. Spelling was about the only thing the Scots and the Irish would get to keep from their own waters after the EEC had dealt with them.

Eventually, we arrived at the end of a long single track road, all the way up the other side of the lough, almost all the way to the open sea. It didn't strike me as being particularly suited for access to the border, unless remoteness was its own virtue. Approaching it by stealth would certainly be difficult.

Sweeney stopped by a sentry hut and put a call through to someone inside the base. He drove on and we pulled up in a small car park, probably at one time the parade ground of the Napoleonic-era fort perched on the sea-cliff.

'Here we go,' he said quietly. 'Remember again, you're here officially to see how we observe the border for incursions and illegal activities like smuggling. Keep your questions neutral, no smart aleck comments. Which really piss me off, by the way Lenkeit, especially as your people are meant to be boring as fuck.'

Better he finished getting his frustration out now in the

car, rather than in front of the army. At least his head seemed to be clearer, after the drive.

After this little lecture we all stepped smartly out of the car and walked the short distance over the tiny footbridge and the foaming water in the chasm below. A young lieutenant met us just through the gate and took us to the Commanding Officer's office.

Captain Fleming was leaning back on two legs of the commander's chair, feet crossed on the desk, looking out to sea through the window. I was as much taken aback by the disrespect as by seeing him here again.

He turned towards us and Brigid immediately cast her eyes to the ground. Looking sharply at Sweeney and myself, he came to a decision.

'Leave me alone with Mister Lenkeit, if you please.'

The other two got out as fast as they could.

Fleming gave me another good long stare, before bringing himself back to the task in hand.

'Some of your new associates, whom you met on Saturday, have indicated you know of sources of deniable weapons and explosives on mainland Europe which we need for our covert operations here on this island.'

I wondered who had been speaking to whom and whether he'd been told about the conversation in Kelly's house by the captain himself.

'Yes, but my other associates on the Continent, also want to know what use such material would be put to, to see if the risk of exposure is worth it. So what are you going to tell me about the users and their sponsors within the Irish intelligence services?'

He didn't reply but got out his Browning pistol and started to disassemble it on the desk. Then he carefully put it back together, checking that all the components fitted snug and true. Still sitting tilted back on the chair, he took up the gun in a two-handed grip and sighted a black-and-white photograph of some kind of flag-raising ceremony, hanging on the opposite wall, closing an eye as he squinted along the barrel.

'The users you will meet in Dublin on Saturday when you go back there. They'll get in touch with you to arrange a time. Their sponsors won't make themselves known in the current climate of Cabinet ministers and Army officers being arrested. I'm the only person prepared to put their head above the parapet for the time being. Someone has to try something.'

'You're a real hero of Ireland, aren't you?'

'Send in Miss O'Cuacach and go and meet some of the men. Take your time about it,' he said smugly.

I found them by one of the gun casements. Sweeney was leaning over, pointing out something to Brigid in the water, down by the foot of the rocks. The lieutenant was hovering uncertainly nearby.

'He's asked for you, Brigid.'

She pursed her lips, got off the wall and went.

Sweeney continued to stare out to sea, as if yesterday's trip had reminded him where he'd rather be, instead of counting pigs in and out of cattle trucks parked furtively in farmyards near the border - or maybe that was just his cover story if he got stopped by the British, when he was over on their side.

I asked the lieutenant what his unit did, whilst keeping one eye on Sweeney.

'We patrol the border, watch for incursions.'

'Really?' I said.

'In February this year, the UVF blew up a radio transmission tower not far from here, inside Donegal. We think they might have had help from the local Protestants.'

'So why are you based here? It's a long way from anywhere.'

'It's not that far from Derry. Last year we enlisted nine Derrymen into the reserve forces, the FCA, and gave them weapons training in small arms. It was in the papers the other month.'

'What was this place, before.'

He puffed out his chest. 'Last place in the Twenty-Six to be liberated from the British, they gave it up in nineteen thirty-eight, outwitted by de Valera.'

'And the artillery pieces? What were they defending?'

'That,' he pointed at the grey lough, hazy now with fog which had been gradually rolling in off the sea from when we arrived. 'It was the reserve anchorage of the British fleet in the First World War.'

'So this was one of the bases the British wished they had kept for the Second World War?'

'Yes, but there was nothing here. Just deep water. Anyway, on the other side of the peninsula, in Derry, they already had a big naval base for their anti-submarine ships, theirs and the Americans. They kept using the base in Derry after the Emergency too; still had an anti-submarine warfare school there up until June of this year, until the volunteers made it too hot for them.'

'And how long have you been stuck up here yourself, watching the seals?'

'I was appointed adjutant to the commander last year, just as things got interesting.'

He glanced at his watch. 'If you come back across to the main camp, you can meet a few of the lads. They're getting ready to go out on a forty-eight-hour patrol later today.'

We recrossed the footbridge, back to the car park. A bunch of lean young men in plain green uniforms were just arriving, dropping rucksacks along the low boundary wall and propping up rifles next to them.

'Where did Mister Sweeney say you were from again?' asked the adjutant.

'Hamburg,' I told him.

'CJ, over here, this lad's from Germany too.'

One of the men came over. '*Wie geht's mit Ihnen?*' he

asked.

Despite the warning, I still did a double-take. It was the first sentence in German I'd heard in Ireland so far. I responded in kind, to a few odd looks from the other soldiers.

'How come you speak German?'

'My father was Irish, emigrated to America, was drafted into the US Army in 'forty-five. But he missed the war, got deployed to Germany just afterwards. He met my mother, got her pregnant with me and then married her - all in that order.'

'So like a boomerang, you came back here?'

'No, I grew up in the States - got I drafted too. Went to Vietnam and did some shit there. When I left the US Army, my cousin said the Paddy army was looking for ex-soldiers with combat experience.'

'Vietnam, eh? I knew someone who fought for the French there.'

'We could be there for another twenty years yet, and still the gooks would keep coming south.'

'So what is the "Paddy" army like?' I assumed it was a slang word for 'Irish'.

He glanced from side to side, but people had tuned out from the German dialogue and were looking past us, probably because Brigid had reappeared, back from her *tête-à-tête* with Fleming. She was sitting on the wall, next to the rucksacks with a growing swarm of soldiers around her, like Erika in the song I'd taught the CPI.

'They call us "Rangers" but we ain't no special forces. Not as we know them in the US Army, anyway. This army has jack - no armour, no artillery, no helicopters - nothing to speak of, anyway. I think we're only called "Rangers" because the regular grunts are fat REMFs. And the pay is shit too.'

The American soldier slang words dropped into the middle of a German sentence made him hard to follow, especially as his mother was probably Bavarian from the intonations of his strange accent, but I got the gist.

'So what do they have you doing up here, at the very end of the world?'

'Waiting for something to happen in Northern Ireland, to give us an excuse to go in. But it's as boring as hell. Plus, part of me is guilty that I have Vietnam buddies who've returned for a second tour.'

'Is it as tough out there as they say?'

His eyes glazed over, as if he saw himself riding in a Huey again, skimming the jungle canopy, ready to drop down into a hot LZ.

'Hell yeah, but I never felt more alive. I'll give these guys until the fall, then I'm off back to the States, before the start of the Irish rainy season.'

On impulse, I asked him a question, which was prompted by Sweeney's excursion yesterday, although maybe it was also put into my head by the Vietnam talk.

'You been over the border into yet? Just for reconnaissance, into Laos, so to speak?'

At this he paused, reined in his hitherto open expression and answered noncommittally.

'Sometimes, when we're on exercise close to border, map-reading mistakes get made.'

I grinned at him. 'That sort of thing never used to happen to us in the Bundeswehr. Except for the time we did a mock attack on the wrong dummy village because Fat Albert got us lost. We couldn't understand why Blue Force weren't firing back. Thanks to him, we all got put onto double sentry duty for two weeks afterwards, to teach us a lesson. So we had to teach him one in return.'

It was a weak story, compared to the ones he must have collected, after spending twelve months in South-East Asia.

'If something doesn't happen in Northern Ireland to give us a reason to go there, there's enough crazies among the officers here who want to make that something happen. I've heard some of them talk. And the map-reading mistakes are sometimes deliberate, a dare, or perhaps a test to see how long we can be over there without being detected.'

'How far do you think they will try to push it?'

'Lately, we've been taking short-cuts when we go to County Monaghan on exercise. We drive through the back roads of Fermanagh.'

The names didn't mean much to me.

'We travel in civilian cars with hiking jackets over our combats,' he added.

I looked at the rucksacks lined up against the wall and the FN FAL rifles next to them - the same as used by the British.

He was dressed too, in the same plain olive drab as issued by every other European army. Add a British Army camouflage pattern jacket over the top and the two sets of infantry would be indistinguishable at a distance. Someone could make a lot of mischief that way, if they wanted to.

The adjutant came over to break up our little chat, probably also worried that he'd have a mutiny on his hands if he didn't move Brigid on.

'I'm sorry but the lads are off in thirty minutes. Have you seen enough here, Mister Lenkeit? Are there any more questions you need answered?' He didn't sound like he'd be delighted to answer them if I did.

I did indeed have a few, but none he could answer. When they'd first told me about it, the trip to Donegal had sounded like a way for the Irish to use up my time until I left at the end of the week. But I didn't know that Fleming was going to have a cameo role on tour too. Much as I disliked him, I tended to believe him when he said he was the only one prepared to take semi-official action to assist the IRA. Skorzeny would have approved of his decisiveness. I wondered if I had finished in Ireland already and had found the man I needed to bring back to Fiedler. I didn't think he would be very corruptible, though.

I wondered as well, if the visit had been a way for Fleming to get to see Brigid again, before he went off to do whatever training he had planned for his men this weekend. I'd bet they were just loving him for that right now.

He didn't seem that close to Sweeney, though. Still, they could have met up yesterday. Sweeney had certainly been away from Bundoran for long enough to get over here and back again.

Sweeney drove us back to Dublin. On the way here across Donegal, he'd switched on the two-way radio as we got near the border, and keeping one hand on the steering wheel had tried different frequencies, to see what he could find.

Now he did so again, and as he turned the dial back and forth, for a second or two I heard an exchange in strange English accents.

'British Army net - some Geordie soldiers from Newcastle or some such place,' he explained. The names didn't mean much to me.

He kept tuning the radio, until he found what he was looking for.

'Garda channel,' he announced. For a minute I heard a soft Irish voice, presumably at some control centre, giving out instructions. Then he turned the volume way down low again and left it playing on in the background.

Sweeney had told us, when we checked out of the hotel in Bundoran, that he would take the long way round back to Dublin, skirting the border. But now he was becoming impatient again, and couldn't resist showing off his knowledge of the back lanes. For my part, I was glad to see the old Jim returning.

After a good hour or so into our journey, he turned off the main road and down a couple of narrow lanes, one not much wider or better surfaced than a farm track. He twisted around to look at Brigid.

'We just crossed into Fermanagh.'

It was an international frontier, but not as I knew them.

'What?' she said angrily. 'He can't be caught here. If we take an EEC official on a tour of Ireland to the North, that will cause a diplomatic incident.'

'Right you are,' he replied pointedly. 'How could it be worse than your boss, Patrick Hillery, going uninvited to the Falls in Belfast?'

'Turn back, you fool.'

He ignored her, so I tried to calm things down before there was a real explosion.

'Don't worry, Brigid,' I said. 'I'll say I was reading the map and gave the wrong directions. I'm sure it happens all the time.'

We drove on for a couple of minutes without meeting any traffic. Despite Brigid's fears, we didn't seem to be at much risk of discovery, early on a Friday afternoon.

Sweeney relented now.

'I'm sorry, Brigid. I don't normally do this in case my plates get known to the RUC - their police,' he said for my benefit. 'But it saves us an hour off our journey.'

'How far are we into Northern Ireland now?' I asked.

'About two miles or so,' came his reply.

'What does happen if we get stopped?'

'Nothing. The police or army will ask us where we've come from, where we're going to and ask to look in the boot. They won't like the CB radio, but nothing can be traced to our government.'

'How about your pistol? What's the chances of your being caught with that?'

'Only if we're unlucky. There's a hidden compartment behind the dashboard.'

Just as on my very first trip to East Germany, I was most struck by how similar the fields and farm buildings looked on either side of the border. In fact, I couldn't tell the difference between the two countries apart from the different number plates on the few vehicles we did pass on the way through the villages.

After another forty-five minutes, we crossed back into Ireland proper again.

'How was that?' asked Sweeney expectantly.

'Not the kind of border I know.'

As we crossed over, something caught Sweeney's attention and he turned up the volume on the radio.

I couldn't make out everything that was being said through the static, but his ear was more attuned. He turned to me again and said, 'Some kind of games going on, back in Donegal. Seems like some Protestants from the UVF set up a checkpoint, just over the border on our side, on the way to Pettigo but then drove off when the Guards arrived.'

'How do they know they were Protestants?

'Probably by the way their eyes were set close together.' He said this quite casually, as if it wasn't a crude joke, but meant half-seriously.

Ignoring this for now, I asked, 'And what reason would they have to do that?'

'Retaliation for something or other. I'd drive over there and speak with the Guards myself to find out what happened exactly, but I've got to get the pair of you back to Dublin.'

'How long to go now?'

'About three hours. If you want another go driving on the left, just say.'

Driving down from the north, we got to my drop-off at the Gresham first. But Brigid got out too. 'I'm seeing a friend for dinner in town tonight,' she explained to Sweeney. 'Thanks for arranging the trip to Gola.'

'Good-bye to you then, Brigid. I'll see you on Monday as agreed?' Whatever their plan was for next week, they hadn't told me yet. I wondered how much more I had to do here, before I was done in Dublin. Meet the IRA this weekend, as Fleming had instructed, I supposed.

With a casual wave of the hand, Sweeney drove off, but I didn't put it past him to park up round the corner and sneak back to watch what would happen next.

Brigid hesitated, swaying back and forth on her feet, her cases by her side.

'Do you really have a dinner to go to in town?' I asked.

Instead of an answer, she chewed her lip as if she was weighing up whether she could explain an unexpected night away from home to her parents.

'Would you like to meet for lunch here tomorrow?' I replied for her.

She nodded quickly. 'Yes, I'd like that very much Oskar.'

I picked up her bags and went to the head of the taxi rank to hand the driver a ten pound note. 'Don't worry, I have an unlimited expenses account too.'

She smiled. 'Don't learn pick-up tricks from Jim, please.'

I leaned down and kissed her cheek and she returned it on the lips.

'Until tomorrow, then.'

Chapter Nineteen

I looked up from my seat in the bar of the Gresham to see Brigid standing over me. It was the first time I'd seen her wearing holiday clothes, a long floral-print summer dress with wide straps.

I got to my feet and she raised herself slightly on her toes, tilting her head to kiss me on the lips with a smile.

'Where would you like to go for lunch,' I asked. 'O'Connell Bridge House again?'

She laughed and shyly took my hand in hers. 'I didn't know you were a fan of the seedy side of Irish business life. Anyway, who said anything about lunch?'

The alarm bells which had been ringing faintly in my head ever since she appeared in the doorway of my hotel room in Bundoran stubbornly refused to go off. Nothing in life was this easy - at least that was the way my short career, to date, of double-crossing the Stasi tended to make me think.

'Later, if you behave yourself. Show me some more of Dublin first. Your favourite part. The street with only the old buildings left.'

She looked at me somewhat blankly. 'It's nothing to do with architecture. The fabric of Dublin is the history of Ireland, it records the struggles we've been through over the centuries. Why do you think the GPO was rebuilt exactly as it had been before, after the British burned it to a shell?'

'And now the free Irish are destroying their own memories?' The irony of me calling Kramer, to discuss the

284

entrapment of Ireland in the EEC, from the very cradle of their independence revolt, struck me now.

'Why do you think I'm desperate to get out of here? The country gives the impression it doesn't want to be saved. Maybe it's no longer really worth it,' she said.

'You don't know what you have until it's gone. I assure you, Brussels is no picture postcard - architecturally or otherwise. I know what goes on there underneath.'

'Show it to me one day, Oskar. I'll come and visit, if you want me to.'

I gripped her hand more tightly. 'Show me your Dublin first, before it disappears.'

We made our way to Phoenix Park, walked along the wooded paths and had lunch in a cafe by the lake.

Afterwards, we went a little way off the path and sat side by side on the grass with our backs to a tree. As we talked, she occasionally flicked her wrist to look at the time.

'I thought I was your only appointment for today?' I asked.

She gave a faint grin. 'I have to go to confession after, you know.'

'How does that work, morally?' Because Germans naturally tend to the light, conversational topics, all the easy questions of life.

'If we say confession and do penance the priest gives us absolution from our sins.'

'So what's to stop you going away and committing the same sin again, and then just going back to confession again?'

'I think the more times you go to confession, the less you feel like sinning.'

'But that's illogical. If you feel more holy, you'll sin less and won't need to go to confession so often. The other way, which you described, is like Rasputin telling his harem that the more times they did it with him, the greater the forgiveness they would receive.'

Irish whimsy was powerless in the face of German reasoning.

'So what do Protestants believe? That you don't need to go through any guilt or suffering to earn absolution? That seems lazy to me, as well as being wrong.'

She had decided to put up a semblance of a struggle, even though her head was now resting on my shoulder. I grimaced, verbal sparring was fine until the topics stopped being in the abstract.

'I think they believe that you have to forgive others and repent of your sins to God, but just the once. But it's more difficult than you think, especially if you're convinced that the person who did you wrong deserved what they got.'

'Are you speaking from your own personal experience?'

I was silent at this. 'But if you only repent the once, it has to be real. Maybe the Catholics have the right idea after all, one step at a time.'

She smiled again, seeing the faraway look in my eyes.

'How could it hurt to try, if it gives you some comfort?' she suggested.

We took a taxi back to the hotel. On the way, I asked her what time confession was and she told me five o'clock, an hour before Mass.

When we got to the Gresham, she virtually dragged me by the hand across the foyer to the lifts. The concierge I'd spoken with on that first afternoon in Dublin was on duty again, barely suppressing a smirk at us.

But if Brigid saw it, she didn't care. With a satisfied smile, she led me to my room. And once inside, this time she really let herself go, as if it was going to be her last chance for a while.

At four o'clock, the phone by the side of the bed rang. We were sharing a cigarette, puff for puff. She was lying on her side, facing me, the sheets bunched in her fist in front of her chest. She took the cigarette once more as I rolled over to lift the receiver.

'Yes?'

Dermot from the CPI was on the other end of the line.

'Mister Lenkeit, there's some people here who we talked about last Saturday night. People who you wanted to meet. Do you recall how to get to the bar where we went after the meeting on Cuffe Street?

'Yes.'

'If you want to meet them, you need to come right away.'

I looked over. Brigid had already got out of bed to get dressed so she could confess her sins and receive absolution for what she'd got up to this afternoon.

'Okay,' I said, putting the receiver down.

'Will I see you tomorrow?' I asked Brigid.

She leant down for a goodbye kiss. 'Tomorrow, God willing.'

When she was gone, I got dressed myself. For the first time since coming here, I regretted leaving the Makarov in Brussels.

Still, my sixth-sense only moved properly into gear, when the taxi driver asked me if I was certain I wanted to go to the pub I'd named.

'That's an IRA pub. Are you sure you know what you're doing?'

'It's okay, I know some people there.' So not a CPI pub, after all.

The taxi driver wasn't convinced a West German tourist would know any of the regulars, but kept his counsel and his chances of a tip.

The half-empty bar was just as dingy before, but somehow a lot more menacing in the fading afternoon than when it was packed with comrades and others at midnight.

The barman looked up and stopped polishing the glass in his hand. The whole room fell silent as the few drinkers present all turned as one to inspect the new arrival. And the men weren't the ones giving the most threatening looks, either.

'Don't worry, boys. He's with me,' said a man in a leather jacket that had many fewer pins of international liberation movements than Dermot's friend, Nolan, had been wearing on the stage at Bricklayers' Hall. Maybe they were like badges of rank, I thought flippantly to myself.

But it was lucky he'd recognised me because I'd never seen him before.

'Mister Lenkeit?' he asked softly, just to make sure, once the hubbub had started up again.

'Yes.'

'The people you want are through here,' he gestured to a door at the side of the bar counter, leading to the rear of the building.

My thumbs were pricking as I followed him through the door and down a passageway which led out through a fire-door to a yard at the back.

Parked at an angle blocking the gate was a dark green panel van. It felt really wrong now.

'Not here. I'll talk to them in the bar.'

'No you won't.' He drew a knife and sidled round to block the door back into the pub. I tracked him as he moved, my eyes on the knife, which was my mistake because I was grabbed by the arms from behind by the occupants of the van. I thrashed right and left, kicking out. A black hood was thrust over my head. Someone fetched me a crack on the side of my skull, above the ear, and I went down for long enough for them to cuff me. When I came back to full consciousness, I was in the back of the van. From the vibrations of the metal floor under my fingertips, we were on the move at speed.

The Stasi course on agent handling hadn't said anything about what the Americans in Vietnam called escape and evasion.

Those false friends, my unreliable instincts, said not to waste time trying to speak with the abductors. Better to show no fear, like when confronting a strange dog. Nonetheless, as the journey went on and on, I thought I needed to try something, to provoke them even a little, to see what they said, and see what I could work out about my situation. It must have been after the time of Brigid's Mass and I hoped she'd said a prayer for me.

'How far are we going? I need to piss.'

There was a curse from someone in the back with me. So there were at least two of them, probably three. It wasn't to be a short journey either, because the man in the back didn't fancy putting up with the smell of urine for long.

'Tell him to piss himself where he is,' came a shout from the front.

'Feck. You come and sit here then,' said my companion.

So I had some small power over him, but I wasn't that desperate yet. Still, as the minutes seemed to turn into hours, my abductors showed no signs of breaking their vow of silence. Eventually, I really did need to go and told them so.

There was a muttered conversation in the front and the van pulled off the road and stopped. Wherever we were, it was far enough from Dublin that they had no fear of detection.

I was thrust out of the van, still cuffed and hooded, directed to the verge and my trousers yanked down.

'Jaysus, look at the tiny size of that, it's a wonder they make any babies at all in Belgium.'

I'd have given the speaker a spray if he hadn't been standing directly behind me.

There was still a glimmer of light from the gap at the bottom of the hood. Night fell around ten here, which felt about right for the length of the journey. Assuming we'd driven in a straight line, and not round and round, as the

Stasi had done to Sophie and me in Rostock, then we were either back up north, close to Donegal, or right at the other end of the country, in the south west.

I was shoved back into the van and we set off once more. I had been trying to work out for a while now what had happened, to try to prepare myself for whatever was coming next. Several possibilities presented themselves. These people could have been a reactionary, loyal faction of the Irish intelligence agencies, either police or army, who were unhappy at my suggestions of supplying arms to the volunteers. Maybe they were going to work me over in secret, somewhere outside Dublin, to find out what I knew of their rogue colleagues favouring the illegal organisations.

Or they could be the British who wanted the same information, except that they sounded Irish to my ears, unless the Brits were using Protestant proxies.

But then again, as Johannes had said to me when leaving Bad Belzig that day, things were sometimes just what they were, and the kidnap van really had been driven away from Dublin at high speed by the IRA, of one flavour or another. What they might want with me, I couldn't tell. If they were IRA, then perhaps I was on the safest ground of all, for I'd be able to bargain with them using my French and East German intelligence contacts.

My wait wasn't to be much longer. The van suddenly slowed right down, creeping along a narrow lane, by the sound of scratches and scrapes of vegetation down each side. We came to a complete stop for a few minutes, then proceeded again.

The road seemed to degrade into a badly potholed lane. After a wide swing through ninety degrees, the driver finally brought the van to a halt with a sharp tap of the brakes.

The rear doors were opened and I was bundled out

once again. It was now fully dark and there was an occasional careful flash of torchlight, as I was prodded forward over what felt like a farmyard, by the greasy feel underfoot.

Once inside the building, we went down a short passageway and I was sat down in a room on the left. One guard stayed behind in the room, complaining to the others about being stuck with me once again, so presumably the same person who'd ridden with me in the back of the van from Dublin.

I heard another vehicle pull up outside, the slam of a car door and the sound of greetings in the hallway, if that was what it was. I was truly alone tonight, worse off than after my arrest last year in East Germany, which at least had been by a state actor, the Ministry. My one half-hope was that Brigid would raise the alarm when she got to my hotel tomorrow morning - assuming she wasn't already somehow connected to this abduction. Whoever she might alert, though, would have no more clue as to where I was than I did right now.

From the neighbouring room I now heard raised voices and the hard clink of glass, as if a celebration was in progress - but that didn't seem right. Then the door to my room opened. My guard said 'Finally' and what sounded like a crowd of people trooped in, too many for me to distinguish from the tramp of their feet on the bare boards.

'Go outside and see if the window is fully blacked out.'

A glow started somewhere in the room, its intensity growing. I guessed an oil lamp had been lit. There was a scrape, as something heavy was dragged across the floor and the zipping sound of a bag being opened or closed.

'There, there and there,' someone said. The squeak of a wheel started up, followed by a curse at the time it was taking for whatever it was they were doing.

'This wood is bloody hard to drill. Why can't we tie him to a chair?'

'Shush now, you'll give the game away. Hear that, you Belgian bastard?'

'Talkative cunt, isn't he?' commented another voice.

The cuffs were unlocked and I lashed out with my fists in the direction of the voice, connecting with a throat in a lucky hit. There was a rasping, choking wheeze and then someone punched me hard in the side of the head. I was seized again, by more than two people, it felt. They dragged me across the floor and slammed my arms onto a flat surface, stretching them out, many hands holding them in place.

'Lots of turns. Although it's thin rope he'll never break it.'

The tightness around my wrists and elbows increased as they were tied fast to the surface, a table presumably. A chair was pushed behind me and I was made to sit. I now felt the warmth of the oil lamp growing between my forearms, but try as I might, I couldn't reach to grab hold of it. Not that I could have done anything with it anyway, if I had.

'Hood off or hood on?' asked yet another voice.

'It depends but let's have it off for now, so we can give the lads the full experience.'

The hood came off and I took a deep draught of air, warmed by the lamp. I was sitting in the middle of a pool of light, surrounded by a group of dim figures in the gloom. From what I could make out, the younger ones didn't look much older than the teenagers Brigid and I had seen on the beach two days ago on Thursday afternoon. Some of them probably were teenagers. When I listened carefully to their mutterings, as they took a good look at their Belgian prisoner, they had new, harsher accents too - ones I hadn't heard before.

Someone older approached the lamp, with what I now worked out was a southern Irish accent.

'So fella-me-lad, today you'll do a great service to the Movement by letting a few of the new volunteers get a taste for interrogating prisoners. Normally, we'd have a few opening rounds of cracking ribs and stamping on balls, but we've got someone coming over later who especially wants to be the first to do that.'

He looked around the room at the others.

'I'm going to initiate fella here into a holy order of pain. The first thing you do is to let them see your tools. The anticipation is almost as bad as the pain itself, and sometimes can loosen tongues even more quickly.'

He placed a canvas holdall on the table.

'Everything you need can easily be carried in this. If you get stopped by the Brit forces, they're only the completely innocent tools which any workman would normally have.'

He took them out, one by one, laying them down in a neat line, describing each one as he did so.

'So, what do we have here? Hammer and nails - into the elbow and knee joints. Bolt cutters - fingers and toes, you cut them off at the knuckles, segment by segment. Stanley knife - has the same uses as a butcher's skinning knife, so the name speaks for itself. Pliers - teeth and fingernails, also good for holding the tongue whilst you cut it out.'

My eyes had adjusted better by now to the light in the room. Some of the younger faces, who really were not much older than the kids we'd seen on the beach in Donegal, looked a little revolted, but not as much as I was at that moment.

'When I last looked, fella here had ten fingers, so you'll all get a chance to have a go on him. We'll start with a traditional method, removal of the fingernails - because we love our traditions. You need to make enough space under the nail, to get a grip with the pliers, so you can lever it off. Needles are good, because they slip in underneath the nail easily and then you can move them from side to side to loosen it just enough. But today we'll use a hammer and tacks. No, let's see. Here's something better.'

He looked round the table at his students as he fished out a couple of slender brass woodscrews with sharp, widely-spaced cutting threads.

'Any questions lads, before we begin?'

They were really going to do this and there was nothing I could do. They weren't even suggesting they wanted information from me. I had to ask, though, in case it was part of their game.

'Please, why are you doing this? What do you want to know?' I asked.

'Speak up, fella. Can't hear you. Here, you, hold his wee finger still.'

I turned away as he picked up the hammer and one of the woodscrews.

'No, everyone watches. You too.' He pointed to the boy next to me. 'You there, big lad. Make him watch. Hey, Tintin, which hand shall we do first? *Droite* or *gauche*?'

He looked around the room. 'Whichever hand he says, that's the one we'll do. It's important for them to realise your word can be trusted, so they know you're serious about what's coming later.'

I got a punch in the side of my head as an encouragement to answer. My field of vision collapsed to a point in the middle, and everything went black for a split second.

'Hurry up and choose, fella.'

'The left.'

I watched aghast, as he carefully positioned the point of the woodscrew at the tip of my left-hand little finger, under the lip of my nail, and then began to gently tap with the hammer. I yelled with each jolt, as the screw went in under my nail, half way up its length. He stopped, and my cries tailed off into sobs. The pain was so intense, I felt as if I was watching it being done to someone else.

'Now as I said before, if we had used a needle we could have gone back and forward underneath to loosen the nail enough so that you can get a proper grip with the pliers.'

He waggled the screw to demonstrate, and it really did feel like a needle - one which was red-hot, reaching all the way down the length of my finger, up my arm and into my brain.

'But as this is only the wee finger, we can take it off right now.'

He roughly yanked out the woodscrew, causing me to shout out again, then opened the thin, sharp-nosed pliers and forced the bottom jaw into the bloody hole left by the screw.

'So lads, the trick is to do it as slowly as possible, to stretch out fella here's enjoyment. Hey, you, we were told you were a Belgian Nazi. I bet your daddy enjoyed doing this to Jews when he was a guard in the camps.'

He closed the jaws of the pliers, levered down on my finger and pulled off the nail, in a slow deliberate action.

I bucked my head back and forth, free from the grip of the person holding it and screamed to high heaven.

'For fuck's sake, hold him and make sure he gets a good look. I'll tell you lads, this soft Belgian wouldn't have lasted a week at the Industrial School. Not under the tender mercies of the Christian Brothers he wouldn't.'

Where the nail had been was a bloody mess. Bizarrely, my first thought was how repulsive the finger looked naked, like the nightmare tentacle of a pink octopus. Logically, I should have been preparing myself for what came next.

'Okay, you, Derryman, you're up. Yes, why not, next finger along.'

'What in God's name do you want from me?'

'Don't blaspheme, Proddy.'

'I'm not a Proddy. I'm not even a Belgian. What do you want from me?'

'Shut up. Hold his head properly this time.'

I yanked my head from side to side, anything to delay what was coming next.

'By the time we're finished, he'll be begging us to chop

off the tips of his fingers.'

There were sniggers around the table, which I took as a bad sign that they were losing their inhibitions. The new recruit positioned the same bloodied screw, with small pieces of flesh still in the grooves of its threads, under the nail of my ring finger. To keep my hand still while he did so, the leader pressed down on the first ripped up nail bed with the point of the pliers.

As the screw was driven in again, I felt myself approach the edge of a new, uncharted abyss of pain. And by the time the pliers had been handed over and the nail slowly levered off - 'that's the proper way to do it lads. Derryman is a natural,' - I was ready to let myself go over.

But something prevented me. Somehow, I knew that to survive now. I had to stop with all the screaming. I didn't know what to do after that, though. I had no clue. *Herr, rette mich.*

The mood was changing, and the leader was already getting bored of pulling nails. I knew that from the way he started to play the drums with the hammer and pliers on my two ruined fingers, now. I gritted my teeth and slammed my head on the table to kill the pain.

I must have hit the table so hard that I blacked out for a few seconds. When I came to, he'd decided to take things to the next level, to really stretch the volunteers' tolerance to squeamishness.

I couldn't tell what he was doing at first. He seemed to be trying to pinch my eye.

'Keep your head still, I need to cut off your eyelid. Do you want to lose your whole eye now? It's not time for that yet.'

I paid him no attention, straining every muscle in my neck and shoulders to get away from the Stanley knife, which I could just about see on the edge of my vision. With a final, immense effort, I broke free of the hold of the person pressing down on me and I jerked back. As I did so, in frustration the leader slashed down hard at the corner of my eye socket, cutting the flesh to the bone, or so it felt, in a long streak of ragged fire.

I couldn't believe my life was going to end here, bleeding out in a broken-down farmhouse, to the sound of rats under the floorboards.

Maybe the blow to the head cleared my brain. I knew the only way I would be leaving here would be by talking my way out, and suddenly the right words had fallen into place.

'Where are we, North or South?

'Wouldn't you just like to know?'

This was it. Skorzeny had said that any decision was better than no decision.

'Because if we're in the North, no-one is coming here to cut off my balls.'

'Listen to this lads, we have a joker on our hands.'

'Because if we're in the North, you've been betrayed by the Irish Army. Captain Fleming isn't coming here. He's using you as bait for the British forces.'

The mention of an Army officer by name chilled the atmosphere instantly. The leader's eyes were hard and cold where the blood fever had been before.

'Right lads, outside. This isn't for you to hear. This is a security matter.'

The younger men trooped out of the room, the leader and an older sidekick stayed. I wondered, if even the leader wasn't trusted to speak on his own to players in this game.

He took out a switchblade and I instinctively shrank back. He thumbed it open with a flick, tossed it into the air, caught it by the handle and drove it down hard through the back of my left hand. I was almost catatonic with pain. I wanted to scream again, but any ability to do so was gone, sucked away, along with my breath.

Feeling returned after a few seconds, I clenched my teeth and felt the tears of pain trickle down my face, mixed with blood.

I let out a few deep, rasping gasps, and from

somewhere I summoned up the strength to speak.

'You're being used. I've seen the Irish Rangers in Donegal. They've surrounded this place and Captain Fleming has told the British you're here.' I was making it up as I went along, but it seemed approximately right. Fleming had set me up, and surely it hadn't been done just to provide his northern friends with practice at torture, or even to teach me a lesson on who owned Brigid.

I paused to catch my breath and also to see if they would let me carry on speaking.

'He wants the Brits to come to rescue me, and then for them to run into the Irish Army so he can start a war. He's prepared to try anything, he told me so himself, in a pub in Ballsbridge.'

'We're the only true Army of Ireland,' he growled. I was nonplussed for a moment, but cast my confusion to one side.

'He's wired this building for sound. The British police in Belfast are listening to our conversation, as we speak.'

In response, the hammer flew across the room and embedded itself into the flaking plaster by the claw-end.

'Double-crossing bastard,' the leader said in a low voice. He looked at me, weighing up what to do next. A thin smile spread over his face.

'We're going to find you in Belgium one day and finish you off. But you're not leaving this place in a hurry. Who knows, we might be able to come back here and pick you up later.'

He yanked out the switchblade.

'Bring back the Derryman,' he shouted through the door.

His star pupil returned. The leader took out two thick, fifteen-centimetre-long nails from the tool bag and ripped the claw hammer free from the wall behind me.

'Nail his hands to the table.'

The young apprentice placed the first nail at the entry of the wound left by the knife and drove it down into the wood. He picked up the second one, uncertain where to place it on my right hand.

'Just there. It will slip down between the bones. Lots of little taps with the hammer, so he has plenty of time to enjoy it.'

I tried to catch the eye of the youngster, to plead with him for mercy, but his face was a mask. I passed out as the tip exited from my palm, just before the nail bit into the surface of the table.

Chapter Twenty

When I came to, a pale silver-grey light was ghosting in under the filthy hessian sacking at the window. By the way it was carefully tacked all around the edges, I guessed it had been put up by the people from last night to blackout the room. The gash in the corner of my eye was still weeping blood and fluid, as were my fingers and the holes in my hands. I leant over and was sick on the floor next to the chair, even a slight shift in position pulling on the thick steel nails, hammered deep into the table. Whether it was a rational fear or not, I dreaded that the wounds would never close up.

I started chewing at the baler twine around my wrists and elbows, spitting out the tiny fragments of plastic, as the strands broke. At least they'd helped slow the blood flow to my wounded hands, but at the rate I was going, it would take me many hours to get through all the turns of the rope.

The light slowly strengthened, and my hope faded, fearing they would come back. I laughed nervously to myself at the notion I'd talked my way out of death through torture last night, only to expire from thirst in three days' time in some forgotten, broken-down farmhouse. I realised I'd have to pull my hands up over the nails, if it came to that.

Who would know, or could even guess where I was? If my shot in the dark had been right and there had been a cordon of Rangers around the house on the wrong side of the border, they wouldn't have been there for long. That didn't preclude Fleming coming back here later himself, to find out what had happened, and maybe finish me off personally to cover up what he'd done.

I started shouting, a few seconds every couple of minutes, and kept it up for half an hour before giving it up as pointless. At least the shouting had scared off the rat in the corner for a while, his nose twitching as he sniffed blood, wondering when it would be safe to come up on the table for a nibble at my torn fingertips.

It was the return of the rat which prompted me to see if I could at least get outside the farmhouse. Using one knee to lift the table off the floor and pulling on the ropes to shuffle it along, I managed to get as far as the door, despite the red-hot pain and the fresh flow of blood from my hands. But to my despair, it wouldn't fit through, not with me tied down at one side.

Herr, höre mich in meinem Elend.

I guessed it was almost mid-morning when I heard a car engine stop a way off, followed by the sound of voices. I spat out a mouthful of rope fibres and started shouting once more. As the voices came closer, I knew it might well be Fleming or the IRA who'd come back, but I was right out of other options.

CJ appeared cautiously around the edge of the doorway, dressed in civilian clothes and with Browning in hand. I almost wept with relief.

He scanned the rest of the room, still in gloom, but too light now for the rat. The pistol was holstered inside his jacket and he drew a knife to cut the cords.

'Jesus,' he said, when he came closer and realised why I couldn't move my hands.

He shouted to someone outside, to bring a toolbox from their vehicle, and pulled my head back by the hair to take a proper look at my face.

'You look like shit,' were his words of welcome, spoken in harsh East Coast accent, the first time I'd heard him say something in English, I realised.

The other plain-clothed soldier came back, carrying a small red metal box with a folding lid.

CJ had a quick rummage inside and fished out some pliers for electrical wire.

'This is going to hurt,' he said, as he got a grip with the jaws under the nail head.

His forehead knotted with strain as he slowly pulled out each nail, as smoothly as he could manage. A film of blood covered their surfaces as they came up, out of the backs of my hands, and I wanted to vomit again.

'If you were wounded in Vietnam, and your sergeant was a lazy bastard, he might pop smoke and call for Dust Off. But I wouldn't have, not for that scratch.'

I gave a faint grin at the soldier humour as he helped me to my feet and out of the torture room. He kept hold of my arm as we made our way across the muddy churned-up farmyard, to where his companion was waiting by the gate, their car parked up under the cover of the trees in the lane outside.

We drove for about six or seven minutes maximum, taking a couple of turns down some other lanes. We crossed a small bridge and he looked across at me.

'You're safe back in the South now.' Inner German border this was not.

'Ten minutes further, and there's an old friend waiting for you. We'll sort out you out there,' he said, turning around to look at me sitting in the back, my hands lying painfully on my lap.

We pulled into the yard of yet another farmhouse, looking pretty much like the one I'd just left but with the ground floor windows nailed up with boards. Inside, this one looked just as forlorn.

But that wasn't my first impression, on being taken upstairs into one of the old bedrooms. That would have been Captain Fleming, handcuffed to a chair in the middle of the floor. He was being watched by Chief Superintendent Mullen from another beaten-up chair in the bay window, looking at his prisoner over cupped hands as he lit a new cigarette - a Smith & Wesson Police Special, just like Sweeney's, lying on his lap.

Fleming looked a mess. His cheeks were bruised, his lips were swollen and bloodied, and a dried brown streak ran down from his earhole. So not much different to me, then. Not that it was a competition.

'What are you doing, bringing him up here?' roared Mullen at CJ. 'Get him out and try to patch him up.'

'I'll see what I can do. Depends on what we have.'

He took me downstairs again and round to the boot of the car. What he had, proved to be a tube of iodine and some pre-packed field dressings. He squirted the ointment on the slash below my eye and used a fabric strip to try to hold the sides of the cut together. He slapped a dressing around each hand and gave my fingers a squirt too, but I begged him not to cover them. The freshly-applied iodine was agony enough.

'Okay, we've done our job and we're out of here now. Don't hang around here buddy, Ireland ain't healthy for you, or for me,' he said, as he and the other soldier got into their car.

'How did you find me?' I asked, just before he closed the driver's door.

He rolled down the window, glanced up the lane and switched back to German. 'We knew you'd been taken there, but didn't know you hadn't left. We were watching the house the whole time, as part of the exercise.'

He turned around again at the sound of an approaching vehicle. A civilian Land Rover drove into the yard and came to a stop. Sweeney and someone new got out.

As the doors of the Land Rover slammed, CJ gunned his engine and made off through the gate the others had just come through.

'Jaysus, Oskar, what did they do to you?' asked Sweeney.

I silently shook my head, refusing an answer.

We all trooped back inside and upstairs to the bedroom. I sat with Sweeney on the edge of an old metal bed frame, facing Fleming. The new man stayed standing, leaning on the wall with its peeling paper, just inside the doorway.

'Jesus, Mary and Joseph, what's he's doing back up here again?' Mullen said to Sweeney as I sat down. 'If we're going to deal with all our problems at once, then bring that other chair over and put him next to our dear Captain Fleming.'

With a toss of his head, Sweeney motioned me over to sit on the chair he placed beside the beaten-up captain.

When everything had been arranged to his satisfaction, Mullen got slowly to his feet, walked over and stubbed out his cigarette on the crown of Fleming's head. The captain stared straight ahead, not acknowledging Mullen or flinching, even at the acrid whiff of burning keratin.

'Captain Kelly, sitting at home on bail in the bosom of his family, doesn't know how lucky he is,' said Mullen. 'But then he never tried on the caper you did, and all on your own too. Or so you keep telling us, no matter how much we encourage you to say more.'

He swung around to me. 'And what's your story, man of a thousand faces? You arrive in Dublin just over a week ago and blaze a trail of fire for everyone down there to see. Don't think you're getting away with your nonsense either - we'll come to you later.'

I stared grimly ahead, but inside I was burning with shame. Mullen looked for a moment as if he was about to spit in my direction.

He turned to face the others. 'Dearly beloved, we are gathered here today to consider the attempt by Captain Fleming to start a real shooting war with the British: rifles, mortars, tanks the lot, to pass the rightful judgement on his crime and to decide on his sentence.'

I got the sense that today wasn't going to end with an arraignment for another Arms Trial.

'Before we start,' said Mullen, pointing at me again, 'what happened to him?'

Fleming spat bloodily on the ground, a fragment of tooth winking up from the floorboards. 'He wanted to meet the IRA, and he did.'

'Did you ask them to take him apart, piece by piece?'

'He was collateral damage,' he replied.

'Just like Ireland would have been, if your plan had come off,' shouted Mullen back at him.

The new man raised a forefinger to pause the proceedings.

'How was Fleming found out, and what's his explanation?'

'He went to the duty officer at Dundalk barracks and said there was an Army unit in trouble over in Fermanagh, tried to get them to move a company up to the border and throw up checkpoints under one of the Army's contingency plans for a mistaken incursion by our troops.'

'How was he caught?'

'The duty officer called it into GHQ. The Minister asked me to deal with it and make the problem go away. So, we did throw up some Guards checkpoints between here and Dundalk, but ones specially for him, because we knew where he was headed, thanks to the people back at Fort Dunree. He was almost at the far side of Monaghan before we lifted him.'

'How did he end up like that?'

'Rumours of a "Heavy Gang" in the Garda Siochana are completely unfounded. Heard enough?' he asked.

I decided to call the new man the Politician, because it seemed the right label for him, also because I was wondering if I'd seen him before. He might have been one of the junior hangers-on, following the important figure across the hallway of the Department of External Affairs the day I arrived, as I sat waiting on Brigid to descend from on high.

Mullen got back to business. 'So, time presses on and justice delayed is justice denied. My next question is for the other fella looking the worse for wear here.' He gave me a stinging blow on the side of the head with the flat of his hand.

'What's your story, young fella-me-lad? Whatever it is, I'm sure this time yesterday it didn't include losing some of your fingernails, no matter what else might have been on your mind just then,' he leered. In my mind's eye, far off in the distance, I saw a train growing slowly larger, as it came down the track, hauling a load of truth pills. Coming to smack me in the mouth for my wilful inattentiveness, because part of me had always known it was there.

'Why did you offer to Sweeney here, to supply deniable arms to the Irish Army, for them to channel to the illegal organisations? Reading the papers about the Arms Trial, were you? Some kind of fantasist, are you? Or some kind of agent provocateur?'

I could choose to say nothing, but then I might end up kneeling in the same ditch as I suspected Fleming was going to find himself in later, shot whilst attempting to escape.

Acting as agent for a freelance continental arms dealer would have been the easiest and safest story for me to tell. But not after the whole rigamarole of coming here to speak to them under the guise of the EEC. I was left with trying to shift the blame onto the EEC itself, or even the SDECE or the Stasi. Only by fingering the first would I avoid another whole different heap of trouble back at home. And a simple story about the EEC spying on Ireland they would never believe - they simply had no frame of reference to understand the organisation's long-term ambitions.

I'd have to find someone else they could latch onto, to rationalise for themselves why I was in Ireland, and do it quickly if I wanted to avoid what the Soviets would call the 'final ration' or the 'nine grammes' - of lead. Just like a prisoner of the KGB in the basement of the Lubyanka, I would give them what I thought they wanted to hear.

'My name is Oskar Lenkeit. My mother was a nurse in Hamburg just after the war. There she met my father, a junior British Army intelligence officer stationed on denazification duties, and fell pregnant. But he was a Catholic, already married with a wife back in England and either couldn't get a divorce or didn't want to ask for one.'

Mullen's expression told me I'd got a bite on my line.

'He was posted back to Germany in the mid-fifties to BAOR - the British Army of the Rhine - and came to find us and to meet me.'

Here I stopped and swallowed a little, because when I was younger, I had desperately wanted a story like this to be true. I shook my head to clear it of the image of a khaki-clad officer framed in the doorway, holding a bunch of flowers for my mother, and carried on.

'Then he was posted again to Germany in the early sixties. Even back then, the British were seeking to place sleeper agents at the EEC.'

'Is that your original connection to this affair?' asked the Politician.

'Isn't it obvious? I wanted to please my father, to make him proud of me, in the hope he would become a part of our lives.'

Mullen sneered. 'You think we're a bunch of thick Paddies, don't you? British military intelligence would have no interest in a civilian organisation like the EEC. If anyone in London was trying to place people in Brussels it would have been MI6.'

'But the EEC isn't or won't just be a civilian organisation. Its founders tried to create a European Defence Community three years before the EEC even started. An EEC-controlled military force might be on the back-burner for now, but it's never gone away.'

Mullen and the Politician looked at one another.

'I did what I had to do. And earlier this year, they asked me to spy on the Irish negotiators in the accession talks. And then the British got really carried away and asked for more, for me to find out what the Irish government was actually up to with the IRA - all because of the Kelly affair.'

Mullen reverted to his usual state of annoyance with the rest of the world.

'If you trusted a Brit, even your own father, you were badly misled.'

Sweeney was sensibly keeping silent throughout, but I saw wariness in his eyes. The way I'd told my stories about the British firestorm in Hamburg was hard to fake.

'So, were you in cahoots with the British too, Fleming? Are you also a Brit bastard? Did they try to persuade you to treachery, to give them a reason to invade the Republic?'

Fleming looked contemptuously around the room, myself included.

'Captain Kelly is a hero of Ireland. He saw the current opportunity to liberate the whole country and seized it with both hands, but you arrested him for it. Did you think we in the Army were just going to sit back and watch the politicians prevaricate up in the North, and watch a travesty of a legal process in Dublin? Whatever evidence Gibbons presents at Kelly's trial will be perjury, and everyone knows it.'

'We'll let the jury be the judge of that,' said Mullen.

'Kelly simply heard the desire of the nation's heart, and in case you've forgotten, that's the struggle for the freedom of all of the Thirty-Two. That comes first, before anything else. But you have forgotten. All you care about now is patronising applause at the United Nations or sucking up to the Brits and the Europeans to win your subsidies from the Common Market.'

The Politician scowled. Fleming was trying hard to lose

all his friends today. I myself thought that getting the British to put money in the pockets of Irish farmers by way of the CAP would have been a win.

'The nation needs to be awakened from its stupor. Lemass and his crew hardly talked about the situation of the Catholics in the North before the new Troubles. They're still an embarrassment to you, working-class people for whom there's no space in Lynch and Haughey's shiny new Dublin.'

But Mullen wasn't having his patriotism impugned. 'How dare you say that. Don't you think we also know what's going on in the North? Don't you think we also want what you want? Just because we don't intend to invade the Six Counties with the Army doesn't mean we don't intend to keep control of the situation in our own way'

'So what way is that? A nod, a wink, a slap on the wrist to the volunteers you do arrest to show your British overlords that you can still dance to their tune? Fifty years on, you're still trying to play both sides off against each other.'

'It's called politics,' snapped the Politician.

Mullen's tone was cold and flat now.

'Ireland decides for itself what signals to give the illegal organisations, not the British. The legal government of this country decides how much of a threat it can tolerate to the Republic from them, not the Army. The police are the ones who have to live with their day-to-day activities in the Twenty-Six, not you. Did you go to Guard Fallon's funeral in April, look his widow and children in the eye?'

The Politician interjected. 'We've spent almost fifty years trying to build up the rule of law here. We manage to get the IRA to renounce violence as a means of bringing about political change in the southern state and you stir them right up again. If you want to play soldiers, do it elsewhere. Become a mercenary in Africa or somewhere.'

There, I had told Fleming as much back in Dublin. He

couldn't say I hadn't given him good advice.

'And anyway, what did you think would happen when you attacked a NATO member state?' the Politician continued.

'I wanted them to cross the border in retaliation. I wanted to get them to come south to occupy and invade, because then world opinion would turn against them and they'd be forced by the UN to leave the North too. Lynch,' here he turned to one side and spat again, 'would get the blue helmets on the streets of Belfast, just as he'd always wanted.'

'You wanted the British to occupy the Republic? What other madness had you planned, an assassination of Gibbons, a kidnap of Lynch? This is treason. This is a dead man I'm talking to. Who put you up to this nonsense? Blaney, the devil? Or were you taken in by that snake Haughey, doubtless paid off in secret by the Brits with thirty pieces of silver, lover of money that he is? Did the Brit spy sitting next to you promise you something on the side as well?' Mullen was getting redder and redder, as his apoplexy grew.

As Mullen said these last words, I realised, with a deep sense of gloom, that I'd as good as condemned Fleming to death myself, by giving the chief superintendent the necessary fig leaf of testimony, which he needed to bring this kangaroo court to a close.

Mullen walked back to his chair and sank down.

He turned to me again, determined to tie up all the irritating loose ends in one go. 'And how did you make the IRA up and leave? Do they have a British informer in their organisation we should know about?'

I shook my head. 'I guessed what the captain was up to and told them. They didn't appreciate being taken for fools.'

Mullen smiled at me in a self-satisfied way. 'You see, Fleming, now you're in trouble with everyone.'

'Sweeney, stay with these pair, and shoot either or both

of them if they move.'

He indicated the Politician with a nod of the head.

'Him and me need to have a private conversation about the laws of natural justice that govern a nation - the ones we turn to when there's no written precedent for a situation such as the one we find ourselves in now.'

The three of us left in the room looked at one another. Out of all of us, Sweeney was the most uncomfortable.

'You realise that if it comes to it, Sweeney, it will be you who's asked to do the deed,' Fleming stated calmly.

Sweeney looked down and licked his lips.

'Forget what they said about them going off together now, to think of a justification for what comes next. This is about money, it always has been. He knows,' Fleming said, nodding his head at me. 'He's from the EEC, really. Mullen and the other one are going to make sure that no rumours of a hot war between Ireland and the EEC's new cash cow ever get back to Brussels.'

Fleming continued. 'It will be you who's holding the gun, Sweeney, and it will be you who makes the final decision. Can you live with that? Not my death, because that isn't important when set against eight hundred years' worth of sacrifice for freedom. But to live with the knowledge you'll have betrayed your country, your own family too, all so that Midlands farmers can get better prices for their beef.'

Sweeney suddenly looked up now, gazing out of the grimy window, as if far off he could hear the screams of the gulls and the crashing of the great Atlantic waves against the iron-bound coast of Mayo. As if he could see his Da and his eldest brother, bringing onboard a heaving net of silver fish, as the Sweeneys had done for a hundred years.

'If you kill a man, knowing it has been done outside of the authority of the government, the lawful government appointed by God, how do you know you will ever receive absolution for your sin?'

'You think I bother with the nonsense the priests say to keep the people in line?' Sweeney said unconvincingly.

'It's not just the law of the priests. Someone will talk one day - they always do. But if you're given a weapon, you can always use it on the real traitors, all of them here.'

Sweeney looked at me, weighing up a decision in his head.

Mullen and the Politician came back in.

'We're going to do this in stages, Sweeney. Take him downstairs to the cowshed,' the Politician said.

'Which one?'

'Fleming. Take him down, lock him up and wait on us there.'

I felt I should warn them that Fleming was doing his best to talk round Sweeney to the idea of turning the gun on the other two. But I was deep enough into someone else's civil war right now as it was. A small, twisted part of me wanted to see if Fleming could talk his way out of this one - it would be an exploit on the scale of some of Skorzeny's greatest.

The pair of them left, and Mullen turned a baleful eye on me.

'She's a handsome, unobtainable Catholic girl, a real Rose of Tralee, granddaughter of a hero of the War of Independence who lives under the watchful eye of her parents. Her very unattainability drives men crazy. She's had Cabinet ministers after her, so what chance do you think a couple of captains in the Defence Forces had?'

The truth train was filling my range of vision now. The comments of the strangers in the restaurant at the top of O'Connell Bridge House, about the 'O'Cuacach girl' came back to me too.

Mullen continued. 'She's the reason you're going to live. She's the one who told us you had almost certainly been lifted. She's...' here he stopped. 'She's vouched for you as being harmless to Ireland, whatever your real story is, you bastardised Kraut-Brit.'

The Politician tapped his watch.

'However, no Irishman will pull the trigger on Fleming this afternoon. If you want to be on the afternoon flight to Paris, you need to do this thing.'

'Why Paris?' I asked distractedly.

'Because the next flight to Brussels isn't until tomorrow.'

I shook my head in despair.

'Let me make it clear. If you don't, we'll make Sweeney deal with you both. You wouldn't want that on your conscience now?'

Mullen made me walk ahead of him, down the stairs and across the yard to the cowshed. The Politician followed, and we all trooped together into the byre.

Fleming was standing against the back wall, a chain running through his cuffs to an iron ring, set into the mortar. Sweeney was covering him from the door, Smith & Wesson hanging in a loose grip, down by his side.

Mullen rasped out their judgement.

'This mutinous rot goes no further today. We're not going through the humiliation of another Arms Trial. The country won't stand for it. The IRA will be back at the GPO next Easter, and it will be us in the firing line this time.'

Now the Politician spoke up. 'Captain Fleming, you have been found guilty of treason and justice demands the full sentence to be carried out immediately.'

Sweeney stared at us in horror, Fleming stared at us in contempt.

'It's not your sentence,' he said in quiet defiance. 'It's my blood-sacrifice for the soul of the nation, to show people one day that not all Irishmen submitted to the treachery of its leaders.'

Mullen shook his head in despair. 'Send this undead

ghost of Patrick Pearse back to nineteen sixteen, where he belongs,' he said to me bitterly. I knew what he wanted me to do, but I had no idea what the words he was using meant.

I looked up, holding Sweeney's eyes as I spoke. 'I'm to do it, not you. I'm damned already anyway. It's too late for me now.'

Mullen handed me Fleming's Browning, the one I'd seen him strip in Fort Dunree. 'There's one bullet in the magazine. We'll wait outside.'

As they left, Fleming stared at me solemnly. With his strong face, his clear blue eyes and jet-black curly hair he looked how a Goebbels film, trying to rally Ireland to the cause of the New Europe, might have portrayed a Celtic noble savage.

But as I painfully worked the slide of the Browning with my bandaged hand, I saw something else.

This was a man who truly meant the words he'd just spoken, not just as a final act of defiance, but as something he believed in, right to the very last. One way or another, he thought he could win the burning prize of freedom for his whole national territory and rescue his people - no matter how much of their and his blood he caused to be spilled in doing so.

In three days' time in Moscow, Brandt was going to sign away for good the German territory my own family had previously lived in for generations.

I raised the gun to the firing position.

The noonday sun was now shining through a window high in the end-wall. In its beam, dust motes glowed golden as they danced over Fleming's head, like the halo of a saint in a painted icon or even of the Christ, preparing to offer Himself for the salvation of all nations.

The piercing blue eyes, mesmerising in their intensity, looked back at me along the barrel. Unthinkingly, I lowered the weapon down to my side again in a subconscious mark of respect, my grip on the handle over-tight as I pointed the muzzle down at the flagstones. A couple of drops of blood mixed with wound fluid dripped from my left-hand fingertips onto the ground.

Without knowing why, I asked him, 'What would you have done to Brigid when you found out for sure, that she'd...' I struggled to find the right phrase, '... given herself to me?'

He spat on the ground through his bloodied lips again.

'I'd have taken my belt and thrashed her within an inch of her life. With the buckle end.'

An inch was about two centimetres, but it was close enough for me.

'Thanks,' I said, as I raised my arm again and shot him through the eye. There was a spray of blood and fleshy matter onto the back wall, and his lifeless body slumped onto the floor, the arms held above his head by the chain.

From the front, his face looked almost untouched - just the neat hole drilled through the eye socket. My thousand rounds with the Makarov in Bad Belzig had been of some use this summer, after all.

I came out into the yard, gently closing the wooden door behind me. Sweeney stared at me white-faced from the other side of the chasm separating me from the world of decency. Mullen was triumphant.

'Sweeney, wrap him up and get him buried. And pour some petrol on whatever mess is in there and burn it off too. No time for sentimentality - we're all in this together, one way or another,' he snapped, as Sweeney hesitated.

Still on autopilot, I cleared the gun, making to hand it back to Mullen.

'No, keep that,' he said. 'You're taking that out of the country for us when you leave. And you're getting out of Ireland as quick as we can manage it. Finner Camp for you, an Air Corps helicopter to Gormanston Camp, then a fast car to the airport.'

'What about my things at the hotel in Dublin.'

'Oh, don't worry. We'll provide a concierge service and pack everything up neat and tidy - making sure you don't take any materials out of the country you don't need, like lists of contacts or codes.'

They left Sweeney to his task, which I thought was rash of them, because I wasn't at all certain as to his present state of mind. Mullen drove us the forty-five minutes to Finner. There were a few quick words at the gate and we went through, straight up to the lazarette or whatever it was they called it in English.

The medical officer explained when I expressed my surprise at the size of the facility.

'This is a field hospital set up last year to treat the northern refugees fleeing the Prods.'

'How many have you treated so far?'

'You're the second.'

'Second what, batch of patients?'

'No, second patient.'

The doctor carefully removed the first dressing, tutting at the redness glimmering along the cut under my eye which I could see in the mirror, as I perched on the edge of a bed.

He was dispassionate as he unwrapped my hands. His only comment was that I had 'been in the wars.'

'The nurse will give you a tetanus jab and a shot of something for the pain.'

Whatever that last one was, I felt better than I had done for a long time. I experienced a sense of detachment and delightful well-being slowly bloom inside me as the doctor stitched the cut with black thread and rebandaged my hands.

He tutted again at my fingers and placed them in a kind of splint, so he could seal them from the air without touching the bloody mess of the nail bed. He gave me penicillin, made sure I took the first tablet and told me to get everything seen to again, no later than a couple of days' time from now.

'Will the nails grow back?'

'Too early to say. If they do, they may well be deformed. If you're lucky, a first deformed nail might fall off and a second one might then grow back more normally.'

'And my cheek - will there be a scar?'

'Depends if the wound gets infected. The cut is deep but it was made with a sharp blade, so the edges aren't too ragged. A vivid image of the Stanley knife laid out on the table, between the bolt cutters and the pliers, came back to my mind.

'And my hands?'

'Probably scarred for good. If your injuries are on a police file somewhere in the North, they'll be able to identify you for sure.'

An orderly brought us mugs of tea, while we waited in an office inside the hangar, next to the short runway at the side of the base.

We sat on benches around the sides of the room - some kind of crew briefing area perhaps - staring silently at each other. Mullen and the Politician were inscrutable. It was as if they had just come from a departmental meeting, as if absolutely nothing untoward at all had taken place in the cowshed.

It was fine for them, but they hadn't been the ones to pull the trigger. Skorzeny had talked about needing the strength of will to do so, to end a man's life, but now all mine was used up. It had been already, before this trip to Ireland. I was well overdrawn at that particular bank now and on the verge of bankruptcy. Brigid had asked me under the trees in Phoenix Park what harm confession could do, and right now, right at the very end, I was left with nowhere else to go.

I picked up the sound of rotor blades in the distance at the edge of hearing. As the wind blew, they became quieter, then louder again, as the aircraft approached. Dust Off had arrived.

It was my first ride in a helicopter. The take-off was juddery in the crosswind and leaving the ground was disconcertingly slow, unlike in a passenger jet where the transition to smooth flight was almost instantaneous.

As the green fields slipped under us, I thought again about the last thirty-six hours, trying to disentangle in my mind what had happened to me, and to Fleming.

First things first - was Sweeney in the police Special Branch or the Army? He spoke and acted like a policeman, especially in Byrne's pub on the quay of the Liffey, where I'd told him about the firestorm. But Mullen had talked about Brigid deceiving a 'couple' of Army captains. Who was the other one, if it hadn't been Sweeney? Maybe the one she'd been to the summer ball at the Curragh with?

To my thinking, Sweeney was clearly Mullen's man, from the way he'd been bossed around in the farmhouse we'd just left.

They were wary of agent provocateurs and Sweeney had been set to trap one. No wonder he'd gone off from Burtonport to meet somebody - Mullen, I now probably thought - after our mating dance on Gola Island.

However, that still left the thornier question of the Rose of Tralee. What did you do, when your faction no longer knew who to trust - whether it was middle-aged Army intelligence officers living in semi-detached suburbia, Cabinet Ministers or Taoiseachs - who guarded the guards?

Had she been sent by Mullen and her father to go through the whole of the junior ranks of current and former G2 officers? Dating them, eyes fluttering demurely as she sat with them in the back row of cinemas and over drinks at bars in hotels, getting them to boast of what they were ready to do, either for or against Captain Kelly?

How far had she been prepared to go, to get them to

talk? She probably hadn't needed to go very far at all. I'd seen what she'd done to Sweeney and to me, even before that night in Bundoran. For all I knew, Mullen didn't trust Sweeney either. He'd set Jim to watch me when I turned up in the middle of their arms trafficking crisis and maybe set Brigid to watch us both.

So what of Saint Padraig? From the way she talked about knowing his moods, she'd already been involved with him for some time. Had she offered me up to him in the pub in Ballsbridge, just before our trip to Donegal, to see if he'd nibble the bait of illegal arms? Maybe, but he'd might have already made other plans himself by then, to instead use me to keep the IRA squad in one place, as he offered them up in turn as bait for the British. How much of that plan had he secretly shared with her?

A cold hand clutched my heart. Women didn't need liberating from the patriarchy, they already had it wrapped around their little fingers. As we lay in bed in the Gresham yesterday afternoon, she already knew when I'd be taken that day to meet the IRA. Forget getting back to the hotel in the early afternoon because confession was at five o'clock - she'd wanted to make sure I'd be there when they called.

Why else had Mullen been ready to move so quickly? Had she already worked out by then Fleming's deeper plan, even before she came to sit on the low wall of the parade ground at Fort Dunree, understanding, or at least understanding enough, of CJ's complaints in German at his boredom and how his officers were trying to spice up their training?

Fleming thought he was using her, merely to capture me. I was just a handy goat to be staked out for the British tiger. Was that why had he wanted to know if I was a 'big man' at the EEC? Because he wanted to make sure I was worth everybody's while to start fighting over? But, thanks to Brigid, he was the one who'd ended up in the trap, luckily for me.

And why else was Mullen so ready to believe her story about my harmlessness to Ireland and let me go? I was truly lost for words, even when speaking to myself now.

If she ever did turn up in Brussels, having been given the pick of the new jobs on offer to the Irish as her reward, there was no way I was getting involved with her again, no matter how sorry she was for my scars.

All of the women I'd been attracted to since joining the EEC had ended up being a curse on me, one way or another. I'd be safer in a doomed, long-distance relationship with Sigrid Johannes, even if she was a lieutenant in the Stasi.

Ten minutes out of Gormanston, the pilot gestured and jabbed downward with his finger.

We looked out to starboard, and there it was again, the green hill of Tara with its figure-of-eight earthworks, waiting for the rightful king of all Ireland to be proclaimed at their centre, once more. We were flying just low enough for me to make out the Stone of Destiny and the seventeen ninety-eight memorial to the United Irishmen martyrs.

Fleming had been prepared to sacrifice himself for the nation in a corrupted parody of an earlier sacrifice on another hill. I wondered if any of Fleming's blood spray was still on my skin, airborne droplets from the bullet through his eye. If I stretched out of the helicopter, reaching down with my hand to brush the Stone, would his blood cause it to call out, to tell us that Fleming had been the leader the nation had been waiting on?

But that was probably just the morphine talking.

We landed on another short runway and were met by two waiting police cars. Mullen jumped down and strode across, ignoring the crewman's caution about the rotors.

He said a few words to the occupant of one of them and waved me out of the Alouette as the blades finally wound down to a stop.

'This is where our ways part, Lenkeit. Guard Regan here will make sure you get on the five o'clock plane to Paris. We've booked your onward flight to Brussels. Don't ever come back to this country again without a damn good reason or without telling me first. Pray in thankfulness every day for the rest of your life to whoever is your patron saint, that I didn't deal with you the way Michael Collins did to the British spies from Dublin Castle.

I got into the back of another Cortina. The policeman started the engine and drove out onto the main road down to Dublin.

'What happened to you and your face that we need to get you out of here so fast?'

I didn't feel like answering, but it always helped to keep the police sweet.

'I fell into the wrong company in a pub in the docks.'

He shook his head. 'I don't believe Irishmen would do that kind of thing to a European fella. We're too civilised.' I didn't want to disappoint him by telling him that that's what people used to say about the Germans over thirty years and an aeon ago.

We drove the rest of the way to the airport in silence. As we approached the terminal, off to the right I caught sight of the bell tower of the airport church I'd seen straight after I landed last Thursday, a week ago - and, legally speaking, probably a murder ago too.

'Stop, I want to go in there,' I said, pointing at the church.

'What do you want to go in there for?'

'Why do you think?'

Regan turned into the small car park attached to the church. He grumpily slammed his door when he got out and accompanied me in.

'Where do you imagine I'd run off to? I'm as keen to get back as you are to see me go.' I told him.

'Just doing my job. I'll stand at the back if you like, as long as I can see you at all times.'

As I approached the altar, I looked at the painting of Mary on the left, cradling a boy Jesus. The image and that of the adult Jesus on the right looked vaguely Russian or Greek Orthodox in style, not Irish at all, as I had somehow expected.

I didn't really have a clear plan. I was principally seeking some kind of solace by being there. A priest was at the front, a young man in a black cassock. I went over.

'Do you take confession here?' I asked.

'It's not time yet. We do it just before Mass.'

'My plane leaves in a couple of hours. Please, Father.'

With a sigh he pulled aside the curtain of the confessional box for me and installed himself on the other side.

The confessional was gloomy. Once I'd redrawn the curtain, there was no sign of the priest through the grille. He didn't say anything. Maybe he was waiting for me to start. I was at the end of the road. It wasn't just my aching hands or the pull of the stitches on my skin telling me. I had utterly failed in Ireland, let everyone down in both Brussels and Berlin. Everything I touched turned to dust and I knew why. There was a Browning in my luggage and a Makarov in my apartment in Brussels. I was spoilt for choice if the time came. No longer with any ability to suppress my conscience, I could no longer avoid the truth of who I was.

I didn't know what you were meant to say in confession, apart from the dialogue I'd heard in movies. I formed some words in my head and out they brokenly came.

'Forgive me, Father, for I have sinned. I killed a man in my anger.'

Because I couldn't see the priest, as I heard myself say the words, I had the sense I was praying to God Himself. *Vater, vergib mir meine Sünden.*

I half-heard the priest ask if I had been unreasonably provoked, but I ignored him. Suddenly, as I sat there, an image had come into my head and I was transported to a freezing attic room with a tarpaulin cover for a roof. The space was filled with grey light coming through the double sheets of newspaper which had replaced the blown-out glass of the mansard windows. A mockery of a Christmas wreath hung on the door, made from twists of silver cigarette paper. As if from above, I looked down and saw a thin, exhausted mother lying in the grimy bed, curled close around her newborn, trying to warm the baby. Despite her poverty, she exuded dignity, her eyes filled with wonderment and love as she stroked the fine blond birth hair of her son.

I gasped and tried to hold the image, even as it dissolved away. The words of the priest broke through as he tried to get a response from me.

I dimly heard him say something about twenty Hail Marys and going to the police as I stumbled out of the confessional and back along the aisle, tears streaming down my face.

The priest rushed after me, complaining.

'You need to wait until I've given you the Absolution. It doesn't work until then.'

'I killed a man and I felt no remorse, but when I admitted this before God, He showed me that I was loved, sacrificially and unconditionally.'

'You need to say your Hail Marys and take Mass, and then go to the police,' he said impatiently.

I turned away and carried on walking down the aisle towards Guard Regan, wiping my face with my forearm as I did so.

Regan looked at me in disgust but said nothing as we got back into the car for the short drive to the terminal.

'Are you going to make a fool of yourself in here as well?' he asked, as he brought the car to a stop.

I still had the jitters after my revelation in the church and shook my head dumbly. He took me through a door marked *'Diplomatic passports only'* where an official stamped my documents and sat me down to wait in an anteroom with my bags. I stretched out to try to doze, but couldn't settle. A gnawing fear was growing inside of me, some kind of delayed reaction to what had just happened at the border - the events on both sides. My skin flushed and broke into a sweat. I asked for the toilets and made it just in time to vomit into the bowl.

'Jaysus, pull yourself together,' said a voice from the bathroom door. I looked round with angry eyes at Regan.

A curse came to the tip of my tongue, but I bit it back and spat into the bowl instead. Getting to my feet I flushed the pan and washed my fingers as best I could, without getting the dressings wet.

We walked back to the anteroom and he fetched me a glass of water which I took gratefully. Instead of the gnawing fear, a sense of well-being began to slowly come over me again, which could no longer be down to the morphine. I knew that whatever awaited me in Brussels or Berlin, whatever might one day in the future be dredged up from the past, I had a new hope, a new source of confidence. I had seen a vision of God's love and knew it would never go away.

Chapter Twenty-One

My first port of call on Monday morning was Kramer. I ignored the strange glances as I strode in through the glass doors of the Berlaymont, past the front desk and headed for the relative privacy of the lifts at mid-morning.

His office was open, his secretary away from her desk, probably gossiping with friends, and he called me straight in with an '*Entrez*'. His head was down as he sat at his desk, making notes in the margins of some papers.

'*Attendez*,' he said, as he finished off and then looked up, straight into my eyes.

Behind the suave bureaucrat with thinning hair and the vanity which meant we only very occasionally saw his gold-rimmed spectacles, there was a harder man. One forged from France's own undeclared civil war between 'forty and 'forty-four, ending with the *Epuration*, a word which meant something quite different in French from the name 'Liberation' which was used by the Americans and the British.

'If that's what I suspect, then I haven't seen those kinds of injuries for a while,' he said, pointing at my fingers.

'How do you know I didn't trap them in a car door?' I asked.

'Because car doors don't give you knife wounds,' he said, indicating my eye now. 'So, what kind of trouble did you get yourself into this time?'

He got up from his desk, came round and stood in front of me, placing a hand on each of my shoulders, looking more closely at the stitches.

'Well, well. Sit down here,' he said solicitously, guiding me by the elbow to the sofas around his meeting table.

'*Dites-moi.*'

I took a deep breath and began.

'I used the names we had from various sources to start fishing, and got lots of bites from all kinds of directions.'

Kramer held up his hand. 'Stop with the sailor's yarn. Just say what you have to say plainly. No code.'

I waited a couple of long seconds and started again.

'I landed myself in more I bargained for.'

'Yes, I can see that.'

'But the real message back to the Sûreté and the SDECE is that the situation there is completely confused right now. Even the Irish government are struggling to stay on top of the two parts of the IRA, Protestant vigilantes coming south, the British Army on their doorstep and different factions within their own army and possibly their police. What's happening in Northern Ireland is testing loyalties in the South to the limit, shaking people out of their long-held allegiances - whether to their political factions or even to their own uniformed organisations.'

'Did you spot a way into the terrorist groups, for the long term?'

'The IRAs are in a rapid state of flux. I didn't get close enough to them in the time available, for me to work out which individuals are going to come out on top. But here's what I did pick up. Right now they're rapidly learning, training themselves, trying new weapons, new explosives, and new techniques all the time.'

'So, who did that to you?'

'They did. They were told to hold me for a while, and then dispose of me. But they used the opportunity to turn it into prisoner interrogation training for their new recruits.' I shivered as I thought again of the row of tools laid out on the table, I suspected the image would be staying with me for a while yet.

'Who told them to do so?' He looked solemn, and I again had the strong feeling he had more experience in this area than he had ever before hinted at.

I covered my face with my hands for a moment to gather my thoughts, but Kramer misinterpreted the gesture. The wide swaths of bandages, which the nurse in Finner Camp had applied, would have melted the hardest heart.

'Here,' he said, getting up and going over to a small, concealed drinks cabinet. He poured us both a shot of brandy. 'Hennessy cognac, in honour of your Irish adventure,' he said encouragingly.

I took a sip and continued. 'The Irish Sûreté, the Special Branch, suspected other army officers were in on the Kelly plot. I think they already had their eyes on them. When I turned up, I assume they thought from my questions that I was working for a foreign agency, maybe. Possibly for an arms dealer. But don't worry, I fed them a story which they believed in, sufficiently enough anyway, that I was working for the British.'

'So they arranged for that to happen to you, in revenge?' he asked, almost hopefully, as if he was still looking for a *casus belli*.

'So they created a fictitious rogue agent, an arms buyer, a lure, to see what I would reveal. And, at the very same time, they used me as bait in turn, introducing me to IRA supporters in the Irish Army whom they suspected, but had no real evidence against. They used me as an unwitting agent provocateur.'

Despite himself, Kramer was laughing. 'I'm sorry. I know you must have had a narrow escape somehow, but the irony... I imagine a woman was involved?'

My blushing was involuntary. 'Isn't there always? As it turned out, the person whom they tricked, by using me as an agent provocateur, had no intention of buying arms there and then. In fact, he and I argued when we met, and I may even have helped tip him over the edge into staging a border incident with me in a starring role.'

'Well, that can't have been part of your espionage training this summer in the East,' said the man who'd seen every trick in the book from de Gaulle when it came to irritating allies to beyond the point of reason.

'How was this new Gleiwitz meant to come about?' The Gaullists probably saw the false flag attack by the SS on the Gleiwitz radio transmitter, which had been used as the excuse to trigger the Second World War, as an example to be copied rather than avoided.

'One that started by him shipping me off to the IRA, who got creative while they were holding me, just on the wrong side of the border. They let me go when they realised they were being used themselves. They were to be the bait for the British forces who would come to see what was going on and then run into the waiting Irish Army, who were also there.' My hand went instinctively to my stitches.

'So, did you preserve international peace between Britain and Ireland? Are the Irish government's assurances true, that the arrests in the Kelly case really are the end of the matter?'

'I played my part in the police's operation which made sure it was, and I got their thanks - after a fashion.'

The Browning had gone into space below the floor of my wardrobe, along with the Makarov and the box of ammunition Johannes had signed over to me in Berlin.

'It reminds me of a time in the Saarland after the war,' he said, without elaborating.

'But the Communist Party of Ireland could be a danger. They've already asked Moscow for arms - last year in fact. In a world of confusion, if the other side do something, it will likely be through their ideological fellow-travellers, whom they already have a degree of trust in.'

'But the Communist Party aren't the IRA?'

'No, but they have links to the core faction of the IRA, whose move to the left created the fault-line inside the organisation which the events of summer last year then opened up.'

'Let's see how successful Brandt is at changing the climate in Europe. If things do improve, they'd have to either be very bold or very foolish to jeopardise that with any bad behaviour in Northern Ireland. It's only Northern Ireland, after all. There's nothing there that could make it worthwhile for them.'

'Unfortunately I didn't meet any Bretons, sorry. If the IRA stabilise and survive, perhaps they'll support the Bretons too. It's too early to tell right now. If sympathetic fishermen from each country are allowed into one another's waters to fish under the CFP, it would be easy. Lots of secret inlets and harbours along both shattered coastlines which could be used.'

I thought about the U-boat crew photograph on the wall of the bar in Burtonport, but said nothing. Johannes might know more when I saw him next, as I was sure would shortly be arranged.

'*Dommage*,' he swirled the drink in his glass and downed it, not seemingly particularly bothered.

'So what story shall I tell Masson, about this?' I said, pointing to my eye.

Kramer grinned. 'Tell him you were in a bar fight, got knifed and then someone slammed the counter flap down on your fingers, requiring the nails to be surgically removed. Everyone knows the Irish spend all their time drinking and fighting. It's a scientific fact.'

'I wish they had been removed that way, instead of the hammer, screws and pliers they actually did it with.'

'I'll give you the card of a doctor we use here in Brussels for confidential work. Very good guy, worked for us in Algeria. He's dealt with lots of that sort of thing, and worse. Charge it to the French embassy account.'

He fished the card from his desktop roll index and wrote out the details himself in a neat clerical hand while he continued to speak.

'And what did you make of the Irish attitude to accession, from the various people you came across?'

'It's as Sophie von Barten said - they're so desperate for agricultural subsidies that they'll suspend all reasoning about where the EEC is headed, just to grab hold of the cash. If the English had known they could be so easily bought off, the British flag would still be flying over Government Buildings.'

'So, no opposition, then, that you saw?'

I thought some more. There had been at least one person prepared to shake things up for his country, but then I'd killed him for his trouble.

'None to speak of.'

'Speaking of intrigues closer to home, Sophie von Barten asked me when you were coming back from Dublin so she could hear how your CAP meetings went.'

'She came to you direct and not through Masson?' I frowned.

'She makes up her own rules, you know that.'

I gave Masson the bar fight story and he bought it. I realised that because I hadn't been to university and had been a junior policeman on the beat, he somehow didn't expect anything better of me. In fact, it worked in my favour because he could claim I'd somehow failed in the task. Not so badly that it reflected on the department and him, but badly enough to ensure I wouldn't get any star billing in any summing-up report he produced on my Irish visit - which was just the way I liked it.

He'd have had me type up my report to him with my injured hands, there and then, if he hadn't also had a message from Kramer in the middle of last week, relaying Sophie's request for me to meet with Agriculture this very afternoon.

Masson didn't look at all pleased when he had to tell me this. I wondered how fast she was rising in the organisation, if she could get her way with Kramer and him that easily - and what her urgency was.

I was back in Sophie's four-man office. She and Rizzo eyed me cautiously across the two desks which had been moved together to make an ersatz meeting table, the ones that Willem and I had sat at last time.

When I opened the door, she'd glanced my bandages, but when she'd come up close to inspect my stitches, I saw something new in her eyes: an earthy, animal look.

We sat down awkwardly around the double desk arrangement.

'Are you going to get a pirate's patch for that?' she demanded.

Brigid would have taken her time to explain any observation she wanted to make. Sophie's unconscious assumption was that everyone else could immediately see her logic - and then do as she wanted, of course. But I knew Sophie, and I knew she didn't mean it in a malign way - most of the time, I thought.

'I haven't lost the use of my eye. Anyway, I have these to distract people with.' To show her. I put on a pair of wide sunglasses like the ones I'd seen Steve McQueen wearing in *Bullitt* two years ago.

Rizzo clapped his hands. *'Bravo bello.* Now you look like an Italian, apart from the hair of course, although perhaps you could be a South Tyrolean.'

Neither of them had the slightest idea about the stomach-churning fear for my life and the agony of the woodscrews and pliers - let alone what had happened in the cowshed. it was like I'd arrived back from a different planet. They simply had no clue.

'How did your briefings on agriculture and fishing go down?' Sophie asked.

I had to give myself a second or two before responding, as calmly as I could.

'Exactly as you expected,' I said. She smirked at this. 'Good, because Sicco is giving a speech on his Plan in

Ireland at the end of October and I'm going along too.'

'They don't care about fishing. Well, the fishermen I met, did care about the CFP, very much. Nevertheless, the farming lobby has its grip so tight on the politicians in the regions that accession is a sure-fire thing, if we want it.'

'That's interesting. We'll see if we can push the Common Fisheries zone even closer to the coastline.' She was merciless.

'You'll do that? Are you the Agricultural Commissioner now?'

'I'll recommend it,' she snapped. 'Same thing.'

Rizzo had the grace to be embarrassed. Maybe she had changed much more for the worse in the past year than I'd realised, with her greater responsibilities. We were all a year older, if nothing else.

'And the information on fraud which you gave them?'

'I really don't think they needed it. They're more than clever enough to work out all these scams for themselves. Resistance to rules and finding ways to grease their way past regulations is deeply ingrained over there,' I said, thinking partly of the gombeen men at O'Connell Bridge House.

'We asked you here for something else, though.' As she brought me back to the present, the two of them looked at each other.

Rizzo spoke up. 'There's something going on with my family back in Apulia which I need help with. Help which doesn't come from any of the usual sources.'

Here we go again, I thought. If people started using us as a team of private, on-call fixers, at some point soon External Investigations would no longer be a secret.

'There's three of us in our specialist department within Internal Affairs and Sophie must be desperate if it's me you're asking for help,' I said to Rizzo.

'You're the only one I trust,' she snapped again, answering for him. I was taken aback. She corrected herself. 'I mean, you're the only one I know well enough to ask such a delicate question of.'

Genuinely surprised, I riposted, now even more suspicious. 'Why should I help you? Don't you know what seems to happen every time I run political errands for other people? Including the ones I've done with you in the past?'

'I don't, not really Oskar. But I will tell you this - you owe me.' She was brooking no opposition. And if you don't help me, I'm ready to pay you back for getting me into the mess we found ourselves in Rostock, and the even worse things that happened after we got back.'

Rizzo was suspiciously quiet, as if he knew more about that than he felt he should.

But I was heart-sick. I'd just escaped, not only from the permanent loss of different parts of my body, but my life, on Saturday night. And now, not forty-eight hours later, she was proposing some new mischief to get me into trouble.

I much preferred the French approach to man-management, the one involving brandy made by the descendants of Irish emigrants.

How would she pay me back? She certainly had connections to people of influence in West Germany and was perfectly placed to initiate the thing I feared most right now, after an IRA hit squad come for the torture instructor's threatened unfinished business. That would be a BND counter-espionage investigation into a West German citizen working at what they merely knew to be a minor sub-department within EEC Internal Affairs. Moreover, who knew what other investigations might be triggered on the back of the first one?

'There was a time when I'd have walked through fire for you, Sophie. But not anymore.' This stopped now. Blackmail could only be dealt with in one way.

Rizzo shook his head sadly. 'I warned you, Oskar, all those months ago about what Sophie does to men's judgement.'

'I'm sorry, Rizzo.'

'I'm sorry too, Oskar,' said Sophie. 'I really am, for what comes next. This was your final chance to make up for last year.'

My face was dark. Let her do her worst. If my run as a player for both sides across the Iron Curtain had to come to an end, then so be it. Better to deal with the consequences now, rather than be looking over my shoulder for the next three decades. Right now, I was ready to quit anyway.

And in any case, I no longer needed to prove my true self-worth or worry about being abandoned without hope ever again.

Chapter Twenty-Two

For my fifth visit to the East in less than eighteen months, I flew straight into Schönefeld from Brussels and Johannes himself collected me at arrivals. I wondered if it would be the last visit to Berlin I'd ever make, if Sophie followed through on what I thought she might be planning for me.

Regardless, I suspected Johannes might well tell me himself to stop coming for a while, given the high frequency of my visits so far, and the danger that the West Germans would start taking a closer interest, even without any prompting from Brussels. I realised how dependent I had become on these trips, because of the chance they gave me to see my family in Wismar. As I'd said to Brigid that last day in Dublin, you didn't know what you had until it was gone.

During the flight, I'd had a few funny looks from the other passengers, even with my Italian sunglasses, but otherwise they gave me a wide berth. I felt my various dressings and bandages couldn't have said 'Ministry business' more loudly than if I'd borrowed one of Johannes' dress uniforms. Speaking of uniforms, the Interflug stewardesses were at least dressed in colours on the non-psychedelic colour spectrum, unlike the Aer Lingus crew. Karin could take pride in knowing that East Germany was beating at least one airline of the Free World when it came to fashion sense.

Johannes himself was a little subdued when we met. Whether it was the sight of the stitches marching down my cheek or some problem at the office concerning secret imports of Levi jeans and Marlboros, chilling the atmosphere, I couldn't tell. Or maybe one the Stasi's moles at the BND had told them that I was already under suspicion over there.

I got a cursory greeting and not much else as we made our way through arrivals, speeded on by several flashes of his identity card.

It wasn't until we were alone in his Wartburg, about to set off on the short drive into the city, that he turned to stare at my face.

'What happened to the other guy?' he asked tonelessly.

I stared back at him humourlessly, now that the initial excitement of being back in Berlin had worn off. An urge came over me, the words forced themselves up my throat, even though I knew they were the wrong ones to say.

'I shot him through the eye.'

'Um Gottes willen.' He slammed his open palm on the steering wheel. That really was the end of the holiday feeling.

'I knew it,' he said shaking his head. 'You realise we're going straight into a debriefing with my boss, who then has to brief Fiedler himself later today?' Now he really wasn't staring in a friendly way.

'You have to hear my side of the story.'

He covered his face with his hands and breathed deeply. I'd never known him to be at a loss like this.

'Okay.' He switched off the engine. 'Make it quick.'

'I uncovered a plot by rogue elements of the Irish Army to trigger a border clash with the British Army. I helped their police secret intelligence branch find the culprit, and…'

'Go on.'

'There was an impromptu court martial in the field, just like at the end of the war. And they decided on the highest punishment.'

'And you carried it out for them? On the guy who did that to you?' He pointed at my eye and then to my hands.

'I had to, otherwise they would have washed me with the rest of the dirty laundry.'

'How the hell did you get mixed up into all that? You were meant to watch, collect names, get them drunk, listen to their gossip - not this.'

'Because although I went to observe, the very fact that I was there changed the plans of the people around me.'

'What am I to do with you? I don't have a choice right now. I have to take you to this meeting.'

He sat there with slumped shoulders for a few seconds, thinking.

'Don't talk to me for the rest of the drive,' he said, as he switched the engine back on with a cough and a puff of blue smoke. 'Think carefully about the story we're going to rehearse when we get to the office, before we see my boss. Think very carefully about how you're going to tell them, that there was no possibility of this being traced back to the Ministry - for more people's sake than just your own.'

We were sitting back in the office of Johannes' boss. Lieutenant Petzold was there too, ready with his notebook, eager and wistful at the same time, waiting to hear my stories of the Emerald Isle he was unlikely ever to visit.

For the previous ten minutes, Johannes and his boss had already been closeted in here, while Petzold stood guard over me in the corridor outside.

When we were called in, Johannes' boss was looking at me with a sardonic smile.

'Show me their handiwork,' he demanded.

I laid my left hand flat on the table and carefully unwound the bandage from the splint. The ravaged nail bed was an angry pink colour, itching slightly.

'You want to see more?' I asked, offering to unwrap my hands as well.

Johannes and his boss gave the impression of professional curiosity, but my bet was that, even if they had seen this kind of injury before, they'd hadn't seen it performed, because they showed no recognition of the level of pain it inflicted.

But if the two senior officers were looking coolly at the evidence, Petzold was aghast.

'I hope what you're about to tell us made that worth it,' Johannes' boss said, with a nod of his head at my hand.

I wrapped the bandages up again, involuntarily touching the stitches on my cheek, as had become my habit during the past ten days. I cleared my throat and began.

Johannes and I had agreed on a short, terse account, not hiding what had happened, but making it clear it was all an accident of war, an unavoidable hazard of field operations.

'I made contact with the security organ of the civilian police, their so-called Special Branch. My cover story was that I was providing them with consultancy on detecting and combatting fraud in the award of Common Agricultural Policy subsidies, which they will have to administer when they join the EEC.'

'Did they believe you?' he asked sceptically.

'The EEC is a whole new world to them. They were ready to listen, but they didn't just do that. They suspected a rogue faction in the Irish Army and used me to destroy the cover of an officer they had under investigation.'

'And how did you do that?'

Now came the test to see if I could carry off our story, and above all, the test to see if I could tell the same story to the colonel that Johannes had, just before Petzold and I came in.

'Because he knew that I was a former policeman from Hamburg, and started asking questions on whether there were other arms dealers in the city, presumably to replace the one who had let down the Kelly gang earlier this year. He also tried to probe me for underworld names, again presumably to put pressure on the original arms dealer to get their money back.'

'So the exposure - how did that happen exactly?'

'They taped my meeting with him. But as far as the tape will have shown, I was simply an EEC anti-fraud official who happened to have come from Hamburg, and was reminiscing about old times in the police there. He and I were having a private conversation about life in West Germany - nothing more.'

It was a fair enough approximation of the meeting in the pub in Ballsbridge with Fleming. The last part of the story bore no relation to reality, though.

'And?'

'It all got hushed up and he was moved to other duties, put on the next flight to Cyprus, posted to the UN peacekeeping mission on the Greek-Turkish border. I got right inside their organisation, on the police side, anyway. I saw how they dealt with a mutinous situation, and I saw how desperate they are to join the EEC. They won't cause the British more any problems, not ones that will be noticed internationally.'

'So they're going to sit out another war, yet again?' he asked contemptuously.

'No, I didn't say that. They're going to destroy the state in the North, but so slowly it won't be noticed. Like a charcoal burner's fire, the wood appears to simply burn itself out, but all along the *Köhler* is carefully tending to the earth covering which traps the fire underneath.'

'Where did you get that analogy from? You made it up yourself?'

I chose not to rise to the provocation. 'One of their political advisers explained it to me.'

'Okay then, you'll be able to explain this to us.'

Johannes slapped a report down on the table between the four of us.

'This is a report prepared using some material given to us by some friends, shortly after you left. The original was written in May but we only received it in the middle of July. This is the HVA version which we repackaged and sent to the highest authorities on the fifth of August.'

I quickly counted back. That was the day I climbed the Hill of Tara with Brigid, but that wasn't the only realisation that hit me. 'Middle of July? So you wanted me to go to Ireland to check out a West German report, not help Wolf prepare for a conference in Moscow?' I asked grimly.

'We take information from many sources to avoid bias. Just read it, tell us what you think, see if there's something new we can tell Wolf,' said the colonel.

I turned back to the title page:

'Information on the Reflections of West German Governmental Circles on the Relationship Between Great Britain and the Republic of Ireland and the Parallels to Be Drawn for the Shaping of Relations Between the West German Federal Republic and the Democratic Republic.'

Because most Germans liked nothing better than reports with long titles - it was the proof their contents were worth reading.

'What relevance does this report have to working out what the Irish are going to do next in Northern Ireland?'

'Read it first. You're the only one of us who has actually been there.'

So I was finally the one-eyed king in the land of the blind, almost literally.

I carefully leafed through the report with my better hand, licking my finger from time to time to help turn the pages one-handed.

'Repackaged' was a code for 'plagiarised'. I knew that game because Masson made us play it all the time. The problem was, to give an honest appraisal, I needed to know which parts were Petzold's work and which sections were written by someone who might actually have been to the country.

The report had two main themes - a discussion of the legal status of British and Irish citizens in each other's countries, followed by a section on the economic linkages between the two, with a special focus on the single currency and the open border.

One phrase stood out, as I skim read - how everyday life went on, 'as if there had been no political separation.'

'This is wrong,' I said, pointing to the text. 'There is indeed no border in Ireland, but that doesn't mean they have anything to do with each other. Until nineteen sixty-nine, the Irish nomenklatura seem to have forgotten that there even were Catholics in the North. And I didn't meet a single Protestant from Northern Ireland during my trip in the South.'

Petzold scribbled furiously, as if he were taking down notes on a speech being given by Ulbricht himself.

'And this is completely irrelevant,' I said, as I thumbed back to the part on how Irish citizens could vote in British elections. 'I don't believe there's any significance to this, apart from an administrative convenience - it's because these guys don't normally carry papers with them, or have any regular form of identification.'

'As for serving in the British army, again, presumably because in a state without army conscription, the British are happy to fill their ranks with whomever they can get. It's nothing to do with any fellow feelings. They've been doing it for decades.'

'Is anything in this report accurate? Are you trying to make us look like fools?' demanded Johannes' boss of me.

'I'm not the one who forwarded it to Ulbricht,' I said coldly. 'But I'm sure if Mielke quotes from it in a Politburo meeting, Wolf will be able to show him up later using Petzold's brand-new secret addendum, dated today. Count it as a win.'

By their half-hidden smiles I could tell they were.

To give them the best chance of carrying that manoeuvre off, I tried to make sure they understood the real nature of the report they'd been sent.

'The Bonn government is spinning a tissue of lies, but

it's themselves who they are deceiving. They tell a story of how Britain and Ireland have a common social and economic system, and how this somehow means they approximate to a single polity. But I tell you, the Irish hate the British, when they think about them at all. All the practical accommodations referred to are just that - not a sign of a deeper meeting of minds.' Petzold nodded sagely as I carried on.

'Still, if superficial administrative connections can make Bonn believe that East and West Germany are the same country, then make use of that. Fiedler should recommend that Ulbricht squeezes Brandt for all the soft Deutschmark loans the western socialist is ready to give to his fellow-Germans,' I concluded.

Johannes and Petzold looked on, waiting for the colonel's reply.

'The West Germans haven't a clue about us,' he said sourly. 'Twenty-one years after the establishment of the Republic and all these fascists can write about are appeals to the common ethnicity of East and West Germany.'

'You should be proud that they don't understand you,' I said. 'It's the unintended consequences of the Ministry's work.' I nodded toward Johannes. 'It's what Major Johannes said to me before I left for Ireland. Understanding intentions are the real intelligence gold, not counting tanks.'

I scratched the back of my left hand, the unbandaged part, just at the base of my nailless fingers. I saw Johannes watching but he said nothing.

I went back to the start of the report and went through it again, paragraph by paragraph, more for Petzold's benefit, this time. Johannes folded and unfolded his hands whilst Petzold made further notes in the margin of his copy.

'Did you get all that?' asked Johannes' boss to Petzold, when we were done.

'Yes, I believe so. If we are finished here, Comrade

Colonel, I'll start to type it up.' I could tell Petzold would be a lot happier away from the sight of my bandages and stitches.

'Okay, I think we're done. What do you plan for him next, Johannes?'

Johannes looked sombre. 'Nothing more today. I think I should take him to the clinic in the main building. My wife's a doctor and I'm not sure about that dressing.'

The female doctor poked and prodded at my wounds, as I sat before her at her desk. She slapped on some more iodine and changed the dressings again herself.

'It's not too badly inflamed. Come back and I'll give you another course of penicillin if it gets worse.'

She unwrapped a canvas roll containing a selection of scalpels, forceps and other nasty-looking implements.

'But those stitches below your eye are ready to come out. Hold still - this will hurt.'

She snipped and pulled, discarding the fragments of black thread into a basin at her side. I looked in the mirror, the puncture marks stood out pink against my cheek, and the cut was longer than I'd realised, but it seemed to have closed up tightly. I gave a silent vote of thanks to the army doctor at Finner Camp in far-off Donegal, waiting for the northern patients who hopefully never would come.

Johannes saw my solemn expression and tried to cheer me up.

'We've got better drugs here than iodine and penicillin. Perk you up and make you fit to run a marathon in no time.'

'I'll take you to your hotel now, but I can't stay for a drink. You'll need to hang around there today and this evening, in case we have any more questions for you.'

At least the day was ending better than it had started. In any case, after my escape from the IRA, I now understood better what older people who'd been through the war meant when they said they were simply glad to have survived it. Regardless of whether they'd ended up in the East or the West afterwards.

As we walked to the garage, I was glad to see the back of the Normannenstrasse for the time being, and wondered if I'd ever be here again. I'd saved Fiedler's people from complete embarrassment by thoroughly correcting the dossier from Bonn for them, even though it had already been circulated to the upper echelons of the Party. I might even have given the East Germans the other evidence they needed to argue in Moscow against the socialist states from getting involved in another country's civil war.

The tone of the three Stasi officers during the day hadn't suggested I'd be getting a second interview with Fiedler anytime soon, but building credibility took time. The deeper I got into their organisation, the more I would be asked to betray West Germany, but the more valuable my knowledge of the Stasi would be to the SDECE. Even to the BND, despite Sophie's threats. It would be good to hold a few high trumps against her stacked hand of cards.

Who knows, I might even get to go camel riding one day in South Yemen.

When we were alone in the car, I asked him another of the questions that had been troubling me since finishing the course at Bad Belzig a day early, just over a month ago.

'Why did you send me to see Skorzeny?'

'What did you learn there?'

'He had no names. He knew no-one of value to us.'

'I didn't ask what information you collected, *Kunsthandler*. I asked what you learned.'

We pulled up at the lights at the crossroads of Hans-Beimler-Strasse and Karl-Marx-Allee, to stand in a row of smoking Trabants and Wartburgs, interspersed with the odd Western car. Sunny Madrid it was not.

I took a guess. 'You sent me there to show me the real side of fascism? That their star man is no more than a greedy capitalist, still unable to see the misery he helped inflict on the world, including the two thousand sailors of the *Scharnhorst,* still sleeping at the bottom of the ocean?'

I looked at him for an answer, but the lights changed and he busied himself with making the turn.

'Did you and Fiedler make up this Irish task as an excuse to send me to Skorzeny?' I asked incredulously. 'Is that how Markus Wolf plays his games, if that's who Fiedler really is?'

'Fiedler is exactly what he and I told you, a pre-war Communist Party *émigré* now returned, with a long and honourable history of service in the Ministry.'

'Longest,' I muttered under my breath.

'The last time you were here, I locked you in my office and stopped you roaming the corridors. But the locked doors protected you too, from people seeing your face. Too much knowledge is dangerous for everyone.'

And if you tried to breach the biggest locked door in East Germany, the Wall surrounding the capitalist enclave of West Berlin, you got shot. It was the neat logic of the well-meaning technocrat - protect the little people from being exposed to the wrong ideas, protect the system which imprisons them.

He continued. 'You need to trust me on this. You above all.'

I left it there, wary again of the flat tone in his voice.

Part of me wanted him to stay for a drink, if only so I could ask him about the U-boat men, whose photo I'd seen behind the bar of the pub in Burtonport.

But another part of me was glad he didn't. As I got out of the Wartburg to spend an evening alone in my hotel, the anti-climax from a whole day spent in the Normannenstrasse started to creep up on me.

While I'd done them a service in shining the light of truth on the report from Bonn, giving the Ministry the insight into the intentions of the West that was my self-justification for being here, I'd been put through the mangle in Ireland to do so. And also, if I was being cynical again, put through the mangle just to be taught a lesson by Fiedler in Madrid that the Nazis were bad people.

With a final farewell, he told me to be ready with my bags packed at eight tomorrow morning. Where we were going, he didn't say.

Chapter Twenty-Three

Berlin - Friday, 21st August 1970

As Johannes instructed, I got down to the foyer at five minutes to eight, my bag strap over my shoulder to save my hands.

He was already there, but in his formal dress uniform and with an expression to match. Just as with the course director in Bad Belzig, the field-gray tunic with pleated side pockets, metallised buttons and collar patches, made him look like a picture of an old-time Wehrmacht officer.

He was also wearing a black leather holster for his sidearm.

'What's the special occasion?' I asked, as lightly as I could.

The hotel staff and other guests were already giving us a wide berth as they stepped to the side of our little reunion, and the circle was only growing wider.

'You'll see,' he said grimly. 'This way. *Bitte.*'

He extended a hand, indicating the hotel's revolving front door.

My heart was sinking as we stepped outside, but when we got into his Wartburg and I saw Petzold in the back, similarly dressed and also carrying his personal weapon, it dropped to my stomach.

'Where are we going?' I asked uncertainly, as he pulled out into traffic. I glanced at Petzold in rear-view mirror, but he was staring straight ahead, impassive. Even someone wearing ridiculous glasses and with an atrocious haircut carried an air of authority when they were in full uniform - which was the whole point of it, after all.

347

At the crossroads where we'd stopped yesterday evening in the queue of Trabants, instead of taking the Karl-Marx-Allee back to Stasi headquarters, we took the other street, Hans-Beimler-Strasse, up to the north-west.

'Where are we headed?' I asked again, more impatiently this time.

Petzold turned his head to take a better look at me in the mirror as Johannes answered.

'Hohenschönhausen prison.'

My eyes widened.

'It's not what you think,' he said contemptuously.

'So why the honour guard?' I asked.

'Because I know your temper. We're almost here.'

We skirted an abnormally-large city block, just like the Normannenstrasse complex, but surrounded by a four-metre high concrete wall with watchtowers at the corners.

Johannes showed his identity card at the gate and he drove inside to park in the outer courtyard.

'This way,' he said, as we walked to the reception building.

We waited in silence, as a warder was summoned. He led us down a corridor, through a gate set in an iron grille running floor to ceiling and on into the custody area.

Johannes walked ahead of me and Petzold behind, as the warder counted off the cells until he found the one he wanted.

He stood back and let the three of us gather round the cell's grey reinforced steel door.

Johannes turned to face me and said curtly, 'Take a look.'

I slid back the cover of the viewing port, to see a small, thin-shouldered figure hunched over the tiny table, leaning on their elbows.

Johannes reached over and banged open and shut the food-serving hatch a couple of times.

Karin turned round to face the door, her eyes red and

swollen, tear streaks on her grimy cheeks.

I stared savagely at Johannes.

'Come.'

I followed him back with a leaden heart and a deep sense of foreboding to the reception wing.

I simply couldn't imagine what she might have done to warrant her ending up here. Thomas lashing out at his parents in a fit of rage, maybe, just maybe - but not my other cousin.

As we walked some more, the red beast awoke within me and started hunting back and forth, seeking something to sink its teeth into. It was on a leash for the time being, but the chain was straining. No wonder Johannes had dressed up this morning and brought Petzold along for the ride.

A few doors down from the reception there was an office, provided for the use of the HVA. Johannes drew the key and we all trooped inside.

He tossed his cap onto the hatstand, then went and stood behind the desk, facing me over the wooden top.

'Take a seat,' he pointed at a metal-framed chair tucked under my side of the desk. I shook my head, instead standing behind the chair, hands on its back. Petzold watched me carefully from the door to the room, where he had taken up guard in front of it.

'We intercepted some letters. She was planning to leave for the West.'

My heart skipped a beat as the full implications sank in. This was a disaster she would never recover from, and one, not just for her, but the whole of the rest of my aunt's family too. Any hope of a normal life was over. As for her college course at the Fashion Institute, that was gone forever.

'I don't understand. She was happy here. She had a future planned out doing what she loved,' I coldly enunciated each word.

Maybe not as glamorous a career, though, as Sophie thought the West could have offered. An icy hand gripped my heart - oh Karin, what have you done?

I rammed the chair forward under the desk in frustration. My voice rose.

'Where did she get the idea from?'

Johannes slowly nodded, solemnly. 'She had encouragement from the West.'

I closed my eyes for a second as I leant with my hands on the back of the chair, remembering the look of fear on Karin's face at the rattling of the cell door. My grip on the veneer back tightened harder and harder; I was ignorant of the pain.

The beast inside strained and slipped its leash. I swung round with the chair in my hands and flung it hard against the far wall. Its wooden back smashed and splintered. I roared with hurt and rage as I took a flying kick at it, thoroughly wrecking it, bending it well out of shape.

I turned to face Johannes and Petzold.

'I'm going to Brussels and I am going to fucking kill that fucking bitch,' I yelled.

Petzold flinched at my explosion, his hand instinctively clamping onto his holster.

'Shut up! Shut up, Lenkeit!' Johannes was shouting now himself, slamming his fist on the table. 'You can't solve all of your problems by putting a bullet in someone's head. For God's sake, Oskar. Enough of this childishness.'

'You don't know them like I do,' I shouted back. 'The aristocratic von Barten bitch knew exactly what she was doing. Exactly. It was sheer, bloody, cruel spite.'

I inhaled and exhaled deeply, still in a high choler. Where the stitches had been in my cheek, it started to throb, the skin feeling like it was ready to part again. I kicked the broken chair against the wall again, one last time, and came over to lean on the desk, head bowed in front of Johannes. All the parts of my hands were hurting badly now, as if I'd opened up the wounds again.

'Comrade Lieutenant, you can leave us now.'

Petzold left, patting the Makarov in his holster as he went, just to show Johannes he was ready to come back and help, if the craziness returned.

Once the door was closed, Johannes said coldly, 'The first thing you need to do is get back to Brussels and get your woman under control.'

'She's not my woman,' I said bitterly now, ashamed that an East German communist had a stronger moral compass than I did.

'That's not the impression she gave in her letters to your cousin.'

'Letters? How long have they been in contact for?'

'Some months. Well, in one direction at least. Whether she lied in her letters or not, whatever she is to you, Sophie von Barten knows more than you think. And she knew exactly where to hit you. This is as bad as you can imagine - you are compromised. We just don't know yet to what extent.'

'What's going to happen to my cousin?'

'I've really no idea. For someone her age, two, three, maybe four years in prison. Youth detention then adult prison - which might be safer for her than a juvenile institution.' His cheek spasmed involuntarily. A trapdoor opened and for a moment I saw past the fiction of construction battalions for conscientious objectors and a multi-party 'democracy', deep down into the black heart of the police state and what having unlimited power did to people.

'Fuck, Johannes. Get her out.'

He shook his head. 'You know I can't promise you that.'

'I'll go back to Brussels and shut down whatever nonsense von Barten has started. Tell Fiedler that for me.'

He glared at me.

'You have to trust me. You know that? More than ever,

I keep telling you it.'

He punched his hand into his fist for emphasis, as I'd see him do before.

'You cannot stir things up at your end. No letters to the foreign trade office. No representations, threats, exposure of your handler to the Belgian Sûreté - nothing.'

'Okay, I get it,' I said.

'In East Germany, no institution is more powerful than the Ministry. You cannot force it to do something against the will of its leadership. To help your cousin, I am risking all of my own goodwill with them. Goodwill that I've built up over the years, to be used in time of need by me and my own family.'

'She's seventeen.'

'She's old enough to know better,' he retorted.

'How did she plan to escape?'

'Sophie von Barten suggested that she use make-up to give herself an older appearance, so she could pass herself off as her mother and come West using her papers. The travel permission for your aunt which we gave as your reward, Lenkeit.'

'What a miserable, hopeless plan,' I said. 'It's exactly as if von Barten knew she would get caught.'

I choked now, at the pathos of the situation. The old story of a naive young girl led astray by false promises. My hot fury was turning into something cold and bitter.

'She is clever and certainly malicious I accept, but I don't get the impression that's all there is to it. These people always have an agenda,' said Johannes.

I gave a deep sigh and went over to pick up the broken chair, leaning it against the back wall. I sat down heavily, sticking my leg out for balance to stop the chair from wobbling.

I stared at Johannes from across the room.

'Should I go and see my aunt, or will that make things worse?'

'There is no hope you can give her or promise that you

might make which you can keep. Your relationship with the Ministry needs to be more confidential now than ever before.'

I looked past Johannes, out the window, calculating. The sky was completely overcast, heavy with clouds tinted yellow from the capital's filthy lignite power stations.

In some ways, if they followed the legal process to the end, Karin's misfortune could be my escape. The threat of persecution of your loved ones surely no longer worked once the threat had become a reality.

But they knew that too. My first guess was that Fiedler would let a prosecution run, but that there would be a suspended sentence, with the clear implication that it would be carried out if I didn't keep doing what they wanted.

And they had any number of other tricks up their sleeves too, I was sure. Ones that I couldn't even begin to guess at. They'd been doing this kind of thing since Fiedler got off the plane from Moscow in 'forty-five.

'Agreed, I need you to help me, Johannes. As you say, more than before. I know there will be a price for that. And I need to see those letters for myself before I go back.'

'What will you do in Brussels?'

'If you can't get Karin out, I swear to her mother and to mine that I'll do it myself, from my end. By any means necessary.'

IN MEMORIAM
JUDITH COOKE 1950 - 1976

Afterword

The principal conundrum of the 1970 Arms Trial is the apparent bringing to book of the gun runners by the police and judiciary, contrasted with the support to the northern IRA at all levels of the Irish government. 'Apparent', because in the end, the defendants were acquitted of importing arms illegally. Which of course implies that in the eyes of the jury, what Captain Kelly and his merry band did was legal, after all.

To understand why Kelly, Blaney, Haughey and Luykx were arrested in May 1970, it is necessary to understand that other conundrum, the decades-long conflict between the Irish government and the IRA - the glowing embers of the bitter civil war of 1922-3 between the pro- and anti-Treaty factions. The Treaty in question was the Anglo-Irish Treaty, which provided for the withdrawal of the southern twenty-six counties from the Union. But the withdrawal was not complete enough for a large number of the independence fighters, the so-called 'Old IRA', who then rebelled against the Provisional Government.

The anti-Treaty rebels lost the bitter Civil War, but later coalesced politically around Fianna Fail, the governing party in Ireland from 1957-73. The founder of Fianna Fail, Eamon de Valera, was Prime Minister from 1937-48, 1951-54 and finally 1954-59. During the war years, he had some of his former comrades in the IRA interned and one of their number was executed for the murder of a member of the Garda Siochana.

So in August 1969, when Captain Kelly found himself in Northern Ireland, observing, but also participating in the riots too - 'All the men were needed up front, she indicated severely' - the Irish were faced with a new balancing act.

A government relief fund for the humanitarian needs of northern Catholics was set up, run by Charles Haughey and Neil Blaney. They promptly diverted part of these funds to buy arms for the IRA instead. Haughey's brother went further, helping to physically move arms brought into Dublin Airport.

The government tried to square the circle of supporting the efforts of their old-time Republican opponents by attempting to direct the flow of arms to new groups, other than the socialist-leaning legacy IRA (not described as 'Official' until the end of 1970). Captain Kelly's concern, described in 'The Lost Revolution' (see bibliography) was that 'arms and support seem to have got into the wrong hands in Belfast', that was, elements hostile to Dublin. Whether inadvertently or not, this preference in supply effectively engineered a split in the IRA. But, as everyone knows, to make omelettes you have to break eggs.

Another Irish conundrum of the '70s is the harsh treatment of both IRAs by the Garda - the 'Heavy Gang' really existed, IRA men jumped out of second floor windows, attempting suicide rather undergoing further police beatings - alongside local collusion with the terrorists by individual Gardai.

For the Troubles could not have carried on as long as they did without the safe haven provided by the Republic of Ireland - freedom from extradition, supply of arms and funds, training, engineering, weapons testing, medical support, and the undermining of Britain's position abroad by the Irish government, especially through working with the Irish-American lobby to place restrictions on the freedom of action of the British Army and RUC. The irony being of course, that post-9/11 and the various Wars on Terror, 'kill or capture' missions and remotely-controlled drone strikes make a mockery of the restraint the US imposed on the British in Northern Ireland.

And here is the final geopolitical absurdity of the Troubles - in 1972, the Official IRA, at least, was receiving funds and support from both sides in the Cold War - Irish America ('Goulding was introduced to the actor Gene Kelly, who made it clear he would make a financial contribution as long as it was for arms') and the KGB.

Described in Jérôme aan der Wiel's book, *East German Intelligence and Ireland 1949-90*, the 1972 'Operation Splash' involved a Soviet spy trawler dumping arms overboard on the Stanton shoals, marked with a buoy for pickup later by an Irish fishing vessel.

Aan der Wiel's book gives some fascinating insights to exactly how important Ireland was to East Germany (not very), and the sources of information available to them.

The East German view of the IRA seems to have become more and more unfavourable over the years - Aan der Wiel describes this through the changing descriptions of the organisation in various East German official publications. By 1976 they were described as 'increasingly of a Maoist and anti-Communist orientation', and by 1987, when the IRA bombed a Remembrance service for soldiers who had died fighting fascism in Europe, the romance of the Irish anti-imperialist *Partisanenaktionen* mentioned in the 1969 Meyers Neues Lexikon was over.

The overwhelming impression of the activities of the Stasi's foreign intelligence branch, the HVA - led by Markus Wolf from 1952-86 - is one of deep and almost complete penetration at all levels of the West German intelligence community and of the government itself.

To give a sense of the quality of their access, Günter Guillaume, exposed in 1974, was the personal secretary to the West German chancellor Willy Brandt. In the '80s Gaby Gast, the deputy head of the BND's Soviet section, even sent Wolf analysis by the Western intelligence agencies of a Reagan-Gorbachev summit. The HVA couldn't merely see to 'the other side of the hill', they were fighting in the other general's army.

In one sense, West Germany provided the Democratic Republic with more than enough information on any of the minor European countries they might have been interested in. When Lenkeit returns to Berlin, he finds the Stasi already have a comprehensive report on Ireland. There really was such a document, dated 5th August 1970 with a long, 40-word title. Aan der Wiel found it in both East and West German archives - whole passages in the Stasi file simply transcribed from the West German one.

Ireland's neutrality during WW2 is a debate that won't go away. Robert Fisk, in his 1983 book 'In Time of War' tried to assess and debunk some of the more incendiary claims of direct local Irish support to U-boats of the Kriegsmarine made by Nicolas Monserrat in his book 'The Cruel Sea'.

But Fisk does make it clear that there was some limited contact, and he did manage to find one eyewitness account of a U-boat crew arriving off their submarine by rowing boat, to pick up exactly the list of fresh food items recounted to Lenkeit in the pub.

Fisk also describes the daily flights by Focke-Wulf Condors up the west coast, witnessed by Sweeney as a child, and also newspaper photographs of German U-boat aces, pasted up in the wheelhouses of Kerry fishermen.

The logistical endurance of a submarine is limited by fuel, supply of torpedoes and fresh food. Of these three, only the latter would have been available in Ireland. All three were available, to a degree, from the specialist resupply U-boats, the Type XIV *Milchkuh*. If the war had continued, the Type XXI, with its refrigerated long-life food storage would increasingly have come into service, and the risk of approaching the Irish coast would not have been worth it for the cabbages and pork in Fisk's story.

Of course, the one rock on which all attempts to

rationalise Ireland's neutrality founder, is that of de Valera's visit to the German Legation in Dublin on 2nd May 1945 to pay his condolences to the ambassador on Hitler's death. It doesn't matter (or maybe it makes it worse) that the Secretary to the President of Ireland made the same visit the day after, or that De Valera might have done it out of some personal regard for the ambassador, who was later granted political asylum in Ireland. The condemnation, around the world, was immediate. The US ambassador to Ireland was so disgusted, he asked Truman to recall him.

But it wasn't just de Valera, the Irish envoy in Madrid also paid a condolence visit to the German embassy there, prompting this comment to him from a former Francoist Spanish ambassador to Berlin:

The sympathy which both as Spaniard and as Catholic I have always felt for the noble people that you represent has continually increased during the war before the Christian and dignified attitude of its government. Today, in the presence of the noble gesture of Mr de Valera, ... I desire to manifest to Your Excellency my admiration and respect.'

The fact remains, that abandoning neutrality was a choice open to Ireland, once the tide of war had turned against Hitler, and especially after America took the lead in the European war effort after autumn 1944. Even faraway Brazil declared war on the Axis in 1942 and sent 25,000 men to fight the Nazis in the Mediterranean theatre from September 1944.

The Irish were that lucky they got the arrests of Kelly *et al* out of the way when they did in May 1970. For on 18th June 1970, Heath won the British General Election, rushing Sir Con O'Neill off to Brussels in indecent haste to submit a new accession application only two weeks later, on 30th June - a few hours after what would later be known as the CFP came into being. The discussion on accession took up three short paragraphs of the 1970 Conservative election manifesto, less than 2% of the total text and contained only one commitment in relation to a policy towards the EEC, to '... negotiate, no more, no less.' The irony of someone sharing the surname of the great Earl O'Neill, driven from Ulster, thus enabling the Plantation by Scottish settlers, now responsible for the United Kingdom giving up its own independence to the EEC, would surely have pleased the old rebel.

Of course, the deception practised by Heath upon the British electorate and their Parliament really deserves its own, separate book. But first, Lenkeit has to solve his immediate family crisis, and perhaps resolve an earlier one too.

Miscellany

Firstly, my thanks to Clive Uttley for the advice on the number of 9mm rounds someone might fire off over ten hours or so.

Captain James Kelly is an interesting character. Eldest of ten children, the son of a publican in Bailieborough, he joined the Irish Army in 1949. He joined G2 in 1960, and apart from breaks to serve with different Irish UN peacekeeping missions, served there until his voluntary resignation in 1970. In the late '60s he had been considering a switch to academia - he was more thoughtful than commonly given credit for. His contention in later years, was that the Irish government should indeed have tried to actively shape the rejuvenated republican movement in the North, precisely because it could have then channelled and directed its activities, and stopped the fire burning on there for another 40-or-so years.

Kelly met with a range of players between 1969-70, including what he suspected was a real-life British agent provocateur, who advertised himself as 'Randall-Markham'. This man also claimed to be the offspring of a British Army officer and a local woman (Arab in this case), just as Lenkeit does. The real-life 'Randall-Markham' came to Dublin in November 1969 to try to negotiate an arms sales with Kelly's IRA contact. He aroused suspicions through his liberal use of Kelly's name, just as Lenkeit drops the name of G2 officers too. 'Randall-Markham' claimed to have grown up hating the British (despite serving himself in their army), he asked to be taken to IRA training camps, saying he could pass on his counter-

360

terrorism knowledge. He offered to supply arms at one price, then dropped it by 90% in the same discussion. All this was too obvious to Kelly and the IRA. There was talk of taking 'Randall-Markham' up country to a training camp, killing and disposing of his body there, or as Kelly says in his book 'eliminating' him. Kelly, however, chose to dissuade the IRA from this course, presumably preferring to know where the British agents were, once he'd identified them.

Kelly also declined the offer of the three northern republicans, who turned up on his doorstep one day in May 1970, to assassinate the former defence minister Gibbons too. Gibbons was the minister by whom Kelly had been directed to import arms, and who the northerners felt betrayed by, after Kelly's arrest.

Kelly's resignation from the Army was at his request, so he could be free to defend himself at criminal trial, rather than face an Army court-martial. But one of the alternative suggestions from his superiors at the time, mentioned in his book 'The Thimbleriggers', was indeed a transfer to an unspecified department (presumably the Customs Service) to allow him to continue to operate under official cover, as a pig-smuggling prevention officer - a real thing, apparently.

One of Kelly's defence team was, in fact, Peter Sutherland - later an EEC Commissioner, head of the WTO, chairman of Goldman Sachs International for twenty years - and who sat on the steering committee of the Bilderberg Group.

Wolf's memoirs reference the story of Hosea son of Nun and the prostitute Rahab, in relation to his description of the Stasi 'Romeos', tasked with seducing lonely secretaries, far from home at NATO headquarters. Wolf claims his informers were more often motivated by personal reasons than by money - which was good for him, because at the end, hard currency payments to thousands of informers was something they couldn't easily afford. The Stasi's human empathy also extended to birthday telegrams to agents living in the West - which tripped them up when West German data analysis matched up the dates of these with the birthdays of suspects they had already under surveillance.

Lenkeit's arrival at Iveagh House is taken from a description of two East German officials in the '80s who turned up for an appointment to find no-one there. At least Lenkeit isn't allowed to wander up to the third floor unaccompanied to wait for thirty minutes until someone appeared - the Minister for Foreign Affairs himself - as happened to the real Germans.

Two East German journalists attended the XVII Party Congress of the CPI, and the Irish comrades really had learned '*Wir fahren gegen Engel-land*', singing it to the embarrassment of the Germans, one of whom was Jewish and had escaped the Holocaust through being given asylum in England.

The Department of External Affairs hated 'Irisches Tagebuch', complaining as early as 1961 to the West German foreign ministry about a TV programme based on it. The depiction of poverty and emigration did nothing for Irish attempts to attract inward investment and be allowed to join the EEC. Nor, I am sure, did Böll's description of the Swastika Laundry.

Sometimes Lenkeit imagines scenes as they come to him, not as they actually happened. It may be pedantic, but Skorzeny didn't receive his interview from Hitler in a damp concrete bunker at the Wolfsschanze, but instead in a well-lit wooden map room in the same complex. And he didn't leap out of the glider when rescuing Mussolini with sub-machine gun in hand, but instead left it in the aircraft in the rush to get out, making his achievement a little more impressive - the whole episode captured the imagination of

Europe for at least three decades afterwards.

Skorzeny has problems walking, because unknown to him in summer 1970, he had two tumours at the top of his spine, which had to be operated on in November of that year, in Hamburg. By April 1971 he had learned to walk again and discharged himself from hospital.

In December 1970, the Dublin Airport church saw a more distinguished visitor than the penitent Lenkeit, when it hosted the wedding of a Mary Bourke, who left the building as Mary Robinson, and who twenty years after that, would become President of Ireland.

The American tourist, Kelly, tries to assure his wife that their son in the US Marines artillery won't be in danger serving at a firebase. But of course the TV report which they watch together in the pub is indeed that of an attack on a firebase - the desperate 23-day battle by the 101st Airborne Division to defend Firebase Ripcord, 1-23rd July 1970.

The Wild West-style takeover of the small town the trio drive through on the way to Donegal was the 5th February 1923 raid by anti-Treaty IRA on Ballyconnell.

And finally, the 1964 film, *Polizeirevier Davidwache,* portrays the Salvation Army on the mean streets of Hamburg, singing hymns and taking collections in pubs for their charitable work.

Short Bibliography

Christopher Booker & Richard North, 2005 & 2016: *The Great Deception: The Secret History of the European Union*

Heinrich Böll, 1957: *Irisches Tagebuch*

Mary Daly, 2016: *Sixties Ireland*

Gearóid Ó Faoleán, 2019: *A Broad Church: The Provisional IRA in the Republic of Ireland 1969-1980*

Robert Fisk, 1983: *In Time of War: Ireland, Ulster and the Price of Neutrality, 1939-45*

Anna Funder, 2011: *Stasiland: Stories from Behind the Berlin Wall*

Brian Hanley & Scott Millar, 2010: *The Lost Revolution*

Danny Morrison, 1997: *The Wrong Man*

William Matchett, 2016: *Secret Victory: The Intelligence War that beat the IRA*

James Kelly, 1999: *The Thimbleriggers*

Sicco Mansholt, 1970, *The Mansholt Plan - An Irish Quarterly Review, Vol. 59, No. 236*

Patrick Mulroe, 2017: *Bombs, Bullets and the Border*

Stuart Smith, 2018: *Otto Skorzeny: The Devil's Disciple*

Karl Heinz Weber, 1975: *Auch Tote haben einen Schatten*

Robert Widders, 2017: *Spitting on a Soldier's Grave*

Jérôme Aan De Wiel, 2017: *East German Intelligence and Ireland 1949-90*

Clair Wills, 2008: *That Neutral Island*

Markus Wolf, 1998: *Memoirs of a Spymaster*

Printed in Great Britain
by Amazon